*The Editor*

ERIK GRAY is Professor of English and Comparative Literature at Columbia University and a specialist in Victorian poetry. His books include *The Poetry of Indifference, Milton and the Victorians*, and *The Art of Love Poetry*.

# NORTON CRITICAL EDITIONS
## Victorian Era

For a complete list of Norton Critical Editions, visit
wwnorton.com/nortoncriticals

A NORTON CRITICAL EDITION

Alfred, Lord Tennyson
# IN MEMORIAM

AUTHORITATIVE TEXT
BACKGROUNDS AND CONTEXTS
CRITICISM

**THIRD EDITION**

*Edited by*

ERIK GRAY
COLUMBIA UNIVERSITY

**W. W. NORTON & COMPANY**
*Independent Publishers Since 1923*

W. W. Norton & Company has been independent since its founding in 1923, when William Warder Norton and Mary D. Herter Norton first published lectures delivered at the People's Institute, the adult education division of New York City's Cooper Union. The firm soon expanded its program beyond the Institute, publishing books by celebrated academics from America and abroad. By midcentury, the two major pillars of Norton's publishing program—trade books and college texts—were firmly established. In the 1950s, the Norton family transferred control of the company to its employees, and today—with a staff of five hundred and hundreds of trade, college, and professional titles published each year—W. W. Norton & Company stands as the largest and oldest publishing house owned wholly by its employees.

Manufacturing by Maple Press
Book design by Antonina Krass
Production manager: Stephen Sajdak

Library of Congress Cataloging-in-Publication Data

Names: Tennyson, Alfred Tennyson, Baron, 1809–1892, author. | Gray, Erik
  Irving, 1972– editor.
Title: In memoriam : authoritative text, backgrounds and contexts,
  criticism / Alfred, Lord Tennyson ; edited by Erik Gray.
Description: Third edition. | New York, N.Y. : W.W. Norton & Company,
  [2021] | Series: Norton critical editions : Victorian era | Includes
  bibliographical references and index.
Identifiers: LCCN 2020016975 | ISBN 9780393679236 (paperback)
Subjects: LCSH: Hallam, Arthur Henry, 1811–1833—Poetry. | Tennyson, Alfred
  Tennyson, Baron, 1809–1892. In memoriam. | Hallam, Arthur Henry,
  1811–1833—In literature. | Elegiac poetry, English—History and
  criticism. | Friendship in literature.
Classification: LCC PR5562.A2 G73 2021 | DDC 821/.8—dc21
LC record available at https://lccn.loc.gov/2020016975

ISBN: 978-0-393-67923-6 (pbk.)

W. W. Norton & Company, Inc., 500 Fifth Avenue, New York, N.Y. 10110
          www.wwnorton.com
W. W. Norton & Company Ltd., 15 Carlisle Street, London W1D 3BS

1  2  3  4  5  6  7  8  9  0

FOR KATHERINE

*Dear friend, far off*

# Contents

# Criticism 143

# Preface

This third Norton Critical Edition of *In Memoriam* features several significant revisions. Most notably it includes two new sections: a selection of contextual materials that provide biographical, literary, and historical backgrounds for the poem, and a selection of early reviews. In addition I have updated the selection of modern critical readings as well as the annotated bibliography to reflect recent scholarship.

I have also taken this opportunity to emend the text, notes, and introduction where necessary. In particular, I have corrected a small but persistent error that the previous edition shared with most other modern editions of Tennyson: namely, that of sometimes calling the poem *In Memoriam A.H.H.*, as if that were the true full title. The more correct title is simply *In Memoriam*, which I have used accordingly. (On this topic see my note and the response by Christopher Ricks in the *Tennyson Research Bulletin*, 9.3–4 [2009–10].)

This edition once again follows the text of the poem found in the Eversley edition (see the bibliography), which represents the latest version overseen by the poet. In the notes I have frequently quoted the annotations that Tennyson himself provided for the Eversley edition; these are marked [T.]. For the notes, as well as for much else, I am indebted to the work of earlier editors, especially Christopher Ricks, Susan Shatto, and Marion Shaw. I am also grateful to Thea Goodrich at Norton for her expert guidance.

# Introduction

*Tennyson, Hallam, and the Poem*

In October of 1833, twenty-four-year-old Alfred Tennyson (he would not become "Lord" Tennyson for another fifty years) was living at the rectory in Somersby, Lincolnshire, where he had grown up. His father had died two years before, while Tennyson was studying at Cambridge; Alfred, although he was not the eldest son, had left the university without completing his degree in order to take on the duties of the male head of the household for his mother and numerous younger siblings. Life with Tennyson's gloomy, irritable father had been extremely difficult for the whole family, but it did not get much easier when he died. The Reverend George Tennyson had been the rector at Somersby; after his death his family, which was always in want of money, was faced with the probability that they would have to leave the residence that had always been their home—as eventually they were compelled to do in 1837, an event commemorated in sections 100–105 of *In Memoriam*.

One bright spot in Tennyson's life at this time, and in that of his whole family, was Arthur Henry Hallam. Tennyson had met Hallam in the spring of 1829 at Cambridge, where they were both students at Trinity College, and they immediately formed the deepest and most profound friendship of Tennyson's life. Tennyson's childhood had been dark and unquiet, and he had not liked Cambridge at first, but with his newfound friend he flourished. Hallam was a sensitive and brilliant young man, later remembered not just by Tennyson but by many of his friends (including the future prime minister William Ewart Gladstone) as the member of their circle most clearly destined for greatness. Together he and Tennyson became members of The Apostles, an undergraduate society for intellectual discussion and debate. Hallam fervently admired Tennyson's poetry and encouraged him to publish it. The result was a volume of poems in 1830, which Hallam very ably (and very favorably) reviewed in an article the following year, and then another, larger volume of poems in 1832, which Hallam was instrumental in getting published.

Meanwhile, Tennyson brought Hallam to Somersby, where he became an immediate favorite, particularly with Tennyson's younger sister Emily, with whom he fell in love. The two soon became engaged to be married, a move that angered Hallam's father, who had hoped for a more advantageous match for his son and who forbade the young couple to see each other until Hallam turned twenty-one. But their love survived the separation, and when Hallam did come of age in February 1832, the engagement was renewed; Hallam finished his degree at Cambridge and moved to London to study law, hoping to begin a career that would allow him to marry soon. In the meantime, his friendship with Tennyson continued as close as ever. When Hallam left for a long tour of the Continent with his father in late summer of 1833, Tennyson went down to London to share his final days in England and to see him off.

Such was the situation when, in early October 1833, Tennyson received the following letter from Hallam's uncle:

My dear Sir,

At the desire of a most afflicted family, I write to you because they are unequal from the abyss of grief into which they have fallen to do it themselves. Your friend, sir, and my much-loved nephew, Arthur Hallam, is no more. It has pleased God to remove him from this, his first scene of existence, to that better world for which he was created. He died at Vienna, on his return from Buda, by apoplexy, and I believe his remains come by sea from Trieste. * * * May that Being in whose hands are all the destinies of man, and who has promised to comfort all that mourn, pour the balm of consolation on all the families, who are bowed down by this unexpected dispensation!

Tennyson was faced with the duty of breaking the news to Emily and then of learning to cope with it himself.

Tennyson's reaction was to begin writing poetry that, directly or indirectly, confronted the grief that seemed to have cut his life in two. Within a week of receiving the news of Hallam's death, he composed one of his greatest short poems, "Ulysses," and over the following weeks he began work on other major poems, including "Tithonus" and "Morte d'Arthur." All of these dealt obliquely with his loss. But at the same time Tennyson drafted a more explicitly personal lyric, "Fair ship, that from the Italian shore," addressed to the boat that was bearing Hallam's body back to England for burial in Somerset, near the family estate. (The ship finally arrived and the funeral took place in early January; Tennyson could not bring himself to attend.) This lyric later became section 9 of *In Memoriam*.

So began the drawn-out and piecemeal process of composition that was not to conclude until the elegy was published at last in June 1850, nearly seventeen years after it was begun. Indeed, for many years after Hallam's death Tennyson published very little at all, until in 1842 he came out with a two-volume edition of old and new poems—including "Ulysses" and "Morte d'Arthur"—that securely established his reputation as a major English poet. But although he continued to compose his elegies for Hallam, until by 1845 the poem we know as *In Memoriam* had reached nearly its present length, he remained reluctant to publish them. Eventually, early in 1850, he printed a small number of copies for private distribution to his friends. This so-called trial edition had no title, though Tennyson had considered such possibilities as *Fragments of an Elegy* and *The Way of the Soul*. After some further revisions the poem was finally published a few months later; the author's name was not given, and the title (perhaps suggested by Tennyson's fiancée, Emily Sellwood) was simply *In Memoriam*.

The effect of the poem's publication, both on the reading public and on Tennyson's life, was immediate and enormous. *In Memoriam* was hailed as a masterpiece, and Tennyson, who despite the anonymous publication was quickly identified by most reviewers, was widely celebrated in the press. The practical repercussions for him were twofold. The post of poet laureate, or official poet to the British monarch, had been left vacant by the death of William Wordsworth in April, and Queen Victoria was searching for a worthy successor. Tennyson's name had already been suggested, and his nomination was secured when the queen's husband, Prince Albert, read *In Memoriam* and expressed his admiration. Second, Tennyson was enabled to marry Emily Sellwood, to whom he had been engaged, on and off, for over ten years. The marriage had been delayed both by Tennyson's lack of steady income and by Emily's concerns about his possible lack of religious faith. But *In Memoriam*, although it expresses much doubt as well as faith, apparently allayed her misgivings. And profits from the sale of the poem, which quickly ran through several printings, supplemented soon afterward by the modest stipend attached to the laureateship, provided Tennyson with sufficient income to support a family.

The popularity of *In Memoriam* continued to grow after its initial success. It appealed to the Victorians for a number of reasons, in addition to its sheer poetic beauty. The rituals of mourning were a central feature of Victorian culture: there were elaborate codes concerning everything from dress to stationery for months or years after the death of a loved one. After the death of her husband in 1861, Queen Victoria spent the last forty years of her life in mourning, and she told Tennyson, "Next to the Bible *In Memoriam* is my comfort." It filled a similar role through all levels of society. Contemporary readers also appreciated Tennyson's poem because it frankly confronted the crisis of faith that troubled so many mid-century thinkers. For several decades scientific discoveries had been challenging the Bible's teachings, particularly the account of creation; by 1850 the scientific and technological progress on which the Victorians so prided themselves seemed painfully at odds with the religious beliefs and practices of earlier times. Readers were therefore grateful to Tennyson for combining a poetic exploration of such concepts as evolution with an ultimate affirmation of faith. To understand how he managed to do this, it is important first to consider the form and structure of *In Memoriam*.

## Unity and Division

The *Memoir* of Tennyson written by his son, Hallam Tennyson (see p. 109 below), records a number of the poet's comments about the way he composed *In Memoriam*. "The sections were written," says Tennyson, "at many different places, and as the phases of our intercourse came to my memory and suggested them. I did not write them with any view of weaving them into a whole, or for publication, until I found that I had written so many." This information confirms what the reader of *In Memoriam* feels while moving through the poem: that *In Memoriam* is simultaneously one poem and 133 poems, almost any of which could stand independently as a separate elegy. This fragmentation is one of the most surprising features of Tennyson's poem. Elegies traditionally exhibit a single movement or trajectory: the speaker reacts to the death of a loved one by moving steadily from grief toward consolation. That continuity, however, is shattered in *In Memoriam*. One section will reach some form of consolation, only to be contradicted by the next section, in which the sense of grief is renewed. Most elegies present a reaction to death; *In Memoriam* presents what T. S. Eliot called a "diary" of reactions (see p. 167 below). The fictional time of the poem extends over nearly three years from the moment the speaker learns of his friend's death, and its fragmentary nature reflects the fluctuations that typify such a period: the mourner continues to have good days and bad days, even after the immediate shock of grief has passed.

And yet for all its fragmentation, *In Memoriam* also displays an admirable unity. Although it includes more doubts and setbacks along the way than most other elegies, it contains the same overall movement from near-despair to a sense of consolation. Moreover, its different sections are often tightly woven together: they react to each other, and sections that share particular concerns (those addressing the ship, for instance, or those that speculate on the possibility of seeing the spirit of the dead) are grouped together. Above all, the poem is written throughout in a single, unusual stanza form. Tennyson's claim that each section was written independently of the others is a little misleading: he must have been conscious early on that all of the poems he was writing about Hallam shared a meter and rhyme scheme that he had only rarely used before. The consistent use of a single stanza—what has come to be called the *In Memoriam* stanza—reinforces the sense that, although the speaker may feel himself to be filled with conflicting, even contradictory feelings, nevertheless he retains some integrity, a hope of eventually resolving the disparate impulses he feels.

The conjunction of division and unity is not merely an aspect of the poem's structure but its most pressing concern. Tennyson feels himself to be divided into two: a former self, who was young and happy in Hallam's company, and a new self, who, at twenty-four, feels already aged. His sense of identity is therefore shaken, leaving him asking "Who am I?" or even on one occasion "What am I?" (54.17). This fragmentation of identity is even more painfully acute in the case of Hallam. Tennyson knows that he longs for his friend, but who is his friend? Is he the Hallam so vividly remembered at Cambridge and at the Tennyson home in Somersby? Is he the corpse being brought back on the ship? Is he an angel looking down from above? Or is he the person that Hallam would be had he survived, as section 84 suggests? These are the pieces that the poem must put together again. How can the poet reassure himself that there is some sense in saying "I" or saying "Hallam"?

Even the stanza, the formal feature that provides the greatest unifying force, itself contains elements of brokenness or dividedness. Each line of the *In Memoriam* stanza is shorter than one would expect. The typical meter for long poems in English is iambic pentameter, a line consisting of ten syllables (five "feet"); *In Memoriam* uses a tetrameter line, which is two syllables shorter. Furthermore, what is usually called the "elegiac stanza" in English poetry is a quatrain (a four-line stanza) with interlaced rhymes, *abab*; the stanza of *In Memoriam* rearranges the rhymes *abba*. These may seem like small variations, but they have an immense effect, and together they make the stanza form so unusual that Tennyson thought he was the first to use it: "I believed myself the originator of the metre, until after 'In Memoriam' came out, when some one told me that Ben Jonson and Sir Philip Sidney had used it" (see p. 110 below).

There are several important effects Tennyson achieves by using a tetrameter line rather than the more standard pentameter. The tetrameter or four-beat line is the standard meter for ballads, nursery rhymes, and songs—in other words, for what are considered to be the more spontaneous or immediately appealing forms of poetry. The shorter line allows *In Memoriam* to appear more unpremeditated. The poem often wishes to present itself as inarticulate or unthinking, poured forth as naturally as the lament of a bird that has lost its fledglings (section 21) or as the cry of an infant in the night (sections 54, 124). These assertions are still paradoxical—a poem that claims to be speechless—but the self-deprecation derives credibility from the use of the simpler, abbreviated meter. Pentameter had for centuries been used for long or important poems, such as epics and elegies, because it conveys a sense of confidence; this derives in part from the fact that a ten-syllable line is long enough to contain a complete statement. Consider, for instance, the opening line from a major elegy written in pentameters a few decades before *In Memoriam*, Percy Shelley's "Adonais":

> I weep for Adonais—he is dead!

The theme and motivation of the poem (partially reprinted on pp. 127–29 below) are summed up neatly in a single line. Contrast the opening stanza of section 1 of *In Memoriam*:

> I held it truth, with him who sings
> To one clear harp in divers tones,
> That men may rise on stepping-stones
> Of their dead selves to higher things.
> (1.1–4)

"I held it truth, with him who sings": by itself it is an incomplete and almost meaningless statement. We must wait until the second line to get a sense of who this singer is and until the final two lines to learn what "truth" is being repudiated. Tennyson emphasizes the brokenness of the tetrameter stanza, the way that each line falls short of expressing a complete thought—just as words fall short of expressing his emotion, as he insists throughout the poem. Words "half reveal / And half conceal the Soul within" (5.3–4); they are insufficient, and the shorter line insists on this by being itself insufficient.

Like the meter, the rhyme scheme Tennyson employs expresses the poem's self-doubt, or rather its mixture of faith and doubt. In one sense, the *abba* stanza conveys a sense of fulfillment: it begins with one rhyme sound, which is then temporarily lost as we move on to the couplet in the middle; but in the end the initial rhyme returns, clinching the stanza and seeming to redeem or justify the open-endedness of the beginning. The second stanza of section 1 offers both an example and an image of this forward-looking trustfulness:

> But who shall so forecast the years
>   And find in loss a gain to match?
>   Or reach a hand thro' time to catch
> The far-off interest of tears?
>
>                                    (1.5–8)

Like the expectant hand in line 7 (a symbol that recurs throughout
the poem), the opening rhyme word, *years*, is extended in good faith
and then left waiting, until it is finally rewarded with the satisfying
closure of a matching rhyme at the end.

Yet this hopeful or redemptive reading is only one side of the
*abba* rhyme scheme, and even the stanza just quoted seems doubt-
ful: it is phrased, after all, as a question. The same rhyme scheme
also conveys the opposite sense, a feeling not of looking forward,
but of falling back. It begins surely enough with a progression, *a* to
*b*, but then it seems almost to give up, to turn around and retreat
into what it knows. This sense is conveyed in the third stanza of
section 1:

> Let Love clasp Grief lest both be drown'd,
>   Let darkness keep her raven gloss:
>   Ah, sweeter to be drunk with loss,
> To dance with death, to beat the ground.
>
>                                    (1.9–12)

Instead of moving beyond grief toward some eventual reward, a
"far-off interest," the poet wishes to turn around and "clasp Grief,"
to cling to the familiar past. It is therefore appropriate that the
rhyme scheme itself is one of clasping—the *a* rhyme embracing
the *b*, and the stanza as a whole ending where it began. Both of the
poet's impulses, then—the impulse to move hopefully on and
the desire to circle back—are equally represented by the stanza.

But it is worth pausing to consider the notion of *clasping*, which,
like the hand, reappears as one of the central images of the poem.
The command given at the beginning of the third stanza seems to
be backward: "Let Love clasp Grief lest both be drown'd." Anyone
who has ever taken swimming lessons knows that to grab onto a
fellow swimmer is the most dangerous thing one can do in the
water: rather than prevent one from drowning, it actually causes
both to go under. What does Tennyson mean then by saying that
Love and Grief should clasp each other to prevent their being
"drown'd"? The answer seems to lie in the nature of clasping. To
clasp something implies unity, of course; clasping or hugging is a
way of bringing two things together. But it necessarily implies sep-
arateness or division as well: only two distinct or independent enti-
ties can clasp each other. A hand cannot clasp itself, but must

clasp a different hand; a raindrop cannot "clasp" another raindrop without their melting into each other, because they are not sufficiently individuated. For Tennyson, both aspects of clasping—division as much as unity—are equally important. He strives in his poem to reunify what has been fragmented, to reunite with his lost friend. At the same time, however, he resists the possibility of total union; he seeks to "clasp" his friend, not that they should merge entirely.

Hence the importance of embraces in the poem, beginning with the rhyme scheme. An example of the unifying power of clasping comes in section 89; it is the only representation we are given of a remembered conversation between Tennyson and Hallam—although they are shown, significantly, disagreeing:

> But if I praised the busy town,
>     He loved to rail against it still,
>     For 'ground in yonder social mill
> We rub each other's angles down,
>
> 'And merge' he said 'in form and gloss
>     The picturesque of man and man.'
>     We talk'd: the stream beneath us ran,
> The wine-flask lying couch'd in moss.
>
> (89.37–44)

It has been pointed out that of these eight lines, Tennyson speaks four and Hallam speaks four; none of Tennyson's lines rhyme together, nor do any of Hallam's. This is the threat, as it were, of the rhyme scheme: divide up the quatrains differently and you are left with four unrhymed lines. But Tennyson takes the memory of a simple prose conversation, and by enfolding it within his own words, he turns it into verse.

These lines seem therefore to exemplify the benefits of clasping, which is able to convert unrhymed fragments into a unified whole. But the same lines also express a fear of unity: Hallam decries the tendency of individuals in society to "merge," to become too much like one another. Love may thrive on union, but the poem reminds us that love also requires a certain amount of separation. In section 47, for instance, in which he describes his notion of heaven, Tennyson renounces the idea that the souls of the dead all become so equally perfect as to be indistinguishable:

> That each, who seems a separate whole,
>     Should move his rounds, and fusing all
>     The skirts of self again, should fall
> Remerging in the general Soul,

> Is faith as vague as all unsweet:
>     Eternal form shall still divide
>     The eternal soul from all beside;
> And I shall know him when we meet.
>                              (47.1–8)

Division, then, has its purpose: how else can those who love recognize each other? Tennyson therefore rejects the notion of spirits who, being all infinitely good, are all alike parts of the "general Soul," and he gives instead his own notion of a homelier heaven:

> And we shall sit at endless feast,
>     Enjoying each the other's good:
>     What vaster dream can hit the mood
> Of Love on earth? He seeks at least
>
> Upon the last and sharpest height,
>     Before the spirits fade away,
>     Some landing-place, to clasp and say,
> 'Farewell! We lose ourselves in light.'
>                              (47.9–16)

When Tennyson here asks for the right to "clasp" once more, he is asking for something mundane: angels presumably are no more capable of hugging each other than raindrops are. But "Love on earth" (the only love he knows) demands division.

This concern helps explain the difficulty of the earlier image, "Let Love clasp Grief lest both be drown'd." Tennyson seems to be calling on love and grief to "clasp" in the sense of bracketing each other, limiting each other. Grief must not become infinite, nor must love grow to become an indistinguishable angel-love; both must be kept earthly and distinct, lest they be "drown'd" in a sea of light and infinity. And this is what the *In Memoriam* stanza manages to do, both in its shortened lines and in its clasping rhyme scheme: it stresses its own limits and recognizes the importance of division, even while the consistency of the rhyme scheme lends unity to the poem as a whole.

Section 1 usefully illustrates these effects of the stanza form. It is not, admittedly, the most captivating section of *In Memoriam*: it contains an obscure reference to the German poet Goethe (he is the one "who sings" in line 1), and its argument is not immediately clear. But this section boldly introduces the problem of fragmentation or self-division that will occupy the whole poem. It begins in apparent self-confidence with the word *I*, but then immediately questions what that "I" might mean. Goethe, it is pointed out, believed that people leave behind their former lives, their "dead selves," as they grow older, the way a snake sheds its skin; so "I" is not the same person from year to year.

Tennyson repudiates this view. There is some continuity, he insists, between "me" now and "me" then, before the death of Hallam. But the doubt has already been introduced, and it only grows more acute in the following section. Tennyson may well claim that he is not completely cut off from his former life, but it is far more difficult to say the same of Hallam. Having asserted that "I" exists as a continuous, unified self, Tennyson wishes to say the same of "you." As mentioned, however, Hallam seems to have become many different selves: Hallam the memory, the corpse, the dream, the angel. Wishing to address his friend but at a loss where to direct his speech, Tennyson turns to the yew tree in the graveyard:

> Old Yew, which graspest at the stones
> That name the under-lying dead.
> (2.1–2)

Section 1 began with *I*; section 2 begins with *Yew,* but not the "you" Tennyson wished for. One might call this a pun, but that would be misleading. It is rather an indication of the difficulty of establishing a sense of identity after such a shattering event. The very layout of the poem reinforces the sense of unwanted multiplicity where there ought to be unity. The beginning of the poem looks like an epitaph carved on a headstone: the first numbered section is preceded by a Latin inscription (In Memoriam A.H.H. Obiit MDCCCXXXIII) and headed by a Roman numeral (I). Usually, however, one person gets only one headstone. Here, on the other hand, the original "epitaph" is followed by another, as if the first were insufficient. Even the Roman numerals seem to suggest something amiss: just after the first section has asserted the unity of "I," we are confronted by "II," as if "I" had multiplied.

"You," meanwhile, is even less stable, more difficult to locate. One of the most moving aspects of the opening sections is the difficulty Tennyson has in finding someone or something to address. He begins with "Old Yew" (2.1), then turns to "O Sorrow" (3.1), then "O heart" (4.5), "Dark house" (7.1), and finally "Fair ship" (9.1). When you lose the person you love best, this is the quandary: the very person you would usually turn to in a time of grief is the one person you cannot find. It could be said that the closest Tennyson comes to locating Hallam in these opening sections is in section 1, line 11: "Ah, sweeter to be drunk with loss"—where the sigh that escapes the speaker ("Ah") contains Hallam's initials. Hallam seems to be both everywhere and nowhere, to be divided into so many different selves as to be irrecoverable. The end of section IX suggests just how fragmented he has become:

My friend, the brother of my love;

My Arthur, whom I shall not see
   Till all my widow'd race be run;
   Dear as the mother to the son,
More than my brothers are to me.
        (9.16–20)

Hallam is, within the space of five lines, a friend, a brother, a spouse, a mother, a more-than-brother. But none of these will quite do to represent him, nor can the whole of Tennyson's actual family make up for his loss.

And yet for all the division of "I" and "you" that plagues the speaker here, section 9 also introduces the first note of comfort and consistency in the poem. After searching vainly for an object to whom, or to which, he can direct his lament, the poet here fixes on the ship, which he will continue to address for the following nine sections. This may be a small comfort, but it is a certain one. It gives Tennyson a single point of concentration, and it gives the poem a sense of stability. Just as important, the ship represents a return of some sort: the movement is no longer all outward from the poet; now something is coming back to him, coming home. The newfound (if precarious) stability is evident in the opening stanza of section 18, when the ship finally arrives and delivers Hallam's body to his homeland:

'Tis well; 'tis something; we may stand
   Where he in English earth is laid,
   And from his ashes may be made
The violet of his native land.
        (18.1–4)

We saw earlier, in discussing the opening of section 1, that the eight-syllable line is usually too short to include a complete sentence. Here, however, Tennyson is at last collected enough to fit three complete clauses into the first line. "'Tis well"—no, not quite that; but at least "'tis something; we may stand" by his grave. He goes on in line 5 to say, "'Tis little." It is little, but at least it is more than he had in the beginning; he has begun the process of reassembling the selves shattered by Hallam's sudden death.

## Faith, Science, and Other Critical Concerns

At the end of this volume are reprinted a number of reviews and critical essays representing the range of critical reaction to *In Memoriam*. Some address the question of the poem's unity, while others focus on the poem's form, its erotics, or its place in the elegiac tradition. One of the most persistent concerns is also the one that most interested the first reviewers of *In Memoriam*: the conflict in the poem between religious faith and doubt, specifically doubt resulting from new scientific theories. The poem's framework is distinctly Christian: its time scheme, for instance—the three years of mourning—is marked by the recurrence of Christmas at regular intervals (sections 28–30, 78, and 104–105). Moreover, the great consolation on which the poem depends and concludes is the immortality of the individual soul, the assurance that Hallam is in heaven and that "I shall know him when we meet" (47.8). Within this broad framework, however, there is plenty of room for doubt. Even the Christmas poems seem far more concerned with the loss of Hallam than with possible religious consolations. And Tennyson has little to say for most received doctrine; rather, "There lives more faith in honest doubt," he judges, "than in half the creeds" (96.11–12). But the profoundest moments of religious questioning come when he considers the evidence of science.

Charles Darwin did not publish his treatise *On the Origin of Species By Means of Natural Selection* until 1859, nine years after *In Memoriam* was published, but there was no dearth of troubling scientific theories earlier in the century. Tennyson was particularly aware of these theories: his poetry reflects a deeper concern with scientific developments perhaps than that of any other poet of his time writing in English; the allusions to astronomy and geology in *In Memoriam* reveal a sophisticated understanding of current ideas. It might seem odd for a poem of personal grief to refer to complex scientific concepts, but these allusions do not seem out of place, for two reasons. First, science was increasingly depicting both the universe and the human race as doomed to eventual extinction; yet Tennyson's poem is predicated on an assurance of personal immortality, and such a contradiction could scarcely be ignored. Second, an evolutionary model of development is central to *In Memoriam* starting from the first section, which speculates whether or not individuals leave behind their "dead selves" in a constant progression forward. These questions lead naturally to broader speculations about similar evolutions in the natural world.

Doubts about the eternal nature of the world and of the soul had always existed and had been steadily accruing in Europe since the eighteenth century; hence there is no single scientist whose work can be specified as the source of the doubts expressed in *In Memoriam*. But we do know that Tennyson was particularly affected by reading Scottish geologist Charles Lyell's *Principles of Geology* (1830–33) in 1837. (For extracts from Lyell and other contemporary scientific writers, see "Scientific Contexts," p. 131 below.) Lyell suggested that the earth's surface was constantly changing: natural forces such as erosion altered the landscape gradually but eternally.

So whereas other scientists had proposed that extinct species had been wiped out by cataclysmic events that would not necessarily be repeated, Lyell reached quite a different conclusion: the same slow but steady forces that had changed the environment and extinguished earlier species were still in operation and therefore would extinguish humans as well. This is the pitiless view Tennyson represents in sections 55 and 56, some of the most despairing in the poem. Nature tells humankind:

> 'I care for nothing, all shall go.
>
> 'Thou makest thine appeal to me:
>     I bring to life, I bring to death:
>     The spirit does but mean the breath:
> I know no more.'
>
> (56.4–8)

Such destruction not only of individuals but of entire species seems irreconcilable with the Christian concept of a God to whom every life is dear for all eternity. If we, like every other species, are doomed to extinction by impersonal forces, Tennyson concludes, our life is "as futile, then, as frail" (56.25).

Yet there is another way of thinking about this same theory that leads to an opposite conclusion. Lyell, we have noted, disagreed with the "catastrophic" model of change; rather than a series of cataclysmic breaks with the past, he posited a constant series of small changes. In that case, however, nothing is ever left entirely behind, since every stage is part of a continuous progression. So the idea of constant evolution, which posed such a problem, also provides the solution. According to this understanding, there exists a direct and traceable continuity between earlier stages of life and this one, just as there does between childhood and adulthood. This is exactly the reassurance that Tennyson sought in section 1: that what seemed like a catastrophic rupture—the death of Hallam, and therefore the death of Tennyson's former self—could be explained in such a way that those former selves would not seem to be wholly extinct. Nothing wholly dies if it gives rise to the next stage of development, and so on infinitely:

> They say,
> The solid earth whereon we tread
>
> In tracts of fluent heat began,
>     And grew to seeming-random forms,
>     The seeming prey of cyclic storms,
> Till at the last arose the man.
>
> (118.7–12)

Change is "fluent": the "solid earth" or "the man" can change constantly and yet remain the same, just as a river does. Tennyson returns to this reassurance a few sections later:

> There rolls the deep where grew the tree.
>     O earth, what changes hast thou seen!
>     There where the long street roars, hath been
> The stillness of the central sea.
>
> The hills are shadows, and they flow
>     From form to form, and nothing stands;
>     They melt like mist, the solid lands,
> Like clouds they shape themselves and go.
>                                         (123.1–8)

There is certainly something melancholy in this vast, almost cinematic sweep through time; Tennyson recognizes the radical instability of the world he depicts. But it has ceased to be terrifying, as it was in section 56, because at least there is no sudden, irretrievable severance from the past.

Evolution does not of course hold all the answers; it does not dispel the poet's grief. But it does suggest a way of reconciling parts of a life that seemed to be hopelessly fragmented, and also of justifying a God whose workings otherwise seem so careless of individual lives. Evolution therefore features prominently in the Epilogue—a section that, like the Prologue, Tennyson wrote late in the process of composition and left untitled. This final section cannot be taken as a summing up of all that has gone before: the reader has witnessed too many fluctuations and contradictions along the way to accept any point of view as the final word. Moreover, the Epilogue presents itself more as a coda or counterpoint to the rest of the poem than as a representative piece. It is set on a day nine years after the death of Hallam, at the wedding of one of Tennyson's younger sisters; the poem that begins with a funeral ends, suddenly, with a marriage.

Nevertheless, although the Epilogue is in some ways distinct from the body of the poem, it does present the last word, and it chimes well with the hopefulness that predominates in the sections that precede it. Its final vision is one of evolution: Tennyson predicts that on this wedding night, a child will be conceived who, because the human race is constantly progressing, will be slightly more developed than the current generation. But the end point of all this evolution, Tennyson suggests, is a state that Arthur Henry Hallam already achieved when he lived—a form of humanity

> Whereof the man, that with me trod
>     This planet, was a noble type

> Appearing ere the times were ripe,
> That friend of mine who lives in God,
>
> That God, which ever lives and loves,
>     One God, one law, one element,
>     And one far-off divine event,
> To which the whole creation moves.
>                        (Epilogue, 137–144)

The constant progression from one state of being to "higher things" (1.4), which seems so painful and problematic in earlier sections of the poem, here becomes the source of greatest comfort, because it leads toward an eventual reunion with Hallam.

Yet optimistic though this ending may be—Tennyson himself is said to have expressed a concern that it was "too hopeful"—it is also slightly disturbing: it seems to come uncomfortably close to equating Hallam ("That friend") with God ("That God"). We have already seen how much trouble the poet has in finding a fit image to describe his friend: is he a friend, a brother, a parent, or a spouse? A good deal of criticism in recent decades has concentrated on the last of these, the repeated depiction of their relationship as a marriage, and more generally, on what one early reviewer called the tone of "amatory tenderness" that pervades the poem (see p. 158 below). The aim of these critics is not to try to determine whether the actual relationship between Tennyson and Hallam involved a homosexual attraction, but rather to understand the significance in the poem of language Tennyson would not normally use toward a male friend: terms of endearment, expressions of longing, recurrent images of Hallam's body, his hands, his eyes. Queer criticism of the poem is thus not as different from other, earlier schools of criticism as it might seem, since it too centers on the difficulty of finding appropriate words. Tennyson responded to objections to his use of terms like *dearest* (74.5 and 122.1) by saying, "If any body thinks I ever called him 'dearest' in his life, they are much mistaken, for I never even called him 'dear.'" The comment is interesting not because it suggests that Tennyson had unwittingly revealed himself and was anxious to explain away his slip; if that were true he could easily have changed the text after publication, as he was often willing to do in response to criticism. Instead the comment reveals how conscious Tennyson was of his unusually erotic phrasing: Hallam's death, which changed so much, even altered the nature of the language in which he must be addressed.

Queer criticism also helps remind us that *In Memoriam* is not only an elegy but one of the most beautiful love poems in English. Among its chief glories is the way that Tennyson manages to consider great issues of public import—the latest science, and all the questions of faith and doubt to which the contemplation of death leads him—without ever losing the poignancy of an intensely personal lament. Section 129, at the end of the poem, feels the shock and longing of loss as minutely as the opening sections:

> Dear friend, far off, my lost desire,
>     So far, so near in woe and weal;
>     O loved the most, when most I feel
> There is a lower and a higher;
>
> Known and unknown; human, divine;
>     Sweet human hand and lips and eye;
>     Dear heavenly friend that canst not die,
> Mine, mine, for ever, ever mine;
>
> Strange friend, past, present, and to be;
>     Loved deeplier, darklier understood;
>     Behold, I dream a dream of good,
> And mingle all the world with thee.
>                                         (129.1–12)

Tennyson certainly seems at times to "mingle all the world" with Hallam; his poem on Hallam looks to be all-encompassing. The word *all* recurs almost obsessively throughout the poem—157 times in 133 sections. Yet all of those *all*'s cannot dispel the underlying doubt, the sense of something slipping away (the more tentative word *half* also appears persistently). After all his universal speculations, Tennyson still dwells with supreme tenderness on the details, the "sweet human hand and lips and eye." And after so many sections and so many years, Hallam in the final address remains what he was at first: "Strange friend." Those we have loved and lost seem "So far, so near" at once—loved more than ever and yet, at the end of it all, still a mystery.

It is only appropriate, then, that what is often seen as the climactic moment of the poem is also described as "strange." In section 95 Tennyson temporarily achieves the reunion with Hallam for which he has been longing. Sitting alone outdoors one evening he begins to read Hallam's old letters:

> And strangely on the silence broke
>     The silent-speaking words, and strange
>     Was love's dumb cry defying change
> To test his worth; and strangely spoke
>
> The faith, the vigour, bold to dwell
>     On doubts that drive the coward back,
>     And keen thro' wordy snares to track
> Suggestion to her inmost cell.

So word by word, and line by line,
　　The dead man touch'd me from the past,
　　And all at once it seem'd at last
The living soul was flash'd on mine.
　　　　　　　　　　(95.25–36)

These stanzas deploy two devices typical of *In Memoriam*. The first is the immediate repetition of a word: "word by word," "line by line." Here such repetition suggests the certainty, the undeniability of this moment of spiritual contact. But this is balanced by the other device, repetition with a difference: "silence" in the first line becomes "silent," and "strangely" becomes simply "strange." Such verbal mutation, which occurs often in the poem, here serves as a reminder that the glorious experience Tennyson describes is still—like everything else in our world—unstable, fleeting, evolving. This conflict, between the wish to "defy change" and the need to accept it, is the poem's central concern. Its strange and wonderful ability to affirm its faith and yet to alter, to accept the perpetual drift of things, is one reason *In Memoriam* continues to "touch us from the past."

ERIK GRAY

# The Text of
# IN MEMORIAM

# IN MEMORIAM.

LONDON:

EDWARD MOXON, DOVER STREET.

1850.

Facsimile title page of the first edition.

# In Memoriam

## [Prologue][1]

Strong Son of God, immortal Love,
    Whom we, that have not seen thy face,
    By faith, and faith alone, embrace,
Believing where we cannot prove;

5  Thine are these orbs of light and shade;[2]
    Thou madest Life in man and brute;
    Thou madest Death; and lo, thy foot
Is on the skull which thou hast made.

Thou wilt not leave us in the dust:
10    Thou madest man, he knows not why,
    He thinks he was not made to die;
And thou hast made him: thou art just.

Thou seemest human and divine,
    The highest, holiest manhood, thou:
15    Our wills are ours, we know not how;
Our wills are ours, to make them thine.

Our little systems have their day;[3]
    They have their day and cease to be:
    They are but broken lights of thee,
20  And thou, O Lord, art more than they.

We have but faith: we cannot know;
    For knowledge is of things we see;
    And yet we trust it comes from thee,
A beam in darkness: let it grow.

---

1. This introductory poem, which Tennyson left untitled, is dated 1849; it was thus composed after the rest of *In Memoriam* was already completed.
2. "Sun and moon" [Tennyson's note; indicated throughout by "T."].
3. I.e., our humanly conceived systems of thought and behavior.

25  Let knowledge grow from more to more,
        But more of reverence in us dwell;
        That mind and soul, according well,
    May make one music as before,[4]

    But vaster. We are fools and slight;
30      We mock thee when we do not fear:
        But help thy foolish ones to bear;
    Help thy vain worlds to bear thy light.

    Forgive what seem'd my sin in me;
        What seem'd my worth since I began;
35      For merit lives from man to man,
    And not from man, O Lord, to thee.

    Forgive my grief for one removed,
        Thy creature, whom I found so fair.
        I trust he lives in thee, and there
40  I find him worthier to be loved.

    Forgive these wild and wandering cries,
        Confusions of a wasted youth;
        Forgive them where they fail in truth,
    And in thy wisdom make me wise.

                                                1849

---

4. "As in ages of faith" [T.]. I.e., before the religious doubts that resulted from recent
scientific discoveries.

# IN MEMORIAM A.H.H.

## Obiit MDCCCXXXIII[5]

### I

I held it truth, with him who sings
    To one clear harp in divers tones,
    That men may rise on stepping-stones
Of their dead selves to higher things.[6]

5    But who shall so forecast the years
    And find in loss a gain to match?
    Or reach a hand thro' time to catch
The far-off interest of tears?

Let Love clasp Grief lest both be drown'd,
10    Let darkness keep her raven gloss:
    Ah, sweeter to be drunk with loss,
To dance with death, to beat the ground,

Than that the victor Hours should scorn
    The long result of love, and boast,
15    'Behold the man that loved and lost,
But all he was is overworn.'

### II

Old Yew, which graspest at the stones
    That name the under-lying dead,
    Thy fibres net the dreamless head,
Thy roots are wrapt about the bones.

5    The seasons bring the flower again,
    And bring the firstling to the flock;
    And in the dusk of thee, the clock
Beats out the little lives of men.[7]

---

5. "To the memory of A.H.H., died 1833" (Latin). On Tennyson's friendship with Arthur Henry Hallam, see "Tennyson, Hallam, and the Poem," pp. xi–xiv above.
6. These lines refer to the German poet Goethe, who wrote in many different styles ("divers tones") and who believed, Tennyson suggests, that individuals should profit from painful experiences and move on. The following stanzas express doubts about this view.
7. The yew is pictured as growing in the churchyard, the clock as striking the hours from the church tower.

O not for thee the glow, the bloom,
10     Who changest not in any gale,
         Nor branding summer suns avail
To touch thy thousand years of gloom:[8]

And gazing on thee, sullen tree,
         Sick for thy stubborn hardihood,
15     I seem to fail from out my blood
And grow incorporate into thee.

# III

O Sorrow, cruel fellowship,
         O Priestess in the vaults of Death,
         O sweet and bitter in a breath,
What whispers from thy lying lip?

5     'The stars,' she whispers, 'blindly run;
         A web is wov'n across the sky;
         From out waste places comes a cry,
And murmurs from the dying sun:[9]

'And all the phantom, Nature, stands—
10     With all the music in her tone,
         A hollow echo of my own,—
A hollow form with empty hands.'

And shall I take a thing so blind,
         Embrace her as my natural good;
15     Or crush her, like a vice of blood,
Upon the threshold of the mind?

# IV

To Sleep I give my powers away;
         My will is bondsman to the dark;
         I sit within a helmless bark,[1]
And with my heart I muse and say:

8. The dark green foliage of the English yew, an unusually long-lived tree, does not change color with the seasons.
9. "Sorrow" is referring to the hypothesis, then recently put forth, that the sun was burning down and would eventually be extinguished. See the selection from William Whewell, p. 134 below.
1. Like a passenger in a rudderless boat ("a helmless bark"), the speaker cannot control the direction of his thoughts.

5    O heart, how fares it with thee now,
        That thou should'st fail from thy desire,
        Who scarcely darest to inquire,
    'What is it makes me beat so low?'

    Something it is which thou hast lost,
10      Some pleasure from thine early years.
        Break, thou deep vase of chilling tears,
    That grief hath shaken into frost![2]

    Such clouds of nameless trouble cross
        All night below the darken'd eyes;
15      With morning wakes the will, and cries,
    'Thou shalt not be the fool of loss.'

## V[3]

I sometimes hold it half a sin
    To put in words the grief I feel;
    For words, like Nature, half reveal
And half conceal the Soul within.

5    But, for the unquiet heart and brain,
      A use in measured language lies;
      The sad mechanic exercise,
Like dull narcotics, numbing pain.

In words, like weeds,[4] I'll wrap me o'er,
10    Like coarsest clothes against the cold:
      But that large grief which these enfold
Is given in outline and no more.

## VI

One writes, that 'Other friends remain,'
    That 'Loss is common to the race'—
    And common is the commonplace,
And vacant chaff well meant for grain.

---

2. "Water can be brought below freezing-point and not turn to ice—if it be kept still; but if it be moved suddenly it turns into ice and may break the vase" [T.].
3. This is the first of several sections concerning the adequacy or inadequacy of poetry to convey deeply felt human experience. Compare sections XX, XXXVII, XLVIII, LXXV, and XCV.
4. Meaning not only "grass" but also "garments," specifically mourning garments.

<sup>5</sup> That loss is common would not make
    My own less bitter, rather more:
    Too common! Never morning wore
To evening, but some heart did break.

O father, wheresoe'er thou be,
<sup>10</sup>    Who pledgest now thy gallant son;
    A shot, ere half thy draught be done,
Hath still'd the life that beat from thee.

O mother, praying God will save
    Thy sailor,—while thy head is bow'd,
<sup>15</sup>    His heavy-shotted hammock-shroud[5]
Drops in his vast and wandering grave.

Ye know no more than I who wrought
    At that last hour to please him well;
    Who mused on all I had to tell,
<sup>20</sup> And something written, something thought;[6]

Expecting still his advent home;
    And ever met him on his way
    With wishes, thinking, 'here to-day,'
Or 'here to-morrow will he come.'

<sup>25</sup> O somewhere, meek, unconscious dove,
    That sittest ranging[7] golden hair;
    And glad to find thyself so fair,
Poor child, that waitest for thy love!

For now her father's chimney glows
<sup>30</sup>    In expectation of a guest;
    And thinking 'this will please him best,'
She takes a riband or a rose;

For he will see them on to-night;
    And with the thought her colour burns;
<sup>35</sup>    And, having left the glass, she turns
Once more to set a ringlet right;

---

5. A sailor buried at sea would be wrapped in his hammock, which would be weighted down with shot to make it sink.
6. According to his son's notes in the Eversley edition, Tennyson was writing a letter to Hallam at the hour of Hallam's death.
7. Arranging. The young woman addressed in the final five stanzas is a fictitious example, like the father and mother of stanzas 3 and 4.

And, even when she turn'd, the curse
  Had fallen, and her future Lord
  Was drown'd in passing thro' the ford,
40 Or kill'd in falling from his horse.

O what to her shall be the end?
  And what to me remains of good?
  To her, perpetual maidenhood,
And unto me no second friend.

## VII

Dark house, by which once more I stand
  Here in the long unlovely street,[8]
  Doors, where my heart was used to beat
So quickly, waiting for a hand,

5 A hand that can be clasp'd no more—
  Behold me, for I cannot sleep,
  And like a guilty thing I creep
At earliest morning to the door.

He is not here; but far away
10 The noise of life begins again,
  And ghastly thro' the drizzling rain
On the bald street breaks the blank day.

## VIII

A happy lover who has come
  To look on her that loves him well,
  Who 'lights[9] and rings the gateway bell,
And learns her gone and far from home;

5 He saddens, all the magic light
  Dies off at once from bower and hall,
  And all the place is dark, and all
The chambers emptied of delight:

So find I every pleasant spot
10 In which we two were wont to meet,

8. Hallam's house on Wimpole Street, London. This section forms a pair with CXIX, when the speaker returns to the house once more.
9. Alights, i.e., dismounts.

The field, the chamber and the street,
    For all is dark where thou art not.

Yet as that other, wandering there
    In those deserted walks, may find
15      A flower beat with rain and wind,
Which once she fostered up with care;

So seems it in my deep regret,
    O my forsaken heart, with thee
    And this poor flower of poesy
20  Which little cared for fades not yet.

But since it pleased a vanish'd eye,
    I go to plant it on his tomb,
    That if it can it there may bloom,
Or dying, there at least may die.


## IX[1]

Fair ship, that from the Italian shore
    Sailest the placid ocean-plains
    With my lost Arthur's loved remains,
Spread thy full wings, and waft him o'er.

5   So draw him home to those that mourn
    In vain; a favourable speed
    Ruffle thy mirror'd mast, and lead
Thro' prosperous floods his holy urn.

All night no ruder air perplex
10      Thy sliding keel, till Phosphor,[2] bright
    As our pure love, thro' early light
Shall glimmer on the dewy decks.

Sphere all your lights around, above;
    Sleep, gentle heavens, before the prow;
15      Sleep, gentle winds, as he sleeps now,
My friend, the brother of my love;

1. Sections IX to XVIII form a unit in which the speaker imagines (and often, as here,
  addresses) the ship that is bearing Hallam's body back to England. Hallam died in
  Vienna, and the ship left from Trieste (hence "Italian shore" in line 1). This section is
  one of the earliest written in the poem, composed while the body was in fact still at sea.
2. The morning star. See section CXXI.

My Arthur, whom I shall not see
    Till all my widow'd race be run;
    Dear as the mother to the son,
20  More than my brothers are to me.


## X


I hear the noise about thy keel;
    I hear the bell struck in the night:
    I see the cabin-window bright;
I see the sailor at the wheel.

5  Thou bring'st the sailor to his wife,
    And travell'd men from foreign lands;
    And letters unto trembling hands;
And, thy dark freight, a vanish'd life.

So bring him: we have idle dreams:
10    This look of quiet flatters thus
    Our home-bred fancies: O to us,
The fools of habit, sweeter seems

To rest beneath the clover sod,
    That takes the sunshine and the rains,
15    Or where the kneeling hamlet drains
The chalice of the grapes of God;

Than if with thee the roaring wells
    Should gulf him fathom-deep in brine;[3]
    And hands so often clasp'd in mine,
20  Should toss with tangle[4] and with shells.


## XI


Calm is the morn without a sound,
    Calm as to suit a calmer grief,
    And only thro' the faded leaf
The chestnut pattering to the ground:

---

3. Better that Hallam be buried in the churchyard (lines 13–14) or in the church itself, where the congregation receives communion (lines 15–16), than that his body be lost at sea.
4. Seaweed.

5  Calm and deep peace on this high wold,[5]
    And on these dews that drench the furze,
    And all the silvery gossamers[6]
That twinkle into green and gold:

Calm and still light on yon great plain
10    That sweeps with all its autumn bowers,
    And crowded farms and lessening towers,
To mingle with the bounding main:

Calm and deep peace in this wide air,
    These leaves that redden to the fall;
15    And in my heart, if calm at all,
If any calm, a calm despair:

Calm on the seas, and silver sleep,
    And waves that sway themselves in rest,
    And dead calm in that noble breast
20  Which heaves but with the heaving deep.

# XII

Lo, as a dove when up she springs
    To bear thro' Heaven a tale of woe,
    Some dolorous message knit below
The wild pulsation of her wings;[7]

5  Like her I go; I cannot stay;
    I leave this mortal ark behind,
    A weight of nerves without a mind,
And leave the cliffs, and haste away

O'er ocean-mirrors rounded large,
10    And reach the glow of southern skies,
    And see the sails at distance rise,
And linger weeping on the marge,

And saying; 'Comes he thus, my friend?
    Is this the end of all my care?'

---

5. The name for the open, rolling countryside of Tennyson's native Lincolnshire.
6. Spiderwebs. "Furze": a thick shrublike plant.
7. The reference is to a carrier pigeon, impatient to deliver a "message" (line 3). But there is also an allusion to the dove that Noah sends forth from the ark in Genesis 8; like the dove, Tennyson's spirit flies forth from his body ("this mortal ark," line 6) but can find no rest and eventually returns.

15      And circle moaning in the air:
        'Is this the end? Is this the end?'

And forward dart again, and play
        About the prow, and back return
        To where the body sits, and learn
20      That I have been an hour away.


## XIII

Tears of the widower, when he sees
        A late-lost form that sleep reveals,
        And moves his doubtful arms, and feels
Her place is empty, fall like these;

5      Which weep a loss for ever new,
        A void where heart on heart reposed;
        And, where warm hands have prest and closed,
Silence, till I be silent too.

Which weep the comrade of my choice,
10      An awful thought, a life removed,
        The human-hearted man I loved,
A Spirit, not a breathing voice.

Come Time, and teach me, many years,[8]
        I do not suffer in a dream;
15      For now so strange do these things seem,
Mine eyes have leisure for their tears;

My fancies time to rise on wing,
        And glance about the approaching sails,
        As tho' they brought but merchants' bales,
20      And not the burthen that they bring.


## XIV

If one should bring me this report,
        That thou hadst touch'd the land to-day,
        And I went down unto the quay,
And found thee lying in the port;

8. "Time" and "many years" are both being directly addressed.

5    And standing, muffled round with woe,
        Should see thy passengers in rank
        Come stepping lightly down the plank,
     And beckoning unto those they know;

     And if along with these should come
10      The man I held as half-divine;
        Should strike a sudden hand in mine,
     And ask a thousand things of home;

     And I should tell him all my pain,
        And how my life had droop'd of late,
15      And he should sorrow o'er my state
     And marvel what possess'd my brain;

     And I perceived no touch of change,
        No hint of death in all his frame,
        But found him all in all the same,
20   I should not feel it to be strange.


# XV

     To-night the winds begin to rise
        And roar from yonder dropping day:[9]
        The last red leaf is whirl'd away,
     The rooks are blown about the skies;

5    The forest crack'd, the waters curl'd,
        The cattle huddled on the lea;
        And wildly dash'd on tower and tree
     The sunbeam strikes along the world:

     And but for fancies, which aver
10      That all thy motions gently pass
        Athwart a plane of molten glass,
     I scarce could brook the strain and stir

     That makes the barren branches loud;
        And but for fear it is not so,
15      The wild unrest that lives in woe
     Would dote and pore on yonder cloud[1]

---

9. I.e., from the setting sun in the west.
1. If I were not able to picture the ship sailing in calm weather, on a sea as smooth as
   glass, my nerves would not be able to bear the storm I am witnessing (lines 9–13). On
   the other hand (lines 14–16), if I were not still so worried about the ship's progress, my

That rises upward always higher,
   And onward drags a labouring breast,
   And topples round the dreary west,
20  A looming bastion fringed with fire.

# XVI[2]

What words are these have fall'n from me?
   Can calm despair and wild unrest
   Be tenants of a single breast,
Or sorrow such a changeling be?

5  Or doth she only seem to take
   The touch of change in calm or storm;
   But knows no more of transient form
In her deep self, than some dead lake

That holds the shadow of a lark
10   Hung in the shadow of a heaven?
   Or has the shock, so harshly given,
Confused me like the unhappy bark

That strikes by night a craggy shelf,[3]
   And staggers blindly ere she sink?
15   And stunn'd me from my power to think
And all my knowledge of myself;

And made me that delirious man
   Whose fancy fuses old and new,
   And flashes into false and true,
20  And mingles all without a plan?

# XVII

Thou comest, much wept for: such a breeze
   Compell'd thy canvas, and my prayer
   Was as the whisper of an air
To breathe thee over lonely seas.

---

grieving spirit would take pleasure in the sublime appearance of the storm cloud (described
in the final stanza).

2. Tennyson's son wrote that in this section the speaker "questions himself about these
alternations of 'calm despair' and 'wild unrest' [in earlier sections]. Do these changes
only pass over the surface of the mind while in the depth still abides his unchanging
sorrow? or has his reason been stunned by his grief?"

3. Like a boat ("bark") that strikes a reef ("craggy shelf").

5    For I in spirit saw thee move
       Thro' circles of the bounding sky,
       Week after week: the days go by:
    Come quick, thou bringest all I love.

    Henceforth, wherever thou may'st roam,
10      My blessing, like a line of light,
       Is on the waters day and night,
    And like a beacon guards thee home.

    So may whatever tempest mars
       Mid-ocean, spare thee, sacred bark;
15      And balmy drops in summer dark
    Slide from the bosom of the stars.

    So kind an office hath been done,
       Such precious relics brought by thee;
       The dust of him I shall not see
20    Till all my widow'd race be run.[4]

# XVIII

    'Tis well; 'tis something; we may stand
       Where he in English earth is laid,[5]
       And from his ashes may be made
    The violet of his native land.[6]

5    'Tis little; but it looks in truth
       As if the quiet bones were blest
       Among familiar names to rest
    And in the places of his youth.

    Come then, pure hands, and bear the head
10      That sleeps or wears the mask of sleep,
       And come, whatever loves to weep,
    And hear the ritual of the dead.

    Ah yet, ev'n yet, if this might be,
       I, falling on his faithful heart,

---

4. Compare IX.18.
5. Hallam was buried in St. Andrew's Church at Clevedon on January 3, 1834. Tennyson did not actually visit Clevedon until many years later.
6. In his note Tennyson cites the comparable lines spoken by Laertes at the grave of his sister Ophelia in Shakespeare's *Hamlet* (5.1.238–240): "Lay her in the earth, / And from her fair and unpolluted flesh / May violets spring."

15      Would breathing thro' his lips impart
        The life that almost dies in me;

        That dies not, but endures with pain,
            And slowly forms the firmer mind,
            Treasuring the look it cannot find,
20      The words that are not heard again.


## XIX

        The Danube to the Severn gave[7]
            The darken'd heart that beat no more;
            They laid him by the pleasant shore,
        And in the hearing of the wave.

5       There twice a day the Severn fills;
            The salt sea-water passes by,
            And hushes half the babbling Wye,
        And makes a silence in the hills.[8]

        The Wye is hush'd nor moved along,
10          And hush'd my deepest grief of all,
            When fill'd with tears that cannot fall,
        I brim with sorrow drowning song.

        The tide flows down, the wave again
            Is vocal in its wooded walls;
15          My deeper anguish also falls,
        And I can speak a little then.


## XX

        The lesser griefs that may be said,
            That breathe a thousand tender vows,
            Are but as servants in a house
        Where lies the master newly dead;

5       Who speak their feeling as it is,
            And weep the fulness from the mind:

---

7. Vienna, where Hallam died, is on the Danube River, and Clevedon, where he was buried, is on the Severn.
8. The Wye River feeds into the Severn. Twice a day, at high tide, "the rapids of the Wye are stilled by the incoming sea" [T.].

'It will be hard,' they say, 'to find
Another service such as this.'

My lighter moods are like to these,
10      That out of words a comfort win;
        But there are other griefs within,
And tears that at their fountain freeze;

For by the hearth the children sit
        Cold in that atmosphere of Death,
15      And scarce endure to draw the breath,
Or like to noiseless phantoms flit:

But open converse is there none,
        So much the vital spirits sink
        To see the vacant chair, and think,
20      'How good! how kind! and he is gone.'

# XXI

I sing to him that rests below,
        And, since the grasses round me wave,
        I take the grasses of the grave,
And make them pipes whereon to blow.[9]

5      The traveller hears me now and then,
        And sometimes harshly will he speak:
        'This fellow would make weakness weak,
And melt the waxen hearts of men.'[1]

Another answers, 'Let him be,
10      He loves to make parade of pain
        That with his piping he may gain
The praise that comes to constancy.'

A third is wroth: 'Is this an hour
        For private sorrow's barren song,
15      When more and more the people throng
The chairs and thrones of civil power?'[2]

---

9. Here Tennyson imitates classical pastoral elegy, in which the speaker is imagined to be a shepherd or rustic. Where other major English elegies, such as Milton's "Lycidas," adhere to pastoral conventions throughout, Tennyson uses them sparingly.

1. In stanzas 2–5 the poet considers the charges that may be brought against him and his poem: excessive sentimentality (lines 7–8); love of praise (lines 9–12); and selfish, self-imposed isolation from the stirring events of his time (lines 13–20).

2. Perhaps a reference to Chartism, a populist political movement of the 1830s and 1840s.

'A time to sicken and to swoon,
　　When Science reaches forth her arms
　　To feel from world to world, and charms
20　Her secret from the latest moon?'[3]

Behold, ye speak an idle thing:
　　Ye never knew the sacred dust:
　　I do but sing because I must,
And pipe but as the linnets[4] sing:

25　And one is glad; her note is gay,
　　For now her little ones have ranged;
　　And one is sad; her note is changed,
Because her brood is stol'n away.

# XXII

The path by which we twain did go,
　　Which led by tracts that pleased us well,
　　Thro' four sweet years arose and fell,
From flower to flower, from snow to snow:

5　And we with singing cheer'd the way,
　　And, crown'd with all the season lent,
　　From April on to April went,
And glad at heart from May to May:

But where the path we walk'd began
10　To slant the fifth autumnal slope,[5]
　　As we descended following Hope,
There sat the Shadow fear'd of man;

Who broke our fair companionship,
　　And spread his mantle dark and cold,
15　And wrapt thee formless in the fold,
And dull'd the murmur on thy lip,

And bore thee where I could not see
　　Nor follow, tho' I walk in haste,
　　And think, that somewhere in the waste
20　The Shadow sits and waits for me.

3. Referring to recent astronomical discoveries, in which Tennyson was keenly interested.
4. A linnet is a songbird.
5. Tennyson met Hallam at Cambridge in the spring of 1829; Hallam died in September 1833, at the beginning of the fifth autumn of their friendship.

# XXIII

Now, sometimes in my sorrow shut,
    Or breaking into song by fits;
    Alone, alone, to where he sits,
The Shadow cloak'd from head to foot,

5   Who keeps the keys of all the creeds,[6]
    I wander, often falling lame,
    And looking back to whence I came,
Or on to where the pathway leads;

And crying, How changed from where it ran
10      Thro' lands where not a leaf was dumb;
    But all the lavish hills would hum
The murmur of a happy Pan.[7]

When each by turns was guide to each,
    And Fancy light from Fancy caught,
15      And Thought leapt out to wed with Thought
Ere Thought could wed itself with Speech;

And all we met was fair and good,
    And all was good that Time could bring,
    And all the secret of the Spring
20  Moved in the chambers of the blood;

And many an old philosophy
    On Argive heights divinely sang,
    And round us all the thicket rang
To many a flute of Arcady.[8]

# XXIV

And was the day of my delight
    As pure and perfect as I say?

6. This description fits Death ("The Shadow") since "After death we shall learn the truth of all beliefs" [T.].
7. The Greek god of nature, the patron of shepherds (and hence of pastoral poetry), and the inventor of the panpipes (see XXI.4).
8. I.e., Arcadia, the region of Greece that traditionally provides the setting for pastoral poetry. "Argive": Greek. The stanza suggests that Tennyson and Hallam read Greek literature together and also that their own lives echoed the golden age of Greece.

The very source and fount of Day
Is dash'd with wandering isles of night.[9]

5   If all was good and fair we met,
        This earth had been the Paradise
        It never look'd to human eyes
Since our first Sun arose and set.[1]

And is it that the haze of grief
10      Makes former gladness loom so great?
        The lowness of the present state,
That sets the past in this relief?

Or that the past will always win
        A glory from its being far;
15      And orb into the perfect star
We saw not, when we moved therein?

# XXV

I know that this was Life,—the track
        Whereon with equal feet we fared;
        And then, as now, the day prepared
The daily burden for the back.

5   But this it was that made me move
        As light as carrier-birds in air;
        I loved the weight I had to bear,
Because it needed help of Love:

Nor could I weary, heart or limb,
10      When mighty Love would cleave in twain
        The lading of a single pain,
And part it, giving half to him.

# XXVI

Still onward winds the dreary way;
        I with it; for I long to prove

9. I.e., the sun itself is flecked with sunspots.
1. In these stanzas the speaker doubts the recollections of the previous section, since
   such perfection has not existed on earth since humans were created.

No lapse of moons can canker Love,[2]
Whatever fickle tongues may say.

5    And if that eye which watches guilt
        And goodness, and hath power to see
        Within the green the moulder'd tree,
    And towers fall'n as soon as built—

    Oh, if indeed that eye foresee
10       Or see (in Him is no before)
        In more of life true life no more
    And Love the indifference to be,[3]

    Then might I find, ere yet the morn
        Breaks hither over Indian seas,
15       That Shadow waiting with the keys,
    To shroud me from my proper scorn.[4]


## XXVII


    I envy not in any moods
        The captive void of noble rage,
        The linnet born within the cage,
    That never knew the summer woods:

5    I envy not the beast that takes
        His license in the field of time;[5]
        Unfetter'd by the sense of crime,
    To whom a conscience never wakes;

    Nor, what may count itself as blest,
10       The heart that never plighted troth
        But stagnates in the weeds of sloth;
    Nor any want-begotten rest.[6]

    I hold it true, what'er befall;
        I feel it, when I sorrow most;
15       'Tis better to have loved and lost
    Than never to have loved at all.[7]

---

2. I.e., the passage of time cannot destroy love.
3. I.e., if the love I now feel is destined to turn into indifference.
4. My proper scorn: "scorn of myself" [T.], but also with the implication "appropriate."
5. I.e., a man who lives (like a beast) without self-restraint.
6. Rest that springs only from lethargy or dullness.
7. These lines (perhaps the best known in the poem) are repeated in LXXXV.2–4; compare also I.11–16.

## XXVIII[8]

The time draws near the birth of Christ:
    The moon is hid; the night is still;
    The Christmas bells from hill to hill
Answer each other in the mist.

5    Four voices of four hamlets round,
    From far and near, on mead and moor,
    Swell out and fail, as if a door
Were shut between me and the sound:

Each voice four changes on the wind,[9]
10    That now dilate, and now decrease,
    Peace and goodwill, goodwill and peace,
Peace and goodwill, to all mankind.

This year I slept and woke with pain,
    I almost wish'd no more to wake,
15    And that my hold on life would break
Before I heard those bells again:

But they my troubled spirit rule,
    For they controll'd me when a boy;
    They bring me sorrow touch'd with joy,
20    The merry merry bells of Yule.

## XXIX

With such compelling cause to grieve
    As daily vexes household peace,
    And chains regret to his decease,
How dare we keep our Christmas-eve;

5    Which brings no more a welcome guest
    To enrich the threshold of the night
    With shower'd largess of delight
In dance and song and game and jest?

---

8. Sections XXVIII–XXX describe the first Christmas after Hallam's death (1833). This is the first of three Christmases (the others occurring at LXXVIII and CV) that according to Tennyson mark the major divisions in the poem.
9. Sets of bells are pealed in varying sequences, or changes.

Yet go, and while the holly boughs
10     Entwine the cold baptismal font,
        Make one wreath more for Use and Wont,
That guard the portals of the house,

Old sisters of a day gone by,
        Gray nurses, loving nothing new;[1]
15     Why should they miss their yearly due
Before their time? They too will die.

# XXX

With trembling fingers did we weave
        The holly round the Christmas hearth;
        A rainy cloud possess'd the earth,
And sadly fell our Christmas-eve.

5   At our old pastimes in the hall
        We gambol'd, making vain pretence
        Of gladness, with an awful sense
Of one mute Shadow watching all.[2]

We paused: the winds were in the beech:
10     We heard them sweep the winter land;
        And in a circle hand-in-hand
Sat silent, looking each at each.

Then echo-like our voices rang;
        We sung, tho' every eye was dim,
15     A merry song we sang with him
Last year: impetuously we sang:

We ceased: a gentler feeling crept
        Upon us: surely rest is meet:
        'They rest,' we said, 'their sleep is sweet,'
20   And silence follow'd, and we wept.

Our voices took a higher range;
        Once more we sang: 'They do not die

1. Both "sisters" and "nurses" refer to "Use and Wont" (line 11), i.e., custom and tradition.
2. The "Shadow" could refer either to Death, as in sections XXII–XXIII, or to Hallam, who had spent the previous Christmas with the Tennysons. "Awful": literally, "full of awe."

Nor lose their mortal sympathy,
Nor change to us, although they change;

25 'Rapt from the fickle and the frail
    With gather'd power, yet the same,
    Pierces the keen seraphic flame
From orb to orb, from veil to veil.'[3]

Rise, happy morn, rise, holy morn,
30   Draw forth the cheerful day from night:
     O Father, touch the east, and light
The light that shone when Hope was born.


# XXXI[4]

When Lazarus left his charnel-cave,
    And home to Mary's house return'd,
    Was this demanded—if he yearn'd
To hear her weeping by his grave?

5 'Where wert thou, brother, those four days?'
    There lives no record of reply,
    Which telling what it is to die
Had surely added praise to praise.

From every house the neighbours met,
10   The streets were fill'd with joyful sound,
     A solemn gladness even crown'd
The purple brows of Olivet.[5]

Behold a man raised up by Christ!
    The rest remaineth unreveal'd;
15   He told it not; or something seal'd
The lips of that Evangelist.


3. The spirit of the deceased (the "seraphic flame"), removed from this frail world, pene-
trates into ever higher reaches of heaven.
4. Sections XXXI and XXXII refer to the Gospel of John 11–12; John is the "Evangelist" of
line 16. Lazarus, the brother of Mary (not to be confused with the Virgin Mary) and
Martha, all of them followers of Jesus, dies and is buried. After four days Jesus visits
the grave (the "charnel-cave") and raises Lazarus from death. Tennyson is intrigued by
this episode because it implies a state after death but purposely does not describe it.
5. The Mount of Olives, near Jerusalem.

# XXXII[6]

Her eyes are homes of silent prayer,
    Nor other thought her mind admits
    But, he was dead, and there he sits,
And he that brought him back is there.

5   Then one deep love doth supersede
    All other, when her ardent gaze
    Roves from the living brother's face,
And rests upon the Life indeed.

All subtle thought, all curious fears,
10      Borne down by gladness so complete,
    She bows, she bathes the Saviour's feet
With costly spikenard and with tears.

Thrice blest whose lives are faithful prayers,
    Whose loves in higher love endure;
15      What souls possess themselves so pure,
Or is there blessedness like theirs?

# XXXIII[7]

O thou that after toil and storm
    Mayst seem to have reach'd a purer air,
    Whose faith has centre everywhere,
Nor cares to fix itself to form,

5   Leave thou thy sister when she prays,
    Her early Heaven, her happy views;
    Nor thou with shadow'd hint confuse
A life that leads melodious days.

Her faith thro' form is pure as thine,
10      Her hands are quicker unto good:

6. Tennyson pictures the scene in Mary's house after her brother, Lazarus, has returned to life. Stanza 3 refers to John 12:3 ("Then took Mary a pound of ointment of spike-nard, very costly, and anointed the feet of Jesus, and wiped his feet with her hair"). Spikenard is an aromatic oil.
7. With the Lazarus story still in mind, Tennyson here imagines a brother and sister of his own day. The brother ("thou") has been through the "toil and storm" of doubt and developed his own faith, unattached to "form," i.e., any particular religious denomina-tion. The sister retains the more formal doctrines she learned in childhood ("her early Heaven"). The speaker warns the brother that such faith is just as "pure" and true as his own and should not be needlessly disturbed.

Oh, sacred be the flesh and blood
To which she links a truth divine!

See thou, that countest reason ripe
     In holding by the law within,[8]
15      Thou fail not in a world of sin,
And ev'n for want of such a type.


# XXXIV

My own dim life should teach me this,
     That life shall live for evermore,
     Else earth is darkness at the core,
And dust and ashes all that is;

5   This round of green, this orb of flame,
     Fantastic beauty; such as lurks
     In some wild Poet, when he works
Without a conscience or an aim.[9]

What then were God to such as I?
10      'Twere hardly worth my while to choose
     Of things all mortal, or to use
A little patience ere I die;

'Twere best at once to sink to peace,
     Like birds the charming serpent draws,[1]
15      To drop head-foremost in the jaws
Of vacant darkness and to cease.


# XXXV

Yet if some voice that man could trust
     Should murmur from the narrow house,[2]
     'The cheeks drop in; the body bows;
Man dies: nor is there hope in dust:'

5   Might I not say? 'Yet even here,
     But for one hour, O Love, I strive

8. I.e., who consider it more rational to develop one's own understanding of faith.
9. If there is no life after death (stanza 1), then even the beauty of the earth and the sun
   are "fantastic," i.e., meaningless, like an artistic accident.
1. Certain snakes are said to be able to charm birds to fall out of trees.
2. I.e., the grave.

To keep so sweet a thing alive:'
But I should turn mine ears and hear

The moanings of the homeless sea,
10  The sound of streams that swift or slow
  Draw down Aeonian hills, and sow
The dust of continents to be;[3]

And Love would answer with a sigh,
  'The sound of that forgetful shore[4]
15  Will change my sweetness more and more,
Half-dead to know that I shall die.'

O me, what profits it to put
  An idle case? If Death were seen
  At first as Death, Love had not been,
20 Or been in narrowest working shut,

Mere fellowship of sluggish moods,
  Or in his coarsest Satyr-shape
  Had bruised the herb and crush'd the grape,
And bask'd and batten'd in the woods.[5]

# XXXVI

Tho' truths in manhood darkly join,
  Deep-seated in our mystic frame,
  We yield all blessing to the name
Of Him that made them current coin;[6]

5 For Wisdom dealt with mortal powers,
  Where truth in closest words shall fail,
  When truth embodied in a tale
Shall enter in at lowly doors.[7]

---

3. "Aeonian": everlasting. "The vastness of the Ages to come may seem to militate against . . .
Love" [T.]. Compare section CXXIII, which also considers how the latest theories of
geological change undermine faith.
4. The shore of the river Lethe, the boundary of the underworld, the waters of which
cause the dead to forget their former lives.
5. I.e., if we were always conscious of death, no one would ever have bothered to love
beyond mere animal love. "Batten'd": fed.
6. Tennyson audaciously suggests that the truths of Christianity are intuitively though
"darkly" understood by everyone (lines 1–2), but that Christ deserves blessing for hav-
ing made them clearly, generally known (lines 3–4).
7. "For divine Wisdom had to deal with the limited powers of humanity, to which truth
logically argued out would be ineffectual, whereas truth coming in the story of the
Gospel can influence the poorest" [T.].

And so the Word had breath, and wrought
10      With human hands the creed of creeds
        In loveliness of perfect deeds,
More strong than all poetic thought;

Which he may read that binds the sheaf,
        Or builds the house, or digs the grave,
15      And those wild eyes that watch the wave
In roarings round the coral reef.[8]

# XXXVII

Urania speaks with darken'd brow:[9]
        'Thou pratest here where thou art least;
        This faith has many a purer priest,
And many an abler voice than thou.

5       'Go down beside thy native rill,
        On thy Parnassus set thy feet,
        And hear thy laurel whisper sweet
About the ledges of the hill.'[1]

And my Melpomene[2] replies,
10      A touch of shame upon her cheek:
        'I am not worthy ev'n to speak
Of thy prevailing mysteries;

'For I am but an earthly Muse,
        And owning but a little art
15      To lull with song an aching heart,
And render human love his dues;

'But brooding on the dear one dead,
        And all he said of things divine,[3]
        (And dear to me as sacred wine
20      To dying lips is all he said),

---

8. Christ, as the word of God made flesh (line 9), is accessible to everyone. Lines 15–16 refer to "Pacific Islanders" [T.].
9. Urania was the classical muse of astronomy, but in *Paradise Lost* Milton makes her the muse of heavenly or religious poetry. Here she berates the poet for dealing with matters of religion in which he is not skilled.
1. In other words, keep to your own type of poetry. "Parnassus": Greek mountain sacred to the Muses. "Laurel": traditional symbol of the classical poet.
2. Muse of tragic or elegiac poetry.
3. Tennyson greatly admired Hallam's writings about theology.

'I murmur'd, as I came along,
    Of comfort clasp'd in truth reveal'd:
    And loiter'd in the master's field,[4]
And darken'd sanctities with song.'


# XXXVIII

With weary steps I loiter on,
    Tho' always under alter'd skies
    The purple from the distance dies,
My prospect and horizon gone.


5   No joy the blowing[5] season gives,
    The herald melodies of spring,
    But in the songs I love to sing
A doubtful gleam of solace lives.


If any care for what is here
10    Survive in spirits render'd free,
    Then are these songs I sing of thee
Not all ungrateful to thine ear.


# XXXIX[6]

Old warder of these buried bones,
    And answering now my random stroke
    With fruitful cloud and living smoke,[7]
Dark yew, that graspest at the stones


5   And dippest toward the dreamless head,
    To thee too comes the golden hour
    When flower is feeling after flower;
But Sorrow—fixt upon the dead,


And darkening the dark graves of men,—
10    What whisper'd from her lying lips?
    Thy gloom is kindled at the tips,
And passes into gloom again.


4. The master is God; hence "the province of Christianity" [T.].
5. "Blossoming" [T.].
6. Written in 1868 and added to In Memoriam in 1870, this poem closely echoes sections II and III.
7. "The yew, when flowering, in a wind or if struck sends up its pollen like smoke" [T.].

# XL

Could we forget the widow'd hour
    And look on Spirits breathed away,
    As on a maiden in the day
When first she wears her orange-flower![8]

5    When crown'd with blessing she doth rise
    To take her latest leave of home,
    And hopes and light regrets that come
Make April of her tender eyes;

And doubtful joys the father move,
10    And tears are on the mother's face,
    As parting with a long embrace
She enters other realms of love;

Her office there to rear, to teach,
    Becoming as is meet and fit
15    A link among the days, to knit
The generations each with each;

And, doubtless, unto thee[9] is given
    A life that bears immortal fruit
    In those great offices that suit
20    The full-grown energies of heaven.

Ay me, the difference I discern!
    How often shall her old fireside
    Be cheer'd with tidings of the bride,
How often she herself return,

25    And tell them all they would have told,[1]
    And bring her babe, and make her boast,
    Till even those that miss'd her most
Shall count new things as dear as old:

But thou and I have shaken hands,
30    Till growing winters lay me low;
    My paths are in the fields I know.
And thine in undiscover'd lands.

8. An orange blossom was worn by a bride on her wedding day.
9. Hallam.
1. I.e., all they wish to be told.

## XLI

Thy spirit ere our fatal loss
   Did ever rise from high to higher;
   As mounts the heavenward altar-fire,
As flies the lighter thro' the gross.

5   But thou art turn'd to something strange,
   And I have lost the links that bound
   Thy changes; here upon the ground,
No more partaker of thy change.

Deep folly! yet that this could be—
10   That I could wing my will with might
   To leap the grades of life and light,
And flash at once, my friend, to thee.

For tho' my nature rarely yields
   To that vague fear implied in death;
15   Nor shudders at the gulfs beneath,
The howlings from forgotten fields;[2]

Yet oft when sundown skirts the moor
   An inner trouble I behold,
   A spectral doubt which makes me cold,
20   That I shall be thy mate no more,

Tho' following with an upward mind
   The wonders that have come to thee,
   Thro' all the secular to-be,[3]
But evermore a life behind.

## XLII

I vex my heart with fancies dim:
   He still outstript me in the race;
   It was but unity of place
That made me dream I rank'd with him.

5   And so may Place retain us still,
   And he the much-beloved again,

2. Refers to "the eternal miseries of [Dante's] Inferno" [T.].
3. The "aeons of the future" [T.].

A lord of large experience, train
To riper growth the mind and will:

And what delights can equal those
10      That stir the spirit's inner deeps,
          When one that loves but knows not, reaps
A truth from one that loves and knows?

## XLIII

If Sleep and Death be truly one,
          And every spirit's folded bloom
          Thro' all its intervital gloom
In some long trance should slumber on;[4]

5     Unconscious of the sliding hour,
          Bare of the body, might it last,
          And silent traces of the past
Be all the colour of the flower:[5]

So then were nothing lost to man;
10      So that still garden of the souls
          In many a figured leaf enrolls
The total world since life began;

And love will last as pure and whole
          As when he loved me here in Time,
15      And at the spiritual prime
Rewaken with the dawning soul.[6]

## XLIV

How fares it with the happy dead?
          For here the man is more and more;

---

4. "Intervital gloom": "the passage between this life and the next" [T.]. Tennyson specu-
   lates that the souls of the deceased, rather than going straight to heaven, enter a state
   like sleep, until all souls awaken simultaneously at the end of time.
5. "If . . . the spirit between this life and the next should be folded like a flower in a night
   slumber, then the remembrance of the past might remain, as the smell and colour do in
   the sleeping flower" [T.].
6. "Spiritual prime": dawn of the afterlife. "In that case the memory of our love would last
   as true, and would live pure and whole within the spirit of my friend until it was
   unfolded at the breaking of the morn" [T.].

But he forgets the days before
God shut the doorways of his head.[7]

5    The days have vanish'd, tone and tint,
      And yet perhaps the hoarding sense
      Gives out at times (he knows not whence)
A little flash, a mystic hint;

And in the long harmonious years
10      (If Death so taste Lethean springs),[8]
      May some dim touch of earthly things
Surprise thee ranging with thy peers.

If such a dreamy touch should fall,
      O turn thee round, resolve the doubt;
15      My guardian angel will speak out
In that high place, and tell thee all.

## XLV

The baby new to earth and sky,
      What time his tender palm is prest
      Against the circle of the breast,
Has never thought that 'this is I:'

5    But as he grows he gathers much,
      And learns the use of 'I,' and 'me,'
      And finds 'I am not what I see,
And other than the things I touch.'

So rounds he to a separate mind
10      From whence clear memory may begin,
      As thro' the frame that binds him in
His isolation grows defined.

This use may lie in blood and breath,
      Which else were fruitless of their due,
15      Had man to learn himself anew
Beyond the second birth of Death.[9]

---

7. "Closing of the skull after babyhood. The dead after this life may have no remembrance of life, like the living babe who forgets the time before the sutures of the skull are closed, yet . . . though the remembrance of his earliest days are vanished, . . . there comes a dreamy vision of what has been; it may be so with the dead" [T.].
8. I.e., if the dead do indeed forget; see section XXXV, n. 4.
9. The final stanza suggests that "the purpose of the life here [on earth] may be to realise personal consciousness" [T.], as described in the first three stanzas. In that case, the dead

# XLVI

We ranging down this lower track,
  The path we came by, thorn and flower,
  Is shadow'd by the growing hour,
Lest life should fail in looking back.

5    So be it: there no shade can last
  In that deep dawn behind the tomb,
  But clear from marge to marge shall bloom
The eternal landscape of the past;

A lifelong tract of time reveal'd;
10    The fruitful hours of still increase;
  Days order'd in a wealthy peace,
And those five years its richest field.[1]

O Love, thy province were not large,
  A bounded field, nor stretching far;[2]
15    Look also, Love, a brooding star,
A rosy warmth from marge to marge.

# XLVII[3]

That each, who seems a separate whole,
  Should move his rounds, and fusing all
  The skirts of self again, should fall
Remerging in the general Soul,

5    Is faith as vague as all unsweet:
  Eternal form shall still divide
  The eternal soul from all beside;
And I shall know him when we meet:

---

must surely retain some memory of their earthly life; otherwise the individual would have
to "learn himself anew" after death, and the whole of this life would have been "fruitless."

1. On earth the past is not clearly remembered (stanza 1), but in heaven it will be (stanza
  2), and "those five years" of Tennyson's friendship with Hallam will then be clearly seen
  as the "richest field" in the landscape of his life.
2. I.e., but if Love shone only over those five years, its "province" would be restricted;
  therefore, "Look also."
3. Tennyson resists the notion that the soul loses its personal identity in heaven. "Indi-
  viduality lasts after death, and we are not utterly absorbed in the Godhead. If we are to
  be finally merged in the Universal Soul, Love asks [in stanza 4] to have at least one
  more parting before we lose ourselves" [T.].

And we shall sit at endless feast,
10      Enjoying each the other's good:
        What vaster dream can hit the mood
Of Love on earth? He seeks at least

Upon the last and sharpest height,
        Before the spirits fade away,
15      Some landing-place, to clasp and say,
'Farewell! We lose ourselves in light.'

## XLVIII

If these brief lays, of Sorrow born,
        Were taken to be such as closed
        Grave doubts and answers here proposed,
Then these were such as men might scorn:

5   Her care is not to part[4] and prove;
        She takes, when harsher moods remit,
        What slender shade of doubt may flit,
And makes it vassal unto love:

And hence, indeed, she sports with words,
10      But better serves a wholesome law,
        And holds it sin and shame to draw
The deepest measure from the chords:

Nor dare she trust a larger lay,
        But rather loosens from the lip
15      Short swallow-flights of song, that dip
Their wings in tears, and skim away.

## XLIX

From art, from nature, from the schools[5]
        Let random influences glance,
        Like light in many a shiver'd lance
That breaks about the dappled pools:

4. To analyze. "Her" refers to Sorrow.
5. I.e., schools of thought.

5   The lightest wave of thought shall lisp,
        The fancy's tenderest eddy wreathe,
        The slightest air of song shall breathe
    To make the sullen surface crisp.[6]

    And look thy look, and go thy way[7]
10      But blame not thou the winds that make
        The seeming-wanton ripple break,
    The tender-pencil'd shadow play.

    Beneath all fancied hopes and fears
        Ay me, the sorrow deepens down,
15      Whose muffled motions blindly drown
    The bases of my life in tears.


                    L


    Be near me when my light is low,
        When the blood creeps, and the nerves prick
        And tingle; and the heart is sick,
    And all the wheels of Being slow.

5   Be near me when the sensuous frame
        Is rack'd with pangs that conquer trust;
        And Time, a maniac scattering dust,
    And Life, a Fury[8] slinging flame.

    Be near me when my faith is dry,
10      And men the flies of latter spring
        That lay their eggs, and sting and sing
    And weave their petty cells and die.

    Be near me when I fade away,
        To point the term[9] of human strife,
15      And on the low dark verge of life
    The twilight of eternal day.


6. Ripple. As in the previous section, the speaker says that his poetry will respond to all
   sorts of hopes and doubts, but it does not pretend to answer them or to resolve grief
   entirely (stanza 4).
7. Addressed to the reader, according to Tennyson.
8. In classical mythology, a type of vengeful goddess.
9. Show the end.

# LI

Do we indeed desire the dead
    Should still be near us at our side?
    Is there no baseness we would hide?
No inner vileness that we dread?

5    Shall he for whose applause I strove,
    I had such reverence for his blame,
    See with clear eye some hidden shame
And I be lessen'd in his love?

I wrong the grave with fears untrue:
10    Shall love be blamed for want of faith?
    There must be wisdom with great Death:
The dead shall look me thro' and thro'.

Be near us when we climb or fall:
    Ye watch, like God, the rolling hours
15    With larger other eyes than ours,
To make allowance for us all.

# LII

I cannot love thee as I ought,
    For love reflects the thing beloved;
    My words are only words, and moved
Upon the topmost froth of thought.[1]

5    'Yet blame not thou thy plaintive song,'
    The Spirit of true love replied;
    'Thou canst not move me from thy side,
Nor human frailty do me wrong.

'What keeps a spirit wholly true
10    To that ideal which he bears?
    What record? not the sinless years
That breathed beneath the Syrian blue:[2]

---

1. Tennyson explained this: "There is so much evil in me that I don't really reflect you and all my talk is only *words*."
2. I.e., not even the story of the life of Christ (the "record" of the "sinless years") is enough to keep frail humans from occasionally sinning. The "Spirit of true love" (line 6) therefore encourages the speaker not to "fret" about falling short of his ideal of Hallam.

'So fret not, like an idle girl,
   That life is dash'd with flecks of sin.
15     Abide: thy wealth is gather'd in,
When Time hath sunder'd shell from pearl.'

## LIII

How many a father have I seen,
   A sober man, among his boys,
   Whose youth was full of foolish noise,
Who wears his manhood hale and green:

5    And dare we to this fancy give,[3]
   That had the wild oat not been sown,
   That soil, left barren, scarce had grown
The grain by which a man may live?

Or, if we held the doctrine sound
10    For life outliving heats of youth,
   Yet who would preach it as a truth
To those that eddy round and round?[4]

Hold thou the good: define it well:
   For fear divine Philosophy
15    Should push beyond her mark, and be
Procuress to the Lords of Hell.

## LIV[5]

Oh yet we trust that somehow good
   Will be the final goal of ill,
   To pangs of nature, sins of will,
Defects of doubt, and taints of blood;

5    That nothing walks with aimless feet;
   That not one life shall be destroy'd,
   Or cast as rubbish to the void,
When God hath made the pile complete;

---

3. I.e., can we dare believe the following proposition?
4. Even if we believe that sowing wild oats sometimes proves beneficial for some, who would be so bold as to prescribe it to heedless young people?
5. Here Tennyson takes up the theme of the previous section, that good will arise from ill or from suffering. This then leads into the two following sections, in which he looks for confirmation of this doctrine in nature but does not find it.

That not a worm is cloven in vain;
10     That not a moth with vain desire
Is shrivell'd in a fruitless fire,
Or but subserves another's gain.

Behold, we know not anything;
I can but trust that good shall fall
15     At last—far off—at last, to all,
And every winter change to spring.

So runs my dream: but what am I?
An infant crying in the night:
An infant crying for the light:
20     And with no language but a cry.


## LV

The wish, that of the living whole
No life may fail beyond the grave,
Derives it not from what we have
The likest God within the soul?[6]

5     Are God and Nature then at strife,
That Nature lends such evil dreams?
So careful of the type she seems,
So careless of the single life;[7]

That I, considering everywhere
10     Her secret meaning in her deeds,
And finding that of fifty seeds
She often brings but one to bear,[8]

I falter where I firmly trod,
And falling with my weight of cares
15     Upon the great world's altar-stairs
That slope thro' darkness up to God,

6. "The divine in man" [T.].
7. Nature cares only for the continuation of the species ("the type"), not for individual lives. Hence Nature seems to be "at strife" with a God for whom each life is so precious that it survives forever.
8. "'Fifty' should be 'myriad'" [T.]. Tennyson was familiar with contemporary scientific treatises, which noted the ruthlessness of the struggle for survival in nature well before Darwin put forward his theory of natural selection in 1859. See, for instance, the selection from Charles Lyell, p. 131 below.

I stretch lame hands of faith, and grope,
    And gather dust and chaff, and call
    To what I feel is Lord of all,
20  And faintly trust the larger hope.


# LVI

'So careful of the type?' but no.
    From scarped cliff and quarried stone
    She cries, 'A thousand types are gone:
I care for nothing, all shall go.[9]

5  'Thou makest thine appeal to me:
    I bring to life, I bring to death:
    The spirit does but mean the breath.[1]
I know no more.' And he, shall he,

Man, her last work, who seem'd so fair,
10    Such splendid purpose in his eyes,
    Who roll'd the psalm to wintry skies,
Who built him fanes[2] of fruitless prayer,

Who trusted God was love indeed
    And love Creation's final law—
15    Tho' Nature, red in tooth and claw
With ravine,[3] shriek'd against his creed—

Who loved, who suffer'd countless ills,
    Who battled for the True, the Just,
    Be blown about the desert dust,
20  Or seal'd within the iron hills?

No more? A monster then, a dream,
    A discord. Dragons of the prime,
    That tare each other in their slime,
Were mellow music match'd with him.[4]

---

9. From the evidence of fossils found in quarried stone and cliffs cut away so that rock strata are exposed ("scarped"), we know that not only individuals but entire species have become extinct.
1. In Latin *spiritus* means "breath."
2. Temples.
3. More commonly "ravin"; predatoriness or rapacity.
4. If the true order of Nature is destruction and not love, then dinosaurs (the primordial "Dragons" who "tare [i.e., tore] each other in their slime") were more in harmony with Nature than self-deluded humankind.

25    O life as futile, then, as frail!
          O for thy voice to soothe and bless!
          What hope of answer, or redress?
      Behind the veil, behind the veil.


## LVII[5]

      Peace; come away: the song of woe
          Is after all an earthly song:
          Peace; come away: we do him wrong
      To sing so wildly: let us go.

5     Come; let us go: your cheeks are pale;
          But half my life I leave behind:
          Methinks my friend is richly shrined;
      But I shall pass; my work will fail.

      Yet in these ears, till hearing dies,
10        One set slow bell will seem to toll
          The passing of the sweetest soul
      That ever look'd with human eyes.

      I hear it now, and o'er and o'er,
          Eternal greetings to the dead;
15        And 'Ave, Ave, Ave,' said,
      'Adieu, adieu' for evermore.[6]


## LVIII[7]

      In those sad words I took farewell:
          Like echoes in sepulchral halls,
          As drop by drop the water falls
      In vaults and catacombs, they fell;

5     And, falling, idly broke the peace
          Of hearts that beat from day to day,

---

5. These lines are addressed to an unspecified auditor, clearly a fellow mourner.
6. "Ave": hail! (Latin). Tennyson noted that these lines echo the elegy by the Roman poet Catullus for his brother (see p. 123 below), which concludes with the words "*ave atque vale*," "hail and farewell." According to Tennyson, Catullus's lament is particularly poignant because he did not believe in the afterlife; this allusion comes at a point in the poem when the speaker's own faith in eternal life is at its lowest.
7. Tennyson said of the previous section that although it sounds like a conclusion, it was "too sad for an ending." Here the speaker declares his intention to continue in a different vein. The "high Muse" (line 9) is again Urania, as in section XXXVII.

Half-conscious of their dying clay,
And those cold crypts where they shall cease.

The high Muse answer'd: 'Wherefore grieve
10    Thy brethren with a fruitless tear?
        Abide a little longer here,
And thou shalt take a nobler leave.'


## LIX[8]

O Sorrow, wilt thou live with me
    No casual mistress, but a wife,
    My bosom-friend and half of life;
As I confess it needs must be;

5    O Sorrow, wilt thou rule my blood,
        Be sometimes lovely like a bride,
        And put thy harsher moods aside,
If thou wilt have me wise and good.

My centred passion cannot move,
10        Nor will it lessen from to-day;
        But I'll have leave at times to play
As with the creature of my love;

And set thee forth, for thou art mine,
        With so much hope for years to come,
15        That, howsoe'er I know thee, some
Could hardly tell what name were thine.[9]


## LX[1]

He past; a soul of nobler tone:
    My spirit loved and loves him yet,
    Like some poor girl whose heart is set
On one whose rank exceeds her own.

---

8. This section was added in the fourth edition of *In Memoriam* (1851) as the "pendant," or pair, to section III, just as section XXXIX is paired with section II.
9. My love for Hallam will never waver (lines 9–10), but my sorrow, the result or "crea-ture" of that love (line 12), will take different forms, to the point that others may scarcely recognize it as sorrow at all.
1. Sections LX–LXV form one of the most tightly connected groups in the poem, being linked not only thematically but sometimes syntactically as well. The metaphor of this section is particularly poignant, since Tennyson's sister Emily was engaged to Hallam; their wedding was delayed because of the disparity in their social status.

5   He mixing with his proper sphere,
      She finds the baseness of her lot,
      Half jealous of she knows not what,
And envying all that meet him there.

     The little village looks forlorn;
10     She sighs amid her narrow days,
      Moving about the household ways,
In that dark house where she was born.

     The foolish neighbours come and go,
      And tease her till the day draws by:
15     At night she weeps, 'How vain am I!
How should he love a thing so low?'

# LXI

     If, in thy second state sublime,
      Thy ransom'd reason change replies
      With all the circle of the wise,
The perfect flower of human time;[2]

5   And if thou cast thine eyes below,
      How dimly character'd and slight,
      How dwarf'd a growth of cold and night,
How blanch'd with darkness must I grow!

     Yet turn thee to the doubtful shore,
10     Where thy first form was made a man;[3]
      I loved thee, Spirit, and love, nor can
The soul of Shakspeare love thee more.[4]

# LXII

     Tho' if an eye that's downward cast
      Could make thee somewhat blench or fail,[5]
      Then be my love an idle tale,
And fading legend of the past;

2. If you in heaven, with your now higher understanding ("ransom'd reason"), hold conversation with all the wise people who ever lived on earth. "Change": exchange.
3. I.e., this world, now almost indiscernible to you ("doubtful").
4. Shakespeare is specifically cited because he too addressed a series of poems (the Sonnets) to a beloved friend. Both this section and the next contain echoes of Sonnet 116; see p. 125 below.
5. Balk or falter.

5     And thou, as one that once declined,[6]
     When he was little more than boy,
     On some unworthy heart with joy,
But lives to wed an equal mind;

And breathes a novel world, the while
10     His other passion wholly dies,
     Or in the light of deeper eyes
Is matter for a flying smile.

## LXIII

Yet pity for a horse o'er-driven,
     And love in which my hound has part,
     Can hang no weight upon my heart
In its assumptions up to heaven;

5     And I am so much more than these,
     As thou, perchance, art more than I,
     And yet I spare them sympathy,
And I would set their pains at ease.

So mayst thou watch me where I weep,
10     As, unto vaster motions bound,
     The circuits of thine orbit round
A higher height, a deeper deep.

## LXIV

Dost thou look back on what hath been,
     As some divinely gifted man,
     Whose life in low estate began
And on a simple village green;

5     Who breaks his birth's invidious bar,
     And grasps the skirts of happy chance,
     And breasts the blows of circumstance,
And grapples with his evil star;[7]

Who makes by force his merit known
10     And lives to clutch the golden keys,[8]

6. I.e., stooped to love.
7. Bad fortune (of being born "in low estate").
8. Symbols of public office.

To mould a mighty state's decrees,
And shape the whisper of the throne;

And moving up from high to higher,
    Becomes on Fortune's crowning slope
15    The pillar of a people's hope,
The centre of a world's desire;

Yet feels, as in a pensive dream,
    When all his active powers are still,
    A distant dearness in the hill,
20    A secret sweetness in the stream,

The limit of his narrower fate,
    While yet beside its vocal springs
    He play'd at counsellors and kings,
With one that was his earliest mate;

25    Who ploughs with pain his native lea
    And reaps the labour of his hands,
    Or in the furrow musing stands;
'Does my old friend remember me?'

# LXV

Sweet soul, do with me as thou wilt;
    I lull a fancy trouble-tost
    With 'Love's too precious to be lost,
A little grain shall not be spilt.'[9]

5    And in that solace can I sing,
    Till out of painful phases wrought
    There flutters up a happy thought,
Self-balanced on a lightsome wing:

Since we deserved the name of friends,
10    And thine effect so lives in me,
    A part of mine may live in thee
And move thee on to noble ends.

---

9. The grain imagery looks back to LV.11–12 and forward to section LXXXI. The phrase in quotation marks is not found in this form in any known source, but compare Amos 9:9: "I will sift the house of Israel among all nations, like as corn is sifted in a sieve, yet shall not the least grain fall upon the earth."

# LXVI

You thought my heart too far diseased;[1]
    You wonder when my fancies play
    To find me gay among the gay,
Like one with any trifle pleased.

5    The shade by which my life was crost,
    Which makes a desert in the mind,
    Has made me kindly with my kind,
And like to him whose sight is lost;

Whose feet are guided thro' the land,
10    Whose jest among his friends is free,
    Who takes the children on his knee,
And winds their curls about his hand:

He plays with threads,[2] he beats his chair
    For pastime, dreaming of the sky;
15    His inner day can never die,
His night of loss is always there.

# LXVII

When on my bed the moonlight falls,
    I know that in thy place of rest
    By that broad water of the west,[3]
There comes a glory on the walls;

5    Thy marble bright in dark appears,
    As slowly steals a silver flame
    Along the letters of thy name,
And o'er the number of thy years.

The mystic glory swims away;
10    From off my bed the moonlight dies;
    And closing eaves of wearied eyes
I sleep till dusk is dipt in gray:

---

1. Addressed, like section LVII, to an unspecified auditor.
2. Makes cat's cradles to amuse children.
3. "The Severn" [T.].

And then I know the mist is drawn
    A lucid veil from coast to coast,
15     And in the dark church like a ghost
Thy tablet glimmers to the dawn.[4]

# LXVIII

When in the down I sink my head,
    Sleep, Death's twin-brother, times my breath;
    Sleep, Death's twin-brother, knows not Death,
Nor can I dream of thee as dead:

5   I walk as ere I walk'd forlorn,
    When all our path was fresh with dew,
    And all the bugle breezes blew
Reveillée[5] to the breaking morn.

But what is this? I turn about,
10   I find a trouble in thine eye,
    Which makes me sad I know not why,
Nor can my dream resolve the doubt:

But ere the lark hath left the lea
    I wake, and I discern the truth;
15   It is the trouble of my youth
That foolish sleep transfers to thee.

# LXIX

I dream'd there would be Spring no more,
    That Nature's ancient power was lost:
    The streets were black with smoke and frost,
They chatter'd trifles at the door:

5   I wander'd from the noisy town,
    I found a wood with thorny boughs:
    I took the thorns to bind my brows,
I wore them like a civic crown:

I met with scoffs, I met with scorns
10   From youth and babe and hoary hairs:

4. "I myself did not see Clevedon until years after the burial of A.H.H." [T.]; for this rea-
son, the earliest editions of *In Memoriam* mistake the position in the church of Hal-
lam's commemorative "tablet."
5. Bugle call played at dawn in military camps.

They call'd me in the public squares
The fool that wears a crown of thorns:[6]

They call'd me fool, they call'd me child:
    I found an angel of the night;
15    The voice was low, the look was bright;
He look'd upon my crown and smiled:

He reach'd the glory of a hand,
    That seem'd to touch it into leaf:
    The voice was not the voice of grief,
20  The words were hard to understand.

## LXX

I cannot see the features right,
    When on the gloom I strive to paint
    The face I know; the hues are faint
And mix with hollow masks of night;

5  Cloud-towers by ghostly masons wrought,
    A gulf that ever shuts and gapes,
    A hand that points, and palled[7] shapes
In shadowy thoroughfares of thought;

And crowds that stream from yawning doors,
10    And shoals of pucker'd faces drive;
    Dark bulks that tumble half alive,
And lazy lengths on boundless shores;

Till all at once beyond the will
    I hear a wizard[8] music roll,
15    And thro' a lattice on the soul
Looks thy fair face and makes it still.

## LXXI

Sleep, kinsman thou to death and trance
    And madness, thou hast forged at last

---

6. "To write poems about death and grief is 'to wear a crown of thorns,' which the people say ought to be laid aside" [T.]. Compare Jesus' crown of thorns (Matthew 27:29).
7. Shrouded.
8. Magic.

A night-long Present of the Past
In which we went thro' summer France.[9]

5      Hadst thou such credit with the soul?
    Then bring an opiate trebly strong,
    Drug down the blindfold sense of wrong
That so my pleasure may be whole;[1]

While now we talk as once we talk'd
10      Of men and minds, the dust of change,
    The days that grow to something strange,
In walking as of old we walk'd

Beside the river's wooded reach,
    The fortress, and the mountain ridge,
15      The cataract flashing from the bridge,
The breaker breaking on the beach.

## LXXII

Risest thou thus, dim dawn, again,[2]
    And howlest, issuing out of night,
    With blasts that blow the poplar white,[3]
And lash with storm the streaming pane?

5      Day, when my crown'd estate begun
    To pine in that reverse of doom,[4]
    Which sicken'd every living bloom,
And blurr'd the splendour of the sun;

Who usherest in the dolorous hour
10      With thy quick tears that make the rose
    Pull sideways, and the daisy close
Her crimson fringes to the shower;

Who might'st have heaved a windless flame[5]
    Up the deep East, or, whispering, play'd

9. Tennyson has dreamed of the trip he took with Hallam to the Pyrenees in the summer of 1830.
1. I.e., if sleep can revive the past, let it also obliterate the grievous sense of injury.
2. "Hallam's death-day, September the 15th" [T.]. The first anniversary (1834); the second is commemorated in section XCIX.
3. I.e., the wind exposes the white undersides of the poplar leaves.
4. I.e., fortune.
5. I.e., a calm, sunny day.

15      A chequer-work of beam and shade
    Along the hills, yet look'd the same,

    As wan, as chill, as wild as now;
        Day, mark'd as with some hideous crime,
        When the dark hand struck down thro' time,
20   And cancell'd nature's best: but thou,

    Lift as thou may'st thy burthen'd brows
        Thro' clouds that drench the morning star,
        And whirl the ungarner'd sheaf afar,
    And sow the sky with flying boughs,

25   And up thy vault with roaring sound
        Climb thy thick noon, disastrous day;
        Touch thy dull goal of joyless gray,
    And hide thy shame beneath the ground.

## LXXIII

    So many worlds; so much to do,
        So little done, such things to be,
        How know I what had need of thee,
    For thou wert strong as thou wert true?

5     The fame is quench'd that I foresaw,
        The head hath miss'd an earthly wreath:
        I curse not nature, no, nor death;
    For nothing is that errs from law.

    We pass; the path that each man trod
10       Is dim, or will be dim, with weeds:
        What fame is left for human deeds
    In endless age? It rests with God.

    O hollow wraith of dying fame,
        Fade wholly, while the soul exults,
15       And self-infolds the large results
    Of force that would have forged a name.[6]

---

6. I.e., Hallam's soul in heaven still reaps the benefits of talents that would have made him
famous on earth.

# LXXIV

As sometimes in a dead man's face,
   To those that watch it more and more,
   A likeness, hardly seen before,
Comes out—to some one of his race:

5   So, dearest, now thy brows are cold,[7]
   I see thee what thou art, and know
   Thy likeness to the wise below,
Thy kindred with the great of old.

But there is more than I can see,
10   And what I see I leave unsaid,
   Nor speak it, knowing Death has made
His darkness beautiful with thee.

# LXXV

I leave thy praises unexpress'd
   In verse that brings myself relief,
   And by the measure of my grief
I leave thy greatness to be guess'd;

5   What practice howsoe'er expert
   In fitting aptest words to things,
   Or voice the richest-toned that sings,
Hath power to give thee as thou wert?

I care not in these fading days
10   To raise a cry that lasts not long,
   And round thee with the breeze of song
To stir a little dust of praise.

Thy leaf has perish'd in the green,
   And, while we breathe beneath the sun,
15   The world which credits what is done
Is cold to all that might have been.

7. In response to a reviewer's remarks on these lines, Tennyson commented, "If anybody thinks I ever called him 'dearest' in his life they are much mistaken, for I never even called him 'dear.'"

So here shall silence guard thy fame;
>   But somewhere, out of human view,
>   Whate'er thy hands are set to do
20 Is wrought with tumult of acclaim.

## LXXVI

Take wings of fancy, and ascend,
>   And in a moment set thy face
>   Where all the starry heavens of space
Are sharpen'd to a needle's end;[8]

5 Take wings of foresight; lighten thro'
>   The secular abyss to come,[9]
>   And lo, thy deepest lays are dumb
Before the mouldering of a yew;

And if the matin songs,[1] that woke
10    The darkness of our planet, last,
>   Thine own shall wither in the vast,
Ere half the lifetime of an oak.

Ere these have clothed their branchy bowers
>   With fifty Mays, thy songs are vain;
15    And what are they when these remain
The ruin'd shells of hollow towers?

## LXXVII

What hope is here for modern rhyme
>   To him, who turns a musing eye
>   On songs, and deeds, and lives, that lie
Foreshorten'd in the tract of time?

5 These mortal lullabies of pain
>   May bind a book, may line a box,
>   May serve to curl a maiden's locks;[2]
Or when a thousand moons shall wane

---

8. Imagine yourself "so distant in void space that all our firmament would appear to be a needle-point thence" [T.]. The speaker addresses an auditor, or perhaps himself.
9. "The ages upon ages to be" [T.].
1. "The great early poets" [T.].
2. I.e., the pages of this book may someday be used as hair curlers.

A man upon a stall may find,
10    And, passing, turn the page that tells
    A grief, then changed to something else
Sung by a long-forgotten mind.

But what of that? My darken'd ways
    Shall ring with music all the same;
15    To breathe my loss is more than fame,
To utter love more sweet than praise.

# LXXVIII

Again at Christmas did we weave
    The holly round the Christmas hearth;
    The silent snow possess'd the earth,
And calmly fell our Christmas eve:[3]

5    The yule-clog[4] sparkled keen with frost,
    No wing of wind the region swept,
    But over all things brooding slept
The quiet sense of something lost.

As in the winters left behind,
10    Again our ancient games had place,
    The mimic picture's breathing grace,[5]
And dance and song and hoodman-blind.[6]

Who show'd a token of distress?
    No single tear, no mark of pain:
15    O sorrow, then can sorrow wane?
O grief, can grief be changed to less?

O last regret, regret can die!
    No—mixt with all this mystic frame,
    Her deep relations are the same
20    But with long use her tears are dry.[7]

---

3. Compare the opening of the two other Christmas sections (XXX and CV).
4. Yule log (Lincolnshire dialect).
5. "Tableaux vivants" [T.]; a parlor game like charades.
6. Blindman's bluff, another parlor game.
7. Regret remains diffused throughout the deepest parts of the spirit, though no longer
    outwardly visible.

## LXXIX

'More than my brothers are to me,'—
   Let this not vex thee, noble heart![8]
   I know thee of what force thou art
To hold the costliest love in fee.[9]

5   But thou and I are one in kind,
     As moulded like in Nature's mint;
     And hill and wood and field did print
The same sweet forms in either mind.

For us the same cold streamlet curl'd
10   Thro' all his eddying coves; the same
     All winds that roam the twilight came
In whispers of the beauteous world.

At one dear knee we proffer'd vows,
     One lesson from one book we learn'd,
15   Ere childhood's flaxen ringlet turn'd
To black and brown on kindred brows.

And so my wealth resembles thine,
     But he was rich where I was poor,
     And he supplied my want the more
20   As his unlikeness fitted mine.

## LXXX

If any vague desire should rise,
     That holy Death ere Arthur died
     Had moved me kindly from his side,
And dropt the dust on tearless eyes;[1]

5   Then fancy shapes, as fancy can,
     The grief my loss in him had wrought,
     A grief as deep as life or thought,
But stay'd in peace with God and man.

---

8. "The section is addressed to my brother Charles" [T.]. Tennyson had a close relationship with his elder brother Charles (1808–1879) throughout his life. Line 1 quotes IX.20.
9. In possession.
1. I.e., that I had died before Arthur did (and so been buried with "tearless eyes").

I make a picture in the brain;
10     I hear the sentence that he speaks;
        He bears the burthen of the weeks
But turns his burthen into gain.

His credit thus shall set me free;
        And, influence-rich to soothe and save,
15     Unused example from the grave
Reach out dead hands to comfort me.

## LXXXI

Could I have said while he was here,[2]
        'My love shall now no further range;
        There cannot come a mellower change,
For now is love mature in ear.'

5      Love, then, had hope of richer store:
        What end is here to my complaint?
        This haunting whisper makes me faint,
'More years had made me love thee more.'

But Death returns an answer sweet:
10     'My sudden frost was sudden gain,
        And gave all ripeness to the grain,
It might have drawn from after-heat.'

## LXXXII

I wage not any feud with Death
        For changes wrought on form and face;
        No lower life that earth's embrace
May breed with him, can fright my faith.

5      Eternal process moving on,
        From state to state the spirit walks;
        And these are but the shatter'd stalks,
Or ruin'd chrysalis of one.[3]

2. I.e., "I wish I could have said."
3. "These" (i.e., the stages of decomposition, described in lines 2–4) merely represent the
   worn-out husks discarded by the developing soul, as a butterfly discards its "chrysalis"
   or cocoon.

Nor blame I Death, because he bare[4]
10    The use of virtue out of earth:
    I know transplanted human worth
Will bloom to profit, otherwhere.

For this alone on Death I wreak
    The wrath that garners[5] in my heart;
15    He put our lives so far apart
We cannot hear each other speak.


# LXXXIII[6]


Dip down upon the northern shore,
    O sweet new-year delaying long;
    Thou doest expectant nature wrong;
Delaying long, delay no more.

5    What stays thee from the clouded noons,
    Thy sweetness from its proper place?
    Can trouble live with April days,
Or sadness in the summer moons?

Bring orchis, bring the foxglove spire,
10    The little speedwell's darling blue,
    Deep tulips dash'd with fiery dew,
Laburnums, dropping-wells of fire.

O thou, new-year, delaying long,
    Delayest the sorrow in my blood,
15    That longs to burst a frozen bud
And flood a fresher throat with song.


# LXXXIV


When I contemplate all alone
    The life that had been[7] thine below,
    And fix my thoughts on all the glow
To which thy crescent would have grown;

---

4. Bore.
5. Gathers (used especially of grain).
6. This lyric marks the beginning of the second spring since Hallam's death; compare the other springs (sections XXXVIII and CXV).
7. I.e., would have been.

5    I see thee sitting crown'd with good,
       A central warmth diffusing bliss
       In glance and smile, and clasp and kiss,
    On all the branches of thy blood;

    Thy blood, my friend, and partly mine;
10      For now the day was drawing on,
       When thou should'st link thy life with one
    Of mine own house,[8] and boys of thine

    Had babbled 'Uncle' on my knee;
       But that remorseless iron hour
15      Made cypress of her orange flower,[9]
    Despair of Hope, and earth of thee.

    I seem to meet their least desire,
       To clap their cheeks, to call them mine.
       I see their unborn faces shine
20    Beside the never-lighted fire.

    I see myself an honour'd guest,
       Thy partner in the flowery walk
       Of letters, genial table-talk,
    Or deep dispute, and graceful jest;

25    While now thy prosperous labour fills
       The lips of men with honest praise,
       And sun by sun the happy days
    Descend below the golden hills

    With promise of a morn as fair;
30      And all the train of bounteous hours
       Conduct by paths of growing powers,
    To reverence and the silver hair;

    Till slowly worn her earthly robe,
       Her lavish mission richly wrought,
35      Leaving great legacies of thought,
    Thy spirit should fail from off the globe;

    What time mine own might also flee,
       As link'd with thine in love and fate,

8. "The projected marriage of A.H.H. with Emily Tennyson" [T.]. Hallam was engaged to Tennyson's younger sister.
9. The cypress is a symbol of mourning, the orange blossom of a bride.

And, hovering o'er the dolorous strait
40   To the other shore, involved in thee,

Arrive at last the blessed goal,
   And He that died in Holy Land
   Would reach us out the shining hand,
And take us as a single soul.

45   What reed was that on which I leant?
   Ah, backward fancy, wherefore wake
   The old bitterness again, and break
The low beginnings of content.

## LXXXV

This truth came borne with bier and pall,
   I felt it, when I sorrow'd most,
   'Tis better to have loved and lost,
Than never to have loved at all[1]—

5   O true in word, and tried in deed,[2]
   Demanding, so to bring relief
   To this which is our common grief,
What kind of life is that I lead;

And whether trust in things above
10   Be dimm'd of sorrow, or sustain'd;
   And whether love for him have drain'd
My capabilities of love;

Your words have virtue such as draws
   A faithful answer from the breast,
15   Thro' light reproaches, half exprest,
And loyal unto kindly laws.

My blood an even tenor kept,
   Till on mine ear this message falls,
   That in Vienna's fatal walls
20   God's finger touch'd him, and he slept.

1. Compare XXVII.13–16.
2. This whole section is addressed, according to Tennyson, to Edmund Lushington, a close
friend who later (in 1842) married Tennyson's sister Cecilia; their wedding is described
in the Epilogue.

The great Intelligences fair
   That range above our mortal state,
   In circle round the blessed gate,
Received and gave him welcome there;

25    And led him thro' the blissful climes,
   And show'd him in the fountain fresh
   All knowledge that the sons of flesh
Shall gather in the cycled times.[3]

But I remain'd, whose hopes were dim,
30    Whose life, whose thoughts were little worth,
   To wander on a darken'd earth,
Where all things round me breathed of him.

O friendship, equal-poised control,
   O heart, with kindliest motion warm,
35    O sacred essence, other form,
O solemn ghost, O crowned soul!

Yet none could better know than I,
   How much of act at human hands
   The sense of human will demands[4]
40    By which we dare to live or die.

Whatever way my days decline,
   I felt and feel, tho' left alone,
   His being working in mine own,
The footsteps of his life in mine;

45    A life that all the Muses deck'd
   With gifts of grace, that might express
   All-comprehensive tenderness,
All-subtilising intellect:

And so my passion hath not swerved
50    To works of weakness, but I find
   An image comforting the mind,
And in my grief a strength reserved.

Likewise the imaginative woe,[5]
   That loved to handle spiritual strife,

3. The angels or "Intelligences" (line 21) showed Hallam all the knowledge that will be
   gathered on earth in ages to come ("the cycled times").
4. Although bereft (as the two previous stanzas express), the speaker admits "that the
   knowledge that we have free will demands from us action" [T.].
5. I.e., the ability and tendency to sympathize with grief.

55     Diffused the shock thro' all my life,
       But in the present broke the blow.

       My pulses therefore beat again
           For other friends that once I met;
           Nor can it suit me to forget
60     The mighty hopes that make us men.

       I woo your love: I count it crime
           To mourn for any overmuch;
           I, the divided half of such
       A friendship as had master'd Time;

65     Which masters Time indeed, and is
           Eternal, separate from fears:
           The all-assuming months and years
       Can take no part away from this:

       But Summer on the steaming floods,
70         And Spring that swells the narrow brooks,
           And Autumn, with a noise of rooks,
       That gather in the waning woods,

       And every pulse of wind and wave
           Recalls, in change of light or gloom,
75         My old affection of the tomb,
       And my prime passion in the grave:

       My old affection of the tomb,
           A part of stillness, yearns to speak:
           'Arise, and get thee forth and seek
80     A friendship for the years to come.

       'I watch thee from the quiet shore;
           Thy spirit up to mine can reach;
           But in dear words of human speech
       We two communicate no more.'

85     And I, 'Can clouds of nature stain
           The starry clearness of the free?
           How is it? Canst thou feel for me
       Some painless sympathy with pain?'

       And lightly does the whisper fall;
90         ''Tis hard for thee to fathom this;
           I triumph in conclusive bliss,
       And that serene result of all.'

So hold I commerce with the dead;
    Or so methinks the dead would say;
95      Or so shall grief with symbols play
And pining life be fancy-fed.

Now looking to some settled end,
    That these things pass, and I shall prove[6]
    A meeting somewhere, love with love,
100    I crave your pardon, O my friend;

If not so fresh, with love as true,
    I, clasping brother-hands, aver
    I could not, if I would, transfer
The whole I felt for him to you.

105    For which be they that hold apart
    The promise of the golden hours?[7]
    First love, first friendship, equal powers,
That marry with the virgin heart.

Still mine, that cannot but deplore,
110    That beats within a lonely place,
    That yet remembers his embrace,
But at his footstep leaps no more,

My heart, tho' widow'd may not rest
    Quite in the love of what is gone,
115    But seeks to beat in time with one
That warms another living breast.

Ah, take the imperfect gift I bring,
    Knowing the primrose yet is dear,
    The primrose of the later year,
120    As not unlike to that of Spring.

# LXXXVI

Sweet after showers, ambrosial air,
    That rollest from the gorgeous gloom
    Of evening over brake[8] and bloom
And meadow, slowly breathing bare

6. Experience.
7. For what are the things that make youth a time "apart" from all others?
8. Bush or thicket. The "air" (line 1) is meant to be "a west wind" [T.].

5      The round of space, and rapt below
           Thro' all the dewy-tassell'd wood,
           And shadowing down the horned flood[9]
       In ripples, fan my brows and blow

       The fever from my cheek, and sigh
10         The full new life that feeds thy breath
           Throughout my frame, till Doubt and Death,
       Ill brethren, let the fancy fly

       From belt to belt of crimson seas
           On leagues of odour streaming far,
15         To where in yonder orient[1] star
       A hundred spirits whisper 'Peace.'

# LXXXVII

       I past beside the reverend walls
           In which of old I wore the gown;[2]
           I roved at random thro' the town,
       And saw the tumult of the halls;

5      And heard once more in college fanes
           The storm their high-built organs make,
           And thunder-music, rolling, shake
       The prophet blazon'd on the panes;[3]

       And caught once more the distant shout,
10         The measured pulse of racing oars
           Among the willows; paced the shores
       And many a bridge, and all about

       The same gray flats again, and felt
           The same, but not the same; and last
15         Up that long walk of limes I past
       To see the rooms in which he dwelt.[4]

       Another name was on the door:
           I linger'd; all within was noise

---

9. A river "between two promontories" [T.].
1. Rising. "Any rising star is here intended" [T.].
2. "Trinity College, Cambridge" [T.], where Tennyson and Hallam met as undergraduates.
3. I.e., the organ music rattles the stained glass of the college chapels ("fanes").
4. Hallam's rooms "were in New Court" [T.], at the end of Trinity Avenue ("that long walk").

Of songs, and clapping hands, and boys
20    That crash'd the glass and beat the floor;

Where once we held debate, a band
    Of youthful friends, on mind and art,
    And labour, and the changing mart,
And all the framework of the land;[5]

25    When one would aim an arrow fair,
    But send it slackly from the string;
    And one would pierce an outer ring,
And one an inner, here and there;

And last the master-bowman, he,
30      Would cleave the mark. A willing ear
    We lent him. Who, but hung to hear
The rapt oration flowing free

From point to point, with power and grace
    And music in the bounds of law,
35    To those conclusions when we saw
The God within him light his face,

And seem to lift the form, and glow
    In azure orbits heavenly-wise;
    And over those ethereal eyes
40    The bar of Michael Angelo.[6]


## LXXXVIII

Wild bird, whose warble, liquid sweet,
    Rings Eden thro' the budded quicks,[7]
    O tell me where the senses mix,
    O tell me where the passions meet,

5    Whence radiate: fierce extremes employ
    Thy spirits in the darkening leaf,
    And in the midmost heart of grief
Thy passion clasps a secret joy:


5. Hallam and Tennyson were members of the Apostles, a society for intellectual discussion.
6. Like Michelangelo, Hallam had "a broad bar of frontal bone over the eyes" [T.].
7. Hedgerows. The bird addressed is "the Nightingale" [T.].

And I—my harp would prelude woe—
10      I cannot all command the strings;
      The glory of the sum of things
Will flash along the chords and go.


## LXXXIX


Witch-elms that counterchange the floor
      Of this flat lawn with dusk and bright;[8]
      And thou, with all thy breadth and height
Of foliage, towering sycamore;


5    How often, hither wandering down,
      My Arthur found your shadows fair,
      And shook to all the liberal air
The dust and din and steam of town:


He brought an eye for all he saw;
10    He mixt in all our simple sports;
      They pleased him, fresh from brawling courts
And dusty purlieus of the law.[9]


O joy to him in this retreat,
      Immantled[1] in ambrosial dark,
15    To drink the cooler air, and mark
The landscape winking thro' the heat:


O sound to rout[2] the brood of cares,
      The sweep of scythe in morning dew,
      The gust that round the garden flew,
20    And tumbled half the mellowing pears!


O bliss, when all in circle drawn
      About him, heart and ear were fed
      To hear him, as he lay and read
The Tuscan poets[3] on the lawn:


25    Or in the all-golden afternoon
      A guest, or happy sister, sung,

8. The setting is Tennyson's family's home in Somersby, Lincolnshire, where the wych elms checker ("counterchange") the lawn with shade.
9. After leaving Cambridge Hallam studied law in London. "Purlieus": regions.
1. Wrapped.
2. Put to flight.
3. Dante and Petrarch, Hallam's favorites among the Italian poets.

Or here she brought the harp and flung
A ballad to the brightening moon:

Nor less it pleased in livelier moods,
30    Beyond the bounding hill to stray,
    And break the livelong summer day
With banquet in the distant woods;

Whereat we glanced from theme to theme,
    Discuss'd the books to love or hate,
35    Or touch'd the changes of the state,
Or threaded some Socratic dream;[4]

But if I praised the busy town,
    He loved to rail against it still,
    For 'ground in yonder social mill
40  We rub each other's angles down,

'And merge' he said 'in form and gloss
    The picturesque of man and man.'
    We talk'd: the stream beneath us ran,
The wine-flask lying couch'd in moss,

45  Or cool'd within the glooming wave;
    And last, returning from afar,
    Before the crimson-circled star
Had fall'n into her father's grave,[5]

And brushing ankle-deep in flowers,
50    We heard behind the woodbine veil
    The milk that bubbled in the pail,
And buzzings of the honied hours.

## XC

He tasted love with half his mind,
    Nor ever drank the inviolate spring
    Where nighest heaven, who first could fling
This bitter seed among mankind;

4. I.e., discussed idealist philosophy.
5. "Before Venus, the evening star, had dipt into the sunset" [T.]. The sun is "father" to Venus because "according to Laplace," an early-19th-century astronomer, the planets "were evolved from the sun" [T.].

5    That could the dead, whose dying eyes
       Were closed with wail, resume their life,
       They would but find in child and wife
    An iron welcome when they rise:[6]

    'Twas well, indeed, when warm with wine,
10      To pledge them with a kindly tear,
       To talk them o'er, to wish them here,
    To count their memories half divine;

    But if they came who past away,
       Behold their brides in other hands;
15      The hard heir strides about their lands,
    And will not yield them for a day.

    Yea, tho' their sons were none of these,
       Not less the yet-loved sire would make
       Confusion worse than death, and shake
20    The pillars of domestic peace.

    Ah dear, but come thou back to me:
       Whatever change the years have wrought,
       I find not yet one lonely thought
    That cries against my wish for thee.

## XCI

    When rosy plumelets tuft the larch,
       And rarely pipes the mounted thrush;
       Or underneath the barren bush
    Flits by the sea-blue bird of March;

5    Come, wear the form by which I know
       Thy spirit in time among thy peers;[7]
       The hope of unaccomplish'd years
    Be large and lucid round thy brow.

    When summer's hourly-mellowing change
10      May breathe, with many roses sweet,
       Upon the thousand waves of wheat,
    That ripple round the lonely grange;

6. Tennyson's son paraphrases the opening stanzas: "He who first suggested that the dead
   would not be welcome if they came to life again knew not the highest love."
7. I.e., appear to me in the form I remember on earth.

Come: not in watches of the night,
　　But where the sunbeam broodeth warm,
15　　Come, beauteous in thine after form,
And like a finer light in light.


## XCII

If any vision should reveal
　　Thy likeness, I might count it vain
　　As but the canker of the brain;
Yea, tho' it spake and made appeal

5　To chances where our lots were cast
　　Together in the days behind,
　　I might but say, I hear a wind
Of memory murmuring the past.

Yea, tho' it spake and bared to view
10　　A fact within the coming year;
　　And tho' the months, revolving near,
Should prove the phantom-warning true,

They might not seem thy prophecies,
　　But spiritual presentiments,
15　　And such refraction of events
As often rises ere they rise.[8]


## XCIII

I shall not see thee. Dare I say
　　No spirit ever brake the band
　　That stays him from the native land
Where first he walk'd when claspt in clay?

5　No visual shade of some one lost,
　　But he, the Spirit himself, may come
　　Where all the nerve of sense is numb;
Spirit to Spirit, Ghost to Ghost.

O, therefore from thy sightless range
10　　With gods in unconjectured bliss,

8. "The heavenly bodies are seen above the horizon, by refraction, before they actually rise" [T.]. The same might be true of "events"; hence even a correct prediction of the future would not prove that the "vision" (line 1) was really a ghost.

O, from the distance of the abyss
Of tenfold-complicated change,[9]

Descend, and touch, and enter; hear
    The wish too strong for words to name;
15    That in this blindness of the frame
My Ghost may feel that thine is near.


## XCIV

How pure at heart and sound in head,
    With what divine affections bold
    Should be the man whose thought would hold
An hour's communion with the dead.

5    In vain shalt thou, or any, call
    The spirits from their golden day,
    Except, like them, thou too canst say,
My spirit is at peace with all.

They haunt the silence of the breast,
10    Imaginations calm and fair,
    The memory like a cloudless air,
The conscience as a sea at rest:

But when the heart is full of din,
    And doubt beside the portal waits,
15    They can but listen at the gates,
And hear the household jar within.


## XCV[1]

By night we linger'd on the lawn,
    For underfoot the herb was dry;
    And genial warmth; and o'er the sky
The silvery haze of summer drawn;

5    And calm that let the tapers burn
    Unwavering: not a cricket chirr'd:

9. In Dante's *Divine Comedy,* heaven has ten levels or spheres. "Sightless": invisible.
1. The spiritual reunion with Hallam in this section not only represents a culmination to
   the speculations of the previous five sections but has often been seen as a climax of the
   poem as a whole.

The brook alone far off was heard,
And on the board the fluttering urn:[2]

And bats went round in fragrant skies,
10     And wheel'd or lit the filmy shapes
     That haunt the dusk, with ermine capes
And woolly breasts and beaded eyes;[3]

While now we sang old songs that peal'd
     From knoll to knoll, where, couch'd at ease,
15     The white kine glimmer'd, and the trees
Laid their dark arms about the field.

But when those others, one by one,
     Withdrew themselves from me and night,
     And in the house light after light
20    Went out, and I was all alone,

A hunger seized my heart; I read
     Of that glad year which once had been,[4]
     In those fall'n leaves which kept their green,
The noble letters of the dead:

25    And strangely on the silence broke
     The silent-speaking words, and strange
     Was love's dumb cry defying change
To test his worth; and strangely spoke

The faith, the vigour, bold to dwell
30     On doubts that drive the coward back,
     And keen thro' wordy snares to track
Suggestion to her inmost cell.

So word by word, and line by line,
     The dead man touch'd me from the past,
35     And all at once it seem'd at last
The living soul was flash'd on mine,

And mine in this was wound,[5] and whirl'd
     About empyreal heights of thought,

2. Tea urn. "It was a marvellously still night, and I asked my brother Charles to listen to
the brook, which we had never heard so far off before" [T.]. The setting is the lawn at
Somersby (compare section LXXXIX).
3. "Moths" [T.]. "Lit": alighted.
4. The whole time of their friendship.
5. In early editions, these two lines read: "His living soul was flash'd on mine,/And mine
in his was wound." Tennyson changed to the more impersonal reading only in 1872 and

And came on that which is,[6] and caught
40    The deep pulsations of the world,

Aeonian[7] music measuring out
       The steps of Time—the shocks of Chance—
       The blows of Death. At length my trance
Was cancell'd, stricken thro' with doubt.[8]

45    Vague words! but ah, how hard to frame
       In matter-moulded forms of speech,
       Or ev'n for intellect to reach
Thro' memory that which I became:

Till now the doubtful dusk reveal'd
50    The knolls once more where, couch'd at ease,
       The white kine glimmer'd, and the trees
Laid their dark arms about the field:

And suck'd from out the distant gloom
       A breeze began to tremble o'er
55    The large leaves of the sycamore,
And fluctuate all the still perfume,

And gathering freshlier overhead,
       Rock'd the full-foliaged elms, and swung
       The heavy-folded rose, and flung
60    The lilies to and fro, and said

'The dawn, the dawn,' and died away;
       And East and West, without a breath,
       Mixt their dim lights, like life and death,
To broaden into boundless day.

## XCVI

You[9] say, but with no touch of scorn,
       Sweet-hearted, you, whose light-blue eyes

---

later commented, enigmatically, "The first reading . . . troubled me, as perhaps giving
a wrong impression."
6. In Plato's *Phaedrus* (247c) this phrase refers to the true, ideal forms that are percepti-
ble only to the gods and to lovers of wisdom. "Empyreal": celestial.
7. Of the eons, everlasting.
8. "The trance came to an end in a moment of critical doubt, but the doubt was dispelled
by the glory of the dawn of the 'boundless day' [line 64]" [T.].
9. The addressee is a woman—perhaps Emily Sellwood, Tennyson's future wife, who was
troubled by Tennyson's apparent lapses of faith.

Are tender over drowning flies,
You tell me, doubt is Devil-born.

5    I know not: one indeed I knew[1]
In many a subtle question versed,
Who touch'd a jarring lyre at first,
But ever strove to make it true:

Perplext in faith, but pure in deeds,
10    At last he beat his music out.
There lives more faith in honest doubt,
Believe me, than in half the creeds.

He fought his doubts and gather'd strength,
He would not make his judgment blind,
15    He faced the spectres of the mind
And laid them: thus he came at length

To find a stronger faith his own;
And Power was with him in the night,
Which makes the darkness and the light,
20  And dwells not in the light alone,

But in the darkness and the cloud,
As over Sinaï's peaks of old,
While Israel made their gods of gold,
Altho' the trumpet blew so loud.[2]

## XCVII

My love has talk'd with rocks and trees;
He finds on misty mountain-ground
His own vast shadow glory-crown'd;
He sees himself in all he sees.[3]

5    Two partners of a married life—
I look'd on these and thought of thee

1. "A.H.H." [T.]. Compare the two figures in this section to those in section XXXIII.
2. Tennyson cites Exodus 19, in which God appears "in a thick cloud upon the mount [Mount Sinai], and the voice of the trumpet exceeding loud" [T.]. But the stanza also alludes to a later episode (Exodus 32) in which the Israelites build themselves a golden idol to worship while Moses is on the mountain.
3. The speaker's love (here personified) finds a reflection of itself everywhere.

In vastness and in mystery,
And of my spirit as of a wife.[4]

These two—they dwelt with eye on eye,
10      Their hearts of old have beat in tune,
        Their meetings made December June,
Their every parting was to die.

Their love has never past away;
        The days she never can forget
15      Are earnest that he loves her yet,
Whate'er the faithless people say.

Her life is lone, he sits apart,
        He loves her yet, she will not weep,
        Tho' rapt in matters dark and deep
20  He seems to slight her simple heart.

He thrids the labyrinth of the mind,
        He reads the secret of the star,
        He seems so near and yet so far,
He looks so cold: she thinks him kind.

25  She keeps the gift of years before,
        A wither'd violet is her bliss:
        She knows not what his greatness is,
For that, for all, she loves him more.

For him she plays, to him she sings
30      Of early faith and plighted vows;
        She knows but matters of the house,
And he, he knows a thousand things.

Her faith is fixt and cannot move,
        She darkly feels him great and wise,
35      She dwells on him with faithful eyes,
'I cannot understand: I love.'

4. This extended metaphor illustrates "the relation of one on earth to one in the other
and higher world. Not my relation to him here. He looked up to me as I looked up to
him" [T.].

# XCVIII[5]

You leave us: you will see the Rhine,
    And those fair hills I sail'd below,
    When I was there with him; and go
By summer belts of wheat and vine

5    To where he breathed his latest breath,
        That City. All her splendour seems
        No livelier than the wisp that gleams
    On Lethe in the eyes of Death.[6]

Let her great Danube rolling fair
10        Enwind her isles, unmark'd of me:
        I have not seen, I will not see
    Vienna; rather dream that there,

A treble darkness, Evil haunts
    The birth, the bridal; friend from friend
15        Is oftener parted, fathers bend
Above more graves, a thousand wants

Gnarr[7] at the heels of men, and prey
    By each cold hearth, and sadness flings
    Her shadow on the blaze of kings:
20    And yet myself have heard him say,

That not in any mother town
    With statelier progress to and fro
    The double tides of chariots flow
By park and suburb under brown[8]

25    Of lustier leaves; nor more content,
        He told me, lives in any crowd,
        When all is gay with lamps, and loud
    With sport and song, in booth and tent,

---

5. Although Tennyson noted that the "You" of line 1 "is imaginary," he elsewhere said that it referred to his brother Charles, who traveled on the Rhine River during his honeymoon in 1836. Hallam and Tennyson had taken a similar voyage in 1832 (lines 2–3). It was on a trip to Vienna ("That City," line 6) that Hallam died in 1833.
6. "Lethe": a river of the underworld. "Wisp": "ignis-fatuus" [T.]—a thin light sometimes seen at night over swampy ground.
7. "Snarl" [T.].
8. I.e., shadow. "Mother town": "metropolis" [T.].

Imperial halls, or open plain;
30      And wheels the circled dance, and breaks
The rocket molten into flakes[9]
Of crimson or in emerald rain.

## XCIX

Risest thou thus, dim dawn, again,[1]
So loud with voices of the birds,
So thick with lowings of the herds,
Day, when I lost the flower of men;

5      Who tremblest thro' thy darkling red
On yon swoll'n brook that bubbles fast
By meadows breathing of the past,
And woodlands holy to the dead;

Who murmurest in the foliaged eaves
10      A song that slights the coming care,[2]
And Autumn laying here and there
A fiery finger on the leaves;

Who wakenest with thy balmy breath
To myriads on the genial earth,
15      Memories of bridal, or of birth,
And unto myriads more, of death.

O wheresoever those may be,
Betwixt the slumber of the poles,[3]
To-day they count as kindred souls;
20      They know me not, but mourn with me.

## C[4]

I climb the hill: from end to end
Of all the landscape underneath,

---

9. Fireworks.
1. The second anniversary of Hallam's death, September 15; compare LXXII.1.
2. I.e., the hardships of winter.
3. "The ends of the axis of the earth, which move so slowly that they seem not to move, but slumber" [T.].
4. This and the following sections concern the Tennyson family's departure from their home at Somersby to the unfamiliar surroundings of High Beech, north of London. The move took place in 1837, four years after Hallam's death, but the chronology has been altered to fit the poem.

I find no place that does not breathe
Some gracious memory of my friend;

5   No gray old grange, or lonely fold,
      Or low morass and whispering reed,
      Or simple stile from mead to mead,
Or sheepwalk up the windy wold;

Nor hoary knoll of ash and haw
10    That hears the latest linnet trill,
      Nor quarry trench'd along the hill
And haunted by the wrangling daw;

Nor runlet tinkling from the rock;
      Nor pastoral rivulet that swerves
15    To left and right thro' meadowy curves,
That feed the mothers of the flock;

But each has pleased a kindred eye,
      And each reflects a kindlier day;
      And, leaving these, to pass away,
20   I think once more he seems to die.

## CI

Unwatch'd, the garden bough shall sway,
      The tender blossom flutter down,
      Unloved, that beech will gather brown,
This maple burn itself away;

5   Unloved, the sun-flower, shining fair,
      Ray round with flames her disk of seed,
      And many a rose carnation feed
With summer spice the humming air;

Unloved, by many a sandy bar,
10    The brook shall babble down the plain,
      At noon or when the lesser wain[5]
Is twisting round the polar star;

Uncared for, gird the windy grove,
      And flood the haunts of hern and crake;[6]

5. The constellation of Ursa Minor, or the Little Dipper, which revolves around the North Star.
6. A marsh bird. "Hern": heron.

15      Or into silver arrows break
            The sailing moon in creek and cove;

        Till from the garden and the wild
            A fresh association blow,
            And year by year the landscape grow
20      Familiar to the stranger's child;

        As year by year the labourer tills
            His wonted glebe,[7] or lops the glades;
            And year by year our memory fades
        From all the circle of the hills.


## CII

        We leave the well-beloved place
            Where first we gazed upon the sky;
            The roofs, that heard our earliest cry,
        Will shelter one of stranger race.

5       We go, but ere we go from home,
            As down the garden-walks I move,
            Two spirits of a diverse love[8]
        Contend for loving masterdom.

        One whispers, 'Here thy boyhood sung
10          Long since its matin song,[9] and heard
            The low love-language of the bird
        In native hazels tassel-hung.'

        The other answers, 'Yea but here
            Thy feet have stray'd in after hours
15          With thy lost friend among the bowers,
        And this hath made them trebly dear.'

        These two have striven half the day,
            And each prefers his separate claim,
            Poor rivals in a losing game,
20      That will not yield each other way.

        I turn to go: my feet are set
            To leave the pleasant fields and farms;

7. His usual plot of land.
8. "First, the love of native place; second, this enhanced by the memory of A.H.H." [T.].
9. I.e., Tennyson's youthful poetry; compare LXXVI.9.

They mix in one another's arms
To one pure image of regret.


## CIII

On that last night before we went
    From out the doors where I was bred,
    I dream'd a vision of the dead,
Which left my after-morn content.

5    Methought I dwelt within a hall,
    And maidens with me: distant hills
    From hidden summits fed with rills
A river sliding by the wall.[1]

The hall with harp and carol rang.
10    They sang of what is wise and good
    And graceful. In the centre stood
A statue veil'd, to which they sang;

And which, tho' veil'd, was known to me,
    The shape of him I loved, and love
15    For ever: then flew in a dove
And brought a summons from the sea:[2]

And when they learnt that I must go
    They wept and wail'd, but led the way
    To where a little shallop[3] lay
20    At anchor in the flood below;

And on by many a level mead,
    And shadowing bluff that made the banks,
    We glided winding under ranks
Of iris, and the golden reed;

25    And still as vaster grew the shore
    And roll'd the floods in grander space,
    The maidens gather'd strength and grace
And presence, lordlier than before;[4]

---

1. According to Tennyson, the maidens "are the Muses, poetry, arts—all that made life beautiful here, which we hope will pass with us beyond the grave." The hidden summits represent "the divine," and the river, "life" [T.].
2. "Eternity" [T.].
3. A small open boat.
4. This stanza suggests "the progress of the Age" [T.].

And I myself, who sat apart
30      And watch'd them, wax'd in every limb;
I felt the thews of Anakim,
The pulses of a Titan's heart;[5]

As one would sing the death of war,
And one would chant the history
35      Of that great race, which is to be,
And one the shaping of a star;[6]

Until the forward-creeping tides
Began to foam, and we to draw
From deep to deep, to where we saw
40  A great ship lift her shining sides.

The man we loved was there on deck,
But thrice as large as man he bent
To greet us. Up the side I went,
And fell in silence on his neck:

45  Whereat those maidens with one mind
Bewail'd their lot; I did them wrong:
'We served thee here,' they said, 'so long,
And wilt thou leave us now behind?'

So rapt I was, they could not win
50      An answer from my lips, but he
Replying, 'Enter likewise ye
And go with us:' they enter'd in.[7]

And while the wind began to sweep
A music out of sheet and shroud,[8]
55      We steer'd her toward a crimson cloud
That landlike slept along the deep.

# CIV

The time draws near the birth of Christ;[9]
The moon is hid, the night is still;

---

5. The Titans were the giants of Greek mythology. "The thews of Anakim": the strength of "the children of Anak," a biblical race of giants (Numbers 13, Deuteronomy 9).
6. The songs describe "the great hopes of humanity and science" [T.].
7. Tennyson commented that the speaker "was wrong to drop his earthly hopes and powers—they will still be of use to him" in the afterlife.
8. Types of rope on a ship.
9. Compare the opening of section XXVIII, the first Christmas lyric in the poem, with which this section is paired.

A single church below the hill
Is pealing, folded in the mist.

5    A single peal of bells below,
That wakens at this hour of rest
A single murmur in the breast,
That these are not the bells I know.

Like strangers' voices here they sound,
10    In lands where not a memory strays,
Nor landmark breathes of other days,
But all is new unhallow'd ground.[1]

## CV[2]

To-night ungather'd let us leave
This laurel, let this holly stand:
We live within the stranger's land,
And strangely falls our Christmas-eve.

5    Our father's dust is left alone
And silent under other snows:
There in due time the woodbine blows,
The violet comes, but we are gone.

No more shall wayward grief abuse
10    The genial hour with mask and mime;[3]
For change of place, like growth of time,
Has broke the bond of dying use.

Let cares that petty shadows cast,
By which our lives are chiefly proved,
15    A little spare the night I loved,
And hold it solemn to the past.

But let no footstep beat the floor,
Nor bowl of wassail mantle[4] warm;
For who would keep an ancient form
20    Thro' which the spirit breathes no more?

1. "High Beech, Epping Forest (where we were then living)" [T.] (see section C, n. 4).
2. The third Christmas in the poem (compare sections XXX and LXXVIII) and the first in the new home—away from Somersby where, among other things, the grave of Tennyson's father (lines 5–6) has been left behind.
3. I.e., no more shall grief disguised under merriment wrong ("abuse") the holiday.
4. Grow frothy. "Wassail": a traditional Christmas drink.

Be neither song, nor game, nor feast;
　　Nor harp be touch'd, nor flute be blown;
　　No dance, no motion, save alone
What lightens in the lucid east

25　Of rising worlds by yonder wood.[5]
　　Long sleeps the summer in the seed;
　　Run out your measured arcs, and lead
The closing cycle rich in good.


# CVI

Ring out, wild bells, to the wild sky,
　　The flying cloud, the frosty light:
　　The year is dying in the night;
Ring out, wild bells, and let him die.

5　Ring out the old, ring in the new,
　　Ring, happy bells, across the snow:
　　The year is going, let him go;
Ring out the false, ring in the true.

　Ring out the grief that saps the mind,
10　　For those that here we see no more;
　　Ring out the feud of rich and poor,
Ring in redress to all mankind.

Ring out a slowly dying cause,
　　And ancient forms of party strife;
15　　Ring in the nobler modes of life,
With sweeter manners, purer laws.

Ring out the want, the care, the sin,
　　The faithless coldness of the times;
　　Ring out, ring out my mournful rhymes,
20　But ring the fuller minstrel in.

Ring out false pride in place and blood,
　　The civic slander and the spite;
　　Ring in the love of truth and right,
Ring in the common love of good.

---

5. "The scintillating motion of the stars that rise" [T.]. These stars are addressed in lines 27–28, and told to usher in the golden age to come.

25    Ring out old shapes of foul disease;
      Ring out the narrowing lust of gold;
      Ring out the thousand wars of old,
    Ring in the thousand years of peace.[6]

    Ring in the valiant man and free,
30      The larger heart, the kindlier hand;
      Ring out the darkness of the land,
    Ring in the Christ that is to be.[7]

# CVII

    It is the day when he was born,[8]
      A bitter day that early sank
      Behind a purple-frosty bank
    Of vapour, leaving night forlorn.

5    The time admits not flowers or leaves
      To deck the banquet. Fiercely flies
      The blast of North and East, and ice
    Makes daggers at the sharpen'd eaves,

    And bristles all the brakes and thorns
10      To yon hard crescent, as she hangs
      Above the wood which grides and clangs
    Its leafless ribs and iron horns[9]

    Together, in the drifts that pass
      To darken on the rolling brine[1]
15      That breaks the coast. But fetch the wine,
    Arrange the board and brim the glass;

    Bring in great logs and let them lie,
      To make a solid core of heat;
      Be cheerful-minded, talk and treat
20    Of all things ev'n as he were by;

    We keep the day. With festal cheer,
      With books and music, surely we

6. See Revelation 20.
7. "The broader Christianity of the future" [T.].
8. Hallam's birthday, "February 1" [T.].
9. The moon ("yon hard crescent") hangs above trees that grate together ("gride") their "leafless" and frozen branches ("iron horns").
1. Snow flurries that blow into the sea and melt.

Will drink to him, whate'er he be,
And sing the songs he loved to hear.


# CVIII[2]

I will not shut me from my kind,
    And, lest I stiffen into stone,
    I will not eat my heart alone,
Nor feed with sighs a passing wind:

5   What profit lies in barren faith,
        And vacant yearning, tho' with might
        To scale the heaven's highest height,
    Or dive below the wells of Death?

    What find I in the highest place,
10      But mine own phantom chanting hymns?
        And on the depths of death there swims
    The reflex[3] of a human face.

    I'll rather take what fruit may be
        Of sorrow under human skies:
15      'Tis held that sorrow makes us wise,
    Whatever wisdom sleep with thee.


# CIX

Heart-affluence in discursive talk
    From household fountains never dry;
    The critic clearness of an eye,
That saw thro' all the Muses' walk;[4]

5   Seraphic intellect and force
        To seize and throw[5] the doubts of man;
        Impassion'd logic, which outran
    The hearer in its fiery course;

2. Tennyson paraphrases this section: "Grief shall not make me a hermit, and I will not
   indulge in vacant yearnings and barren aspirations [lines 1–6]; it is useless trying to find
   him in the other worlds [lines 6–8]—I find nothing but the reflections of myself [lines
   9–12]: I had better learn the lesson that sorrow teaches [lines 13–16]" [T.].
3. Reflection.
4. Hallam had already published several pieces of very mature literary criticism before he
   died. "Household fountains": i.e., Hallam's ideas sprang from within.
5. Overthrow.

High nature amorous of the good,
10     But touch'd with no ascetic gloom;
    And passion pure in snowy bloom
Thro' all the years of April blood,[6]

A love of freedom rarely felt,
    Of freedom in her regal seat
15     Of England; not the schoolboy heat,
The blind hysterics of the Celt;[7]

And manhood fused with female grace
    In such a sort, the child would twine
    A trustful hand, unask'd, in thine,
20 And find his comfort in thy face;

All these have been, and thee mine eyes
    Have look'd on: if they look'd in vain,
    My shame is greater who remain,
Nor let thy wisdom make me wise.[8]

# CX

Thy converse drew us with delight,
    The men of rathe and riper years:[9]
    The feeble soul, a haunt of fears,
Forgot his weakness in thy sight.

5 On thee the loyal-hearted hung,
    The proud was half disarm'd of pride,
    Nor cared the serpent at thy side
To flicker with his double tongue.

The stern were mild when thou wert by,
10     The flippant put himself to school
    And heard thee, and the brazen fool
Was soften'd, and he knew not why;

While I, thy nearest, sat apart,
    And felt thy triumph was as mine;
15     And loved them more, that they were thine,
The graceful tact, the Christian art;

6. Youth.
7. Referring to Irish uprisings.
8. I.e., "If I do not let thy wisdom make me wise" [T.]; compare Prologue, line 44.
9. I.e., young and old. "Rathe": early.

Nor mine the sweetness or the skill,
 But mine the love that will not tire,
 And, born of love, the vague desire
20 That spurs an imitative will.

# CXI

The churl in spirit, up or down
 Along the scale of ranks, thro' all,
 To him who grasps a golden ball,
By blood a king, at heart a clown;[1]

5 The churl in spirit, howe'er he veil
 His want in forms for fashion's sake,
 Will let his coltish nature break
At seasons thro' the gilded pale:[2]

For who can always act? but he,
10  To whom a thousand memories call,
 Not being less but more than all
The gentleness he seem'd to be,

Best seem'd the thing he was, and join'd
 Each office of the social hour
15  To noble manners, as the flower
And native growth of noble mind;

Nor ever narrowness or spite,
 Or villain fancy fleeting by,
 Drew in the expression of an eye,
20 Where God and Nature met in light;

And thus he bore without abuse
 The grand old name of gentleman,
 Defamed by every charlatan,
And soil'd with all ignoble use.

# CXII

High wisdom holds my wisdom less,
 That I, who gaze with temperate eyes

1. "Churl" (line 1) and "clown" both mean a rude or low-bred person. "Golden ball": the orb held by a king, symbol of power.
2. Fence; here, in the sense of "mask."

On glorious insufficiencies,
  Set light by narrower perfectness.[3]

5   But thou, that fillest all the room
      Of all my love, art reason why
      I seem to cast a careless eye
  On souls, the lesser lords of doom.[4]

  For what wert thou? some novel power
10     Sprang up for ever at a touch,
      And hope could never hope too much,
  In watching thee from hour to hour,

  Large elements in order brought,
      And tracts of calm from tempest made,
15     And world-wide fluctuation sway'd
  In vassal tides that follow'd thought.[5]


# CXIII

'Tis held that sorrow makes us wise;
  Yet how much wisdom sleeps with thee[6]
  Which not alone had[7] guided me,
But served the seasons that may rise;

5   For can I doubt, who knew thee keen
    In intellect, with force and skill
    To strive, to fashion, to fulfil—
  I doubt not what thou wouldst have been:

  A life in civic action warm,
10     A soul on highest mission sent,
      A potent voice of Parliament,
  A pillar steadfast in the storm,

---

3. "Glorious insufficiencies": "Unaccomplished greatness such as Arthur Hallam's" [T.].
Thus "wise" people blame the poet for being more indulgent toward Hallam's promised
greatness than toward others' actual accomplishments, though less great ("narrower
perfectness"). "Set light by": "make light of" [T.].
4. But love for Hallam obscures my perception of those who can act as they wish (are
"lords of doom," i.e., fate) but who remain "lesser." The poet admits that his estimation
of Hallam's extraordinary talents, expressed in sections CIX–CXIII, is biased. But Ten-
nyson was not alone in thinking that Hallam would have been one of the leading fig-
ures of his age; see the selection from William Ewart Gladstone, p. 115 below.
5. I.e., great political issues were marshaled into logical order.
6. Compare CVIII.15–16 (the original reading of which was identical to this).
7. I.e., would have.

Should licensed boldness gather force,[8]
  Becoming, when the time has birth,
15    A lever to uplift the earth
And roll it in another course,

With thousand shocks that come and go,
  With agonies, with energies,
  With overthrowings, and with cries,
20  And undulations to and fro.


# CXIV

Who loves not Knowledge? Who shall rail
  Against her beauty? May she mix
  With men and prosper! Who shall fix
Her pillars?[9] Let her work prevail.

5  But on her forehead sits a fire:
  She sets her forward countenance
  And leaps into the future chance,
Submitting all things to desire.[1]

Half-grown as yet, a child, and vain—
10    She cannot fight the fear of death.
  What is she, cut from love and faith,
But some wild Pallas from the brain[2]

Of Demons? fiery-hot to burst
  All barriers in her onward race
15    For power. Let her know her place;
She is the second, not the first.

A higher hand must make her mild,
  If all be not in vain; and guide
  Her footsteps, moving side by side
20  With wisdom, like the younger child:

8. If a justified social revolution should occur (with the consequent "storm" of complications described in the two final stanzas).
9. Limits. The Pillars of Hercules (the Strait of Gibraltar) represented the limits of the known world in classical geography.
1. In her forward sweep, "Knowledge" subordinates everything to desire (for more knowledge).
2. In Greek mythology, Pallas Athena (goddess of wisdom) was born full-grown from the brain of Zeus. "Cut": cut off.

For she is earthly of the mind,
    But Wisdom heavenly of the soul.
    O, friend, who camest to thy goal
So early, leaving me behind,

25    I would the great world grew like thee,
    Who grewest not alone in power
    And knowledge, but by year and hour
In reverence and in charity.

## CXV

Now fades the last long streak of snow,
    Now burgeons every maze of quick[3]
    About the flowering squares, and thick
By ashen roots the violets blow.

5    Now rings the woodland loud and long,
    The distance takes a lovelier hue,
    And drown'd in yonder living blue
The lark becomes a sightless song.

Now dance the lights on lawn and lea,
10    The flocks are whiter down the vale,
    And milkier every milky sail
On winding stream or distant sea;

Where now the seamew pipes, or dives
    In yonder greening gleam, and fly
15    The happy birds, that change their sky
To build and brood; that live their lives

From land to land; and in my breast
    Spring wakens too; and my regret
    Becomes an April violet,
20  And buds and blossoms like the rest.

## CXVI

Is it, then, regret for buried time
    That keenlier in sweet April wakes,

---

3. Hedgerow (as in LXXXVIII.2). "Burgeons": "buds" [T.]. This is the third spring since Hallam's death.

And meets the year, and gives and takes
The colours of the crescent prime?[4]

5  Not all: the songs, the stirring air,
    The life re-orient[5] out of dust,
    Cry thro' the sense to hearten trust
In that which made the world so fair.

Not all regret: the face will shine
10  Upon me, while I muse alone;
    And that dear voice, I once have known,
Still speak to me of me and mine:

Yet less of sorrow lives in me
  For days of happy commune dead;
15  Less yearning for the friendship fled,
Than some strong bond which is to be.

## CXVII

O days and hours, your work is this
  To hold me from my proper place,
  A little while from his embrace,
For fuller gain of after bliss:

5  That out of distance might ensue
    Desire of nearness doubly sweet;
    And unto meeting when we meet,
Delight a hundredfold accrue,

For every grain of sand that runs,
10  And every span of shade that steals,
    And every kiss of toothed wheels,[6]
And all the courses of the suns.

## CXVIII

Contemplate all this work of Time,
  The giant labouring in his youth;

---

4. "Growing spring" [T.].
5. Rising again.
6. Referring to the hourglass, sundial, and clock, respectively.

Nor dream of human love and truth,
As dying Nature's earth and lime,[7]

5   But trust that those we call the dead
        Are breathers of an ampler day
        For ever nobler ends. They say,
The solid earth whereon we tread

In tracts of fluent heat began,
10      And grew to seeming-random forms,
        The seeming prey of cyclic storms,
Till at the last arose the man;[8]

Who throve and branch'd from clime to clime,
        The herald of a higher race,
15      And of himself in higher place,[9]
If so he type this work of time

Within himself, from more to more;
        Or, crown'd with attributes of woe
        Like glories,[1] move his course, and show
20  That life is not as idle ore,

But iron dug from central gloom,
        And heated hot with burning fears,
        And dipt in baths of hissing tears,
And batter'd with the shocks of doom

25  To shape and use. Arise and fly
        The reeling Faun, the sensual feast;
        Move upward, working out the beast,
And let the ape and tiger die.[2]

---

7. Consider the vast stretches of geological time but without letting it cause you to think
   that the soul is as mortal as the body ("Nature's earth and lime"). The speaker thus
   counters his own doubts in sections LV and LVI, which sprang from his observations of
   nature and particularly of extinction.
8. "They" (line 7) include Georges Cuvier, Pierre-Simon Laplace, Charles Lyell, and Robert
   Chambers, scientists who introduced such theories as the nebular hypothesis (lines
   8–9) and catastrophism (line 11). These theories are revisited in section CXXIII. See
   "Scientific Contexts," p. 131 below.
9. Human development not only presages more highly evolved generations here on earth
   but also hints at what we shall ourselves be in heaven ("higher place").
1. But the human race evolves only if individuals reproduce ("type") its development in
   their own lives, either gradually ("from more to more") or in large steps achieved
   through suffering ("woe"), as described in the lines that follow.
2. The faun (a mythical creature, half-goat and half-human), ape, and tiger all represent sen-
   sual, bestial qualities. Since evolution is partly a matter of individual will (lines 16–25),
   the speaker urges the reader (or himself) to progress ("Move upward") to a higher nature.

# CXIX

Doors, where my heart was used to beat[3]
    So quickly, not as one that weeps
    I come once more; the city sleeps;
I smell the meadow in the street;

5    I hear a chirp of birds; I see
    Betwixt the black fronts long-withdrawn
    A light-blue lane of early dawn,
And think of early days and thee,

And bless thee, for thy lips are bland,[4]
10    And bright the friendship of thine eye;
    And in my thoughts with scarce a sigh
I take the pressure of thine hand.

# CXX

I trust I have not wasted breath:
    I think we are not wholly brain,
    Magnetic mockeries;[5] not in vain,
Like Paul with beasts, I fought with Death;[6]

5    Not only cunning casts in clay:
    Let Science prove we are, and then
    What matters Science unto men,
At least to me? I would not stay.[7]

Let him, the wiser man who springs
10    Hereafter, up from childhood shape
    His action like the greater ape,[8]
But I was *born* to other things.

3. Hallam's old house, as in section VII.
4. Gentle; soothing.
5. I trust that there is more to the soul than electrical impulses in the brain. Tennyson apparently understood "magnetic" and electrical as roughly equivalent; he refers to nerve impulses as "electric" in CXXV.15.
6. Tennyson cites 1 Corinthians 15:32: "If after the manner of men I have fought with beasts at Ephesus, what advantageth it me, if the dead rise not?"
7. If science can prove that we are no more than bodies (and hence that there is no immortality), then life is of no use to me.
8. "Spoken ironically against mere materialism, not against evolution" [T.]. The poet does not abandon the evolutionary model of section CXVIII but reminds the "wiser man" (used ironically of the scientist) that the theory is debasing unless it applies to the soul as well as to the body.

## CXXI[9]

Sad Hesper o'er the buried sun
    And ready, thou, to die with him,
    Thou watchest all things ever dim
And dimmer, and a glory done:

5   The team is loosen'd from the wain,[1]
    The boat is drawn upon the shore;
    Thou listenest to the closing door,
And life is darken'd in the brain.

Bright Phosphor, fresher for the night,
10   By thee the world's great work is heard
    Beginning, and the wakeful bird;
Behind thee comes the greater light:

The market boat is on the stream,
    And voices hail it from the brink;
15   Thou hear'st the village hammer clink,
And see'st the moving of the team.

Sweet Hesper-Phosphor, double name
    For what is one, the first, the last,
    Thou, like my present and my past,
20   Thy place is changed; thou art the same.

## CXXII

Oh, wast thou with me, dearest, then,
    While I rose up against my doom,[2]
    And yearn'd to burst the folded gloom,
To bare the eternal Heavens again,

5   To feel once more, in placid awe,
    The strong imagination roll
    A sphere of stars about my soul,
In all her motion one with law;

9. "The evening star is also the morning star" [T.]. At certain times of the year, the planet Venus is the first "star" visible after sunset; it was then called "Hesper" in ancient astronomy. At other times Venus is the last "star" still shining just before sunrise and was called "Phosphor."
1. The oxen ("the team") are unyoked.
2. "That of grief" [T.]. "Then" does not necessarily refer to any known occasion, but to the time when the speaker first wished to feel joy again. For "dearest," see section LXXIV, n. 7.

If thou wert with me, and the grave
10      Divide us not, be with me now,
      And enter in at breast and brow,
Till all my blood, a fuller wave,

Be quicken'd with a livelier breath,
      And like an inconsiderate boy,
15      As in the former flash of joy,
I slip the thoughts of life and death;

And all the breeze of Fancy blows,
      And every dew-drop paints a bow,[3]
      The wizard[4] lightnings deeply glow,
20 And every thought breaks out a rose.

# CXXIII

There rolls the deep where grew the tree.
      O earth, what changes hast thou seen![5]
      There where the long street roars, hath been
The stillness of the central sea.[6]

5  The hills are shadows, and they flow
      From form to form, and nothing stands;
      They melt like mist, the solid lands,
Like clouds they shape themselves and go.

But in my spirit will I dwell,
10      And dream my dream, and hold it true;
      For tho' my lips may breathe adieu,
I cannot think the thing farewell.[7]

# CXXIV

That which we dare invoke to bless;
      Our dearest faith; our ghastliest doubt;
      He, They, One, All; within, without;
The Power in darkness whom we guess;

---

3. "Every dew-drop turns into a miniature rainbow" [T.].
4. Magical, as in LXX.14.
5. Here, as in section XXXV, Tennyson draws his images of changes in the earth's surface from Charles Lyell, *Principles of Geology* (1830–33); see p. 131 below.
6. "Balloonists say that even in a storm the middle sea is noiseless" [T.].
7. I.e., in spite of all evidence of change, I cannot believe we will never meet again. Compare LVII.15–16 and note.

5     I found Him not in world or sun,
      Or eagle's wing, or insect's eye;
      Nor thro' the questions men may try,
The petty cobwebs we have spun:[8]

If e'er when faith had fall'n asleep,
10      I heard a voice 'believe no more'
      And heard an ever-breaking shore
That tumbled in the Godless deep;

A warmth within the breast would melt
      The freezing reason's colder part,
15      And like a man in wrath the heart
Stood up and answer'd 'I have felt.'

No, like a child in doubt and fear:
      But that blind clamour made me wise;[9]
      Then was I as a child that cries,
20     But, crying, knows his father near;

And what I am beheld again
      What is, and no man understands;
      And out of darkness came the hands
That reach thro' nature, moulding men.

# CXXV

Whatever I have said or sung,
      Some bitter notes my harp would give,
      Yea, tho' there often seem'd to live
A contradiction on the tongue,

5     Yet Hope had never lost her youth;
      She did but look through dimmer eyes;
      Or Love but play'd with gracious lies,
Because he felt so fix'd in truth:[1]

8. Faith comes neither from "natural theology" (which deduced God from evidence in nature) nor from philosophical arguments.
9. His reaction to his doubts was not that of "a man" (line 15), but of a child: the "blind clamour" (described in lines 10–12) inspired fear, but also prompted the recognition that a comforting presence was near. Compare the image in LIV.17–20.
1. Love was so confident that he could afford to entertain hypothetical doubts. "He" in the following lines refers to Love.

      And if the song were full of care,
10        He breathed the spirit of the song;
          And if the words were sweet and strong
      He set his royal signet there;

      Abiding with me till I sail
          To seek thee on the mystic deeps,
15        And this electric force, that keeps
      A thousand pulses dancing, fail.


## CXXVI

      Love is and was my Lord and King,
          And in his presence I attend
          To hear the tidings of my friend,
      Which every hour his couriers bring.

5     Love is and was my King and Lord,
          And will be, tho' as yet I keep
          Within his court on earth, and sleep
      Encompass'd by his faithful guard,

      And hear at times a sentinel
10        Who moves about from place to place,
          And whispers to the worlds of space,
      In the deep night, that all is well.


## CXXVII

      And all is well, tho' faith and form
          Be sunder'd in the night of fear;[2]
          Well roars the storm to those that hear
      A deeper voice across the storm,

5     Proclaiming social truth shall spread,
          And justice, ev'n tho' thrice again
          The red fool-fury of the Seine
      Should pile her barricades with dead.[3]

---

2. Faith can no longer depend on established religious doctrine ("form") that has been
   called into doubt; compare sections XXXIII and XCVI.
3. A reference to the French revolutions of 1789, 1830, and 1848. The Seine River runs
   through Paris, and the revolutionaries of 1789 wore red caps (and were also bloody,
   hence "red"). This section may have been composed before the revolution of 1848; the
   word "thrice" was added only in 1850.

But ill for him that wears a crown,
10    And him, the lazar,[4] in his rags:
They tremble, the sustaining crags;
The spires of ice are toppled down,

And molten up, and roar in flood;
The fortress crashes from on high,
15    The brute earth lightens to the sky,
And the great Aeon sinks in blood,

And compass'd by the fires of Hell;
While thou, dear spirit, happy star,
O'erlook'st the tumult from afar,
20    And smilest, knowing all is well.


## CXXVIII

The love that rose on stronger wings,
Unpalsied when he met with Death,
Is comrade of the lesser faith
That sees the course of human things.[5]

5    No doubt vast eddies in the flood
Of onward time shall yet be made,
And throned races may degrade;[6]
Yet O ye mysteries of good,

Wild Hours that fly with Hope and Fear,
10    If all your office had to do
With old results that look like new;[7]
If this were all your mission here,

To draw, to sheathe a useless sword,
To fool the crowd with glorious lies,
15    To cleave a creed in sects and cries,
To change the bearing of a word,

To shift an arbitrary power,
To cramp the student at his desk,

4. A poor and diseased person. The images in the following stanzas symbolize political upheaval.
5. Faith in the immortality of love "is comrade" to the faith expressed in the previous section, that upheaval in human affairs eventually leads to good.
6. I.e., races now in power may degenerate.
7. If time brought about only superficial change, but no real progress (examples of which are given in the following stanzas).

To make old bareness picturesque
20 And tuft with grass a feudal tower;

Why then my scorn might well descend
    On you and yours.[8] I see in part
    That all, as in some piece of art,
Is toil coöperant to an end.

# CXXIX

Dear friend, far off, my lost desire,
    So far, so near in woe and weal;
    O loved the most, when most I feel
There is a lower and a higher;

5 Known and unknown; human, divine;
    Sweet human hand and lips and eye;
    Dear heavenly friend that canst not die,
Mine, mine, for ever, ever mine;

Strange friend, past, present, and to be;
10    Loved deeplier, darklier understood;
    Behold, I dream a dream of good,
And mingle all the world with thee.

# CXXX

Thy voice is on the rolling air;
    I hear thee where the waters run;
    Thou standest in the rising sun,
And in the setting thou art fair.

5 What art thou then? I cannot guess;
    But tho' I seem in star and flower
    To feel thee some diffusive power,
I do not therefore love thee less:

My love involves the love before;
10    My love is vaster passion now;
    Tho' mix'd with God and Nature thou,
I seem to love thee more and more.

8. The "Wild Hours" and the accompanying "Hope and Fear" (line 9).

Far off thou art, but ever nigh;
  I have thee still, and I rejoice;
15  I prosper, circled with thy voice;
I shall not lose thee tho' I die.


## CXXXI

O living will that shalt endure[9]
  When all that seems shall suffer shock,
  Rise in the spiritual rock,[1]
Flow thro' our deeds and make them pure,

5  That we may lift from out of dust
  A voice as unto him that hears,
  A cry above the conquer'd years
To one that with us works, and trust,

With faith that comes of self-control,
10  The truths that never can be proved
  Until we close with all we loved,
And all we flow from, soul in soul.


## [Epilogue][2]

O true and tried, so well and long,
  Demand not thou a marriage lay;
  In that it is thy marriage day
Is music more than any song.

5  Nor have I felt so much of bliss
  Since first he told me that he loved
  A daughter of our house; nor proved
Since that dark day a day like this;[3]

---

9. "That which we know as Free-will in man" [T.].
1. See 1 Corinthians 10:4, where Christ is compared to the rock that provided water to the Israelites in the desert (Exodus 17): "They drank of that spiritual Rock that followed them: and that Rock was Christ."
2. This concluding section (which, like the Prologue, Tennyson left untitled) is an *epithalamium* or "marriage lay" (line 2), celebrating the wedding of Tennyson's sister Cecilia to his friend Edmund Lushington. The wedding took place in October 1842, nine years after Hallam's death (lines 9–10). Lushington is the person addressed, as he was also in section LXXXV.
3. Lines 6–7 refer to Hallam's engagement to Tennyson's sister Emily; "that dark day" (line 8) refers to the day of Hallam's death. "Proved": experienced.

Tho' I since then have number'd o'er
10      Some thrice three years: they went and came,
        Remade the blood and changed the frame,
And yet is love not less, but more;

No longer caring to embalm
        In dying songs a dead regret,
15      But like a statue solid-set,
And moulded in colossal calm.

Regret is dead, but love is more
        Than in the summers that are flown,
        For I myself with these have grown
20    To something greater than before;

Which makes appear the songs I made
        As echoes out of weaker times,
        As half but idle brawling rhymes,
The sport of random sun and shade.

25    But where is she, the bridal flower,
        That must be made a wife ere noon?
        She enters, glowing like the moon
Of Eden on its bridal bower:

On me she bends her blissful eyes
30      And then on thee; they meet thy look
        And brighten like the star that shook
Betwixt the palms of paradise.

O when her life was yet in bud,
        He too foretold the perfect rose.[4]
35      For thee she grew, for thee she grows
For ever, and as fair as good.

And thou art worthy; full of power;
        As gentle; liberal-minded, great,
        Consistent; wearing all that weight
40    Of learning lightly like a flower.

---

4. I.e., Hallam foretold that she would grow up to be beautiful. Cecilia was eight years younger than her brother. Since their father had died in 1831, Tennyson gave away the bride at the wedding (line 42).

But now set out: the noon is near,
   And I must give away the bride;
   She fears not, or with thee beside
And me behind her, will not fear.

45   For I that danced her on my knee,
     That watch'd her on her nurse's arm,
     That shielded all her life from harm
At last must part with her to thee;

Now waiting to be made a wife,
50     Her feet, my darling, on the dead;
     Their pensive tablets round her head,[5]
And the most living words of life

Breathed in her ear. The ring is on,
   The 'wilt thou' answer'd, and again
55     The 'wilt thou' ask'd, till out of twain
Her sweet 'I will' has made you one.

Now sign your names,[6] which shall be read,
   Mute symbols of a joyful morn,
   By village eyes as yet unborn;
60   The names are sign'd, and overhead

Begins the clash and clang that tells
   The joy to every wandering breeze;
   The blind wall rocks, and on the trees
The dead leaf trembles to the bells.

65   O happy hour, and happier hours
     Await them. Many a merry face
     Salutes them—maidens of the place,
That pelt us in the porch with flowers.

O happy hour, behold the bride
70     With him to whom her hand I gave.
     They leave the porch, they pass the grave
That has to-day its sunny side.

To-day the grave is bright for me,
   For them the light of life increased,

---

5. She stands on the grave of those buried in the church and with their memorial "tablets" on the wall above her.
6. In the parish register, an official record kept in the church.

75      Who stay to share the morning feast,
    Who rest to-night beside the sea.

    Let all my genial spirits advance
        To meet and greet a whiter sun;
        My drooping memory will not shun
80  The foaming grape of eastern France.[7]

    It circles round, and fancy plays,
        And hearts are warm'd and faces bloom,
        As drinking health to bride and groom
    We wish them store of happy days.

85  Nor count me all to blame if I
        Conjecture of a stiller guest,
        Perchance, perchance, among the rest,
    And, tho' in silence, wishing joy.

    But they must go, the time draws on,
90      And those white-favour'd horses wait;
        They rise, but linger; it is late;
    Farewell, we kiss, and they are gone.

    A shade falls on us like the dark
        From little cloudlets on the grass,
95      But sweeps away as out we pass
    To range the woods, to roam the park,

    Discussing how their courtship grew,
        And talk of others that are wed,
        And how she look'd, and what he said,
100 And back we come at fall of dew.

    Again the feast, the speech, the glee,
        The shade of passing thought, the wealth
        Of words and wit, the double health,
    The crowning cup, the three-times-three,[8]

105 And last the dance;—till I retire:
        Dumb is that tower which spake so loud,
        And high in heaven the streaming cloud,
    And on the downs a rising fire:

7. Champagne.
8. I.e., cheers.

And rise, O moon, from yonder down,
110    Till over down and over dale
All night the shining vapour sail
And pass the silent-lighted town,

The white-faced halls, the glancing rills,
And catch at every mountain head,
115    And o'er the friths[9] that branch and spread
Their sleeping silver thro' the hills;

And touch with shade the bridal doors,
With tender gloom the roof, the wall;
And breaking let the splendour fall
120    To spangle all the happy shores

By which they rest, and ocean sounds,
And, star and system rolling past,
A soul shall draw from out the vast
And strike his being into bounds,

125    And, moved thro' life of lower phase,[1]
Result in man, be born and think,
And act and love, a closer link
Betwixt us and the crowning race[2]

Of those that, eye to eye, shall look
130    On knowledge; under whose command
Is Earth and Earth's, and in their hand
Is Nature like an open book;

No longer half-akin to brute,
For all we thought and loved and did,
135    And hoped, and suffer'd, is but seed
Of what in them is flower and fruit;

Whereof the man, that with me trod
This planet, was a noble type[3]

---

9. Waterways.
1. The soul of the child that will be conceived on this wedding night (lines 123–24) will progress through stages in which it resembles lower forms of life. Tennyson was familiar with the theory that the human embryo's development recapitulates the evolution of the species; see, for instance, the selection from Robert Chambers, p. 137 below.
2. The new child will be one step closer to the perfect humanity of the future ("the crowning race"), described in the following stanzas.
3. Archetype; model.

Appearing ere the times were ripe,
140  That friend of mine who lives in God,

That God, which ever lives and loves,
    One God, one law, one element,
    And one far-off divine event,
To which the whole creation moves.

# BACKGROUNDS AND CONTEXTS

# HALLAM, LORD TENNYSON

## *From* Alfred Lord Tennyson: A Memoir[†]

\* \* \*

At first the reviews of the volume were not on the whole sympa-
thetic. One critic in a leading journal, for instance, considered that
"a great deal of poetic feeling had been wasted," and "much shallow
art spent on the tenderness shown to an Amaryllis of the Chancery
Bar." Another referred to the poem as follows: "These touching
lines evidently come from the full heart of the widow of a military
man." However, men like Maurice and Robertson thought that the
author had made a definite step towards the unification of the high-
est religion and philosophy with the progressive science of the day;
and that he was the one poet who "through almost the agonies of a
death-struggle" had made an effective stand against his own doubts
and difficulties and those of the time, "on behalf of those first
principles which underlie all creeds, which belong to our earliest
childhood, and on which the wisest and best have rested through
all ages; that all is right; that darkness shall be clear; that God and
Time are the only interpreters; that Love is King; that the Immortal
is in us; that, which is the keynote of the whole, 'All is well, tho'
Faith and Form be sundered in the night of Fear.'" Scientific lead-
ers like Herschel, Owen, Sedgwick and Tyndall regarded him as a
champion of Science, and cheered him with words of genuine
admiration for his love of Nature, for the eagerness with which he
welcomed all the latest scientific discoveries, and for his trust in
truth. Science indeed in his opinion was one of the main forces
tending to disperse the superstition that still darkens the world.

\* \* \*

"It must be remembered," writes my father,[1] "that this is a poem,
*not* an actual biography. It is founded on our friendship, on the
engagement of Arthur Hallam to my sister, on his sudden death at
Vienna, just before the time fixed for their marriage, and on his
burial at Clevedon Church. The poem concludes with the marriage
of my youngest sister Cecilia. It was meant to be a kind of *Divina
Commedia*,[2] ending with happiness. The sections were written at
many different places, and as the phases of our intercourse came to

---

† From *Alfred Lord Tennyson: A Memoir*, vol. I (New York: Macmillan, 1897), pp. 298–99,
304–6, 308–9, 311–14, 321–23, 327. All notes are the editor's.
1. Hallam Tennyson was the poet's son; throughout the selection, therefore, "my father"
refers to the poet.
2. Dante's *Divine Comedy*, which moves from hell to heaven.

my memory and suggested them. I did not write them with any view of weaving them into a whole, or for publication, until I found that I had written so many. The different moods of sorrow as in a drama are dramatically given, and my conviction that fear, doubts, and suffering will find answer and relief only through Faith in a God of Love. 'I' is not always the author speaking of himself, but the voice of the human race speaking thro' him. After the Death of A.H.H., the divisions of the poem are made by First Xmas Eve (Section XXVIII.), Second Xmas (LXXVIII.), Third Xmas Eve (CIV. and CV. etc.). I myself did not see Clevedon till years after the burial of A.H.H. Jan. 3rd, 1834, and then in later editions of 'In Memoriam' I altered the word 'chancel,' which was the word used by Mr Hallam in his Memoir, to 'dark church.' As to the localities in which the poems were written, some were written in Lincolnshire, some in London, Essex, Gloucestershire, Wales, anywhere where I happened to be."

"And as for the metre of 'In Memoriam' I had no notion till 1880 that Lord Herbert of Cherbury had written his occasional verses in the same metre. I believed myself the originator of the metre, until after 'In Memoriam' came out, when some one told me that Ben Jonson and Sir Philip Sidney had used it."[3]

\* \* \*

That my father was a student of the Bible, those who have read "In Memoriam" know. He also eagerly read all notable works within his reach relating to the Bible, and traced with deep interest such fundamental truths as underlie the great religions of the world. He hoped that the Bible would be more and more studied by all ranks of people, and expounded simply by their teachers; for he maintained that the religion of a people could never be founded on mere moral philosophy: and that it could only come home to them in the simple, noble thoughts and facts of a Scripture like ours.

\* \* \*

His creed, he always said, he would not formulate, for people would not understand him if he did; but he considered that his poems expressed the principles at the foundation of his faith.

He thought, with Arthur Hallam, "that the essential feelings of religion subsist in the utmost diversity of forms," that "different language does not always imply different opinions, nor different opinions any difference in *real* faith." "It is impossible," he said, "to imagine that the Almighty will ask you, when you come before Him in the next life what your particular form of creed was: but the ques-

---

3. The three poets mentioned all used the stanza form found in *In Memoriam* in the 16th and 17th centuries.

tion will rather be, 'Have you been true to yourself, and given in My Name a cup of cold water to one of these little ones?'"

"This is a terrible age of unfaith," he would say. "I hate utter unfaith, I cannot endure that men should sacrifice everything at the cold altar of what with their imperfect knowledge they choose to call truth and reason. One can easily lose all belief, through giving up the continual thought and care for spiritual things."

And again, "In this vale of Time the hills of Time often shut out the mountains of Eternity."

\* \* \*

Assuredly Religion was no nebulous abstraction for him. He consistently emphasized his own belief in what he called the Eternal Truths; in an Omnipotent, Omnipresent and All-loving God, Who has revealed Himself through the human attribute of the highest self-sacrificing love; in the freedom of the human will; and in the immortality of the soul. But he asserted that "Nothing worthy proving can be proven," and that even as to the great laws which are the basis of Science, "We have but faith, we cannot know." He dreaded the dogmatism of sects and rash definitions of God. "I dare hardly name His Name" he would say, and accordingly he named Him in "The Ancient Sage" the "Nameless." "But take away belief in the self-conscious personality of God," he said, "and you take away the backbone of the world." "On God and God-like men we build our trust." A week before his death I was sitting by him, and he talked long of the Personality and of the Love of God, "That God, Whose eyes consider the poor," "Who catereth even for the sparrow." "I should," he said, "infinitely rather feel myself the most miserable wretch on the face of the earth with a God above, than the highest type of man standing alone." He would allow that God is unknowable in "his whole world-self, and all-in-all," and that therefore there was some force in the objection made by some people to the word "Personality," as being "anthropomorphic," and that perhaps "Self-consciousness" or "Mind" might be clearer to them: but at the same time he insisted that, although "man is like a thing of nought" in "the boundless plan," our highest view of God must be more or less anthropomorphic: and that "Personality," as far as our intelligence goes, is the widest definition and includes "Mind," "Self-consciousness," "Will," "Love" and other attributes of the Real, the Supreme, "the High and Lofty One that inhabiteth Eternity Whose name is Holy."

\* \* \*

Everywhere throughout the Universe he saw the glory and greatness of God, and the science of Nature was particularly dear to him. Every new fact which came within his range was carefully weighed. As he exulted in the wilder aspects of Nature (see for instance sect. xv.) and revelled in the thunderstorm; so he felt a joy in her orderliness; he felt a rest in her steadfastness, patient progress and hopefulness; the same seasons ever returned; the same stars wheeled in their courses; the flowers and trees blossomed and the birds sang yearly in their appointed months; and he had a triumphant appreciation of her ever-new revelations of beauty. One of the "In Memoriam" poems, written at Barmouth, gives preeminently his sense of the joyous peace in Nature, and he would quote it in this context along with his Spring and Bird songs:

> Sweet after showers, ambrosial air,
>   That rollest from the gorgeous gloom
>   Of evening over brake and bloom
> And meadow, slowly breathing bare
>
> The round of space, and rapt below
>   Thro' all the dewy-tassell'd wood,
>   And shadowing down the horned flood
> In ripples, fan my brows and blow
>
> The fever from my cheek, and sigh
>   The full new life that feeds thy breath
>   Throughout my frame, till Doubt and Death,
> Ill brethren, let the fancy fly
>
> From belt to belt of crimson seas
>   On leagues of odour streaming far,
>   To where in yonder orient star
> A hundred spirits whisper "Peace."
>
> [LXXXVI]

But he was occasionally much troubled with the intellectual problem of the apparent profusion and waste of life and by the vast amount of sin and suffering throughout the world, for these seemed to militate against the idea of the Omnipotent and All-loving Father.[4]

No doubt in such moments he might possibly have been heard to say what I myself have heard him say: "An Omnipotent Creator Who could make such a painful world is to me *sometimes* as hard to believe in as to believe in blind matter behind everything. The lavish profusion too in the natural world appals me, from the growths of the tropical forest to the capacity of man to multiply, the torrent of babies."

*   *   *

---

4. See section LV.

I need not enlarge upon his faith in the Immortality of the Soul as he has dwelt upon that so fully in his poems. "I can hardly understand," he said, "how any great, imaginative man, who has deeply lived, suffered, thought and wrought, can doubt of the Soul's continuous progress in the after-life." His poem of "Wages" he liked to quote on this subject.

He more than once said what he has expressed in "Vastness": "Hast Thou made all this for naught! Is all this trouble of life worth undergoing if we only end in our own corpse-coffins at last? If you allow a God, and God allows this strong instinct and universal yearning for another life, surely that is in a measure a presumption of its truth. We cannot give up the mighty hopes that make us men."

> My own dim life should teach me this,
>     That life shall live for evermore,
>     Else earth is darkness at the core,
> And dust and ashes all that is.

*  *  *

> What then were God to such as I?
>                                    [XXXIV, 1–4, 9]

I have heard him even say that he "would rather know that he was to be lost eternally than not know that the whole human race was to live eternally"; and when he speaks of "faintly trusting the larger hope" he means by "the larger hope" that the whole human race would through, perhaps, ages of suffering, be at length purified and saved, even those who now "better not with time"; so that at the end of "The Vision of Sin" we read

> God made Himself an awful rose of dawn.

One day towards the end of his life he bade me look into the Revised Version and see how the Revisers had translated the passage "Depart from me, ye cursed, into everlasting fire." His disappointment was keen when he found that the translators had not altered "everlasting" into "æonian" or some such word: for he never would believe that Christ could preach "everlasting punishment."

> "Fecemi la divina potestate
> La somma sapienza, e 'l primo amore,"[5]

were words which he was fond of quoting in this relation, as if they were a kind of unconscious confession by Dante that Love must conquer at the last.

---

5. "Divine power created me [i.e., hell], highest wisdom, and primal love" (*Inferno* III, 5–6); this is inscribed over the gates of hell.

Letters were not unfrequently addressed to him asking what his opinions were about Evolution, about Prayer, and about Christ.

Of Evolution he said: "That makes no difference to me, even if the Darwinians did not, as they do, exaggerate Darwinism. To God all is present. He sees present, past, and future as one."

\*   \*   \*

In the poem "By an Evolutionist," written in 1888 when he was dangerously ill, he defined his position; he conceived that the further science progressed, the more the Unity of Nature, and the purpose hidden behind the cosmic process of matter in motion and changing forms of life, would be apparent. Someone asked him whether it was not hard to account for genius by Evolution. He put aside the question, for he believed that genius was the greatest mystery to itself.

To Tyndall he once said, "No evolutionist is able to explain the mind of Man or how any possible physiological change of tissue can produce conscious thought." Yet he was inclined to think that the theory of Evolution caused the world to regard more clearly the "Life of Nature as a lower stage in the manifestation of a principle which is more fully manifested in the spiritual life of man, with the idea that in this process of Evolution the lower is to be regarded as a means to the higher."

\*   \*   \*

I cannot end this chapter on "In Memoriam" more fitly than by quoting Henry Hallam's[6] letter on receiving in 1850 what he calls "the precious book."

> I know not how to express what I have felt. My first sentiment was surprise, for, though I now find that you had mentioned the intention to my daughter, Julia, she had never told me of the poems. I do not speak as another would to praise and admire: few of them indeed I have as yet been capable of reading, the grief they express is too much akin to that they revive. It is better than any monument which could be raised to the memory of my beloved son, it is a more lively and enduring testimony to his great virtues and talents that the world should know the friendship which existed between you, that posterity should associate his name with that of Alfred Tennyson.

---

6. Arthur Hallam's father.

# Arthur Henry Hallam

## WILLIAM EWART GLADSTONE

### Arthur Henry Hallam[†]

Far back in the distance of my early life, and upon a surface not yet ruffled by contention, there lies the memory of a friendship surpassing every other that has ever been enjoyed by one greatly blessed both in the number and in the excellence of his friends.

It is the simple truth that Arthur Henry Hallam was a spirit so exceptional that everything with which he was brought into relation during his shortened passage through this world came to be, through this contact, glorified by a touch of the ideal. Among his contemporaries at Eton, that queen of visible homes for the ideal schoolboy, he stood supreme among all his fellows; and the long life through which I have since wound my way, and which has brought me into contact with so many men of rich endowments, leaves him where he then stood, as to natural gifts, so far as my estimation is concerned.

But I ought perhaps to note a distinction which it is necessary to draw. Whether he possessed the greatest genius I have ever known is a question which does not lie upon my path, and which I do not undertake to determine. It is of the man that I speak, and genius does not of itself make the man. When we deal with men, genius and character must be jointly taken into view; and the relation between the two, together with the effect upon the aggregate, is infinitely variable. The towering position of Shakespeare among poets does not of itself afford a certain indication that he holds a place equally high among men.

\* \* \*

While intimacy was at this particular time the most delightful note of the friendship between Arthur Hallam and myself, I am

---

† From *The Youth's Companion* 72.1 (January 6, 1898): 1–3. Gladstone, who later served four terms as prime minister of England, was Hallam's best friend when they were schoolboys at Eton. This memoir, published near the end of Gladstone's life, shows that he shared Tennyson's extraordinarily high estimate of Hallam's character and abilities.

bound to say that it had one other and more peculiar characteristic, which was its inequality.[1] Indeed, it was so unequal, as between his mental powers and mine, that I have questioned myself strictly whether I was warranted in supposing it to have been knit with such closeness as I have fondly supposed. * * * It is difficult for me now to conceive how during these years he bore with me; since not only was I inferior to him in knowledge and dialectic ability, but my mind was "cabined, cribbed, confined,"[2] by an intolerance which I ascribe to my having been brought up in what were then termed Evangelical ideas—ideas, I must add, that in other respects were frequently productive of great and vital good.

This he must have found sorely vexing to his large and expansive tone of mind, but his charity covered the multitude of my sins. The explanation is to be found in that genuine breadth of his, which was so comprehensive that he could tolerate even the intolerant. It was a smaller feat than this to tolerate inferiority. But certainly this was one of the points in which he had anticipated what is usually the fruit of mature age.

* * *

* * * When the appalling intelligence of his sudden death at Vienna in the early autumn of 1833, during a holiday tour taken with his father, reached us in England, I felt not only that a dear friend had been lost, but that a great light had been extinguished, and one which was eminently required by the coming necessities of the country and the age. Those who will read the "*Theodicæa Novissima*,"[3] printed among the remains of Arthur Hallam, will be able to surmise the grounds on which my anticipation rested. But I think that of all the characteristics of his mind, perhaps the most peculiar was its moral maturity. What treasures he carried away with him to the grave! How much he had to impart! Something, perhaps, even to the poet and friend[4] who has reared over him the memorial more durable than bronze or stone.

It was one, I think, well warranted by the character of our wonderful century, such as it has been developed before our eyes. It has been an age, at least in Arthur Hallam's country, of characteristics so copious, so varied and so conflicting that it is difficult to sum them up under any one common and connecting phrase. * * * And upon my heightened retrospect, I must advisedly declare that I have never,

---

1. Compare section 42 of *In Memoriam*.
2. Shakespeare, *Macbeth* 3.4.23.
3. Hallam's essay, written while he was at Cambridge, in which he seeks to explain the existence of evil in a divinely ordained world.
4. I.e., Tennyson.

in the actual experience of life, known a man who seemed to me to possess all the numerous and varied qualifications required in order to meet this growing demand and even its fullest breadth, in anything like the measure in which Arthur Hallam exhibited these budding, nay, already flowering gifts. It was to be a sensitive, an exacting, a self-asserting age. To deal with it, to find effectual access to its confidence and the key to its affections, required the combination of breadth with courage, and of firmness with tenderness. * * * The treatment that it needed could only be supplied by one who united an unbounded intellectual insight, and the sure tact which discerns and separates the precious from the vile. His death was, then, a grievous and, humanly speaking, an irreparable bereavement. But He who took him made him, and He who made him can replace him.

* * *

# ARTHUR HALLAM†

## On the Picture of the Three Fates in the Palazzo Pitti, at Florence[1]

None but a Tuscan hand could fix ye here
   In rigidness of sober colouring.
Pale are ye, mighty Triad, not with fear,
   But the most awful knowledge, that the spring
5  Is in you of all birth, and act, and sense.
   I sorrow to behold ye: pain is blent
With your aloof and loveless permanence,
   And your high princedom seems a punishment.
The cunning limner[2] could not personate
10   Your blind control, save in th'aspect of grief;
So does the thought repugn of sovran fate.
   Let him gaze here who trusts not in the love
   Toward which all being solemnly doth move:
More this grand sadness tells, than forms of fairest life.

---

† The following four pieces, some published only after Hallam's death, are reprinted from *The Writings of Arthur Hallam*, ed. T. H. Vail Motter (New York: Modern Language Association, 1943), pp. 3, 45–46, 87, 158–59.
1. The sentiment expressed in this early sonnet (composed 1827 and printed 1830), contrasting a classical belief in absolute Fate with the Christian belief in God's love, would become central both to Hallam's writings and to *In Memoriam*. Tennyson may be recalling the penultimate line of this poem in the final lines of the Epilogue to *In Memoriam*.
2. Painter. As Hallam notes in a subtitle to the poem, the painting was attributed to Michelangelo.

## To A.T.[3]

Oh, last in time, but worthy to be first
    Of friends in rank, had not the father of good
    On my early spring one perfect gem bestowed,
    A friend, with whom to share the best and worst.
5   Him will I shut close to my heart for aye.
    There's not a fibre quivers there, but is
    His own, his heritage for woe, or bliss.
    Thou wouldst not have me such a charge betray.
Surely, if I be knit in brotherhood
10  So tender to that chief of all my love,
    With thee I shall not loyalty eschew.
And well I ween not time with ill or good,
    Shall thine affection e'er from mine remove,
    Thou yearner for all fair things, and all true.

## [To Emily Tennyson][4]

Still here—thou hast not faded from my sight,
    Nor all the music round thee from mine ear:
    Still grace flows from thee to the brightening year,
    And all the birds laugh out in wealthier light.
5   Still am I free to close my happy eyes,
    And paint upon the gloom thy mimic form,
    That soft white neck, that cheek in beauty warm,
    And brow half hidden where yon ringlet lies;
With, Oh! the blissful knowledge all the while
10  That I can lift at will each curved lid,
    And my fair dream most highly realize.
The time will come, 'tis ushered by my sighs,
    When I may shape the dark, but vainly bid
    True light restore that form, those looks, that smile.

3. Hallam wrote this sonnet to Tennyson very early in their friendship (1829, printed 1830). The other friend referred to in the first two quatrains is probably William Ewart Gladstone, Hallam's closest friend before he went to Cambridge (see the selection by Gladstone, p. 115 above).
4. Hallam first met Emily Tennyson, Alfred's younger sister, late in 1829 and, after a period of opposition from his family, became engaged to her in March 1832. This sonnet was probably written early in their relationship (and printed 1834).

## [Manly Love]⁵

\* \* \* Plato saw very early, that to communicate to our nature this noblest kind of love, the love of a worthy object, would have the effect of a regeneration to the soul, and would establish conscience in nearly the same intimacy with the world of the senses, which she already maintains with our interior existence. Hence his constant presentation of morality under the aspect of beauty, a practice favoured by the language of his country, where from an early period the same το καλον⁶ had comprehended them both. Hence that frequent commendation of a more lively sentiment than has existed in other times between man and man, the misunderstanding of which has repelled several from the deep tenderness and splendid imaginations of the Phædrus and the Symposium, but which was evidently resorted to by Plato, on account of the social prejudices which at that time depressed woman below her natural station, and which, even had the philosopher himself entirely surmounted them, would have rendered it perhaps impossible to persuade an Athenian audience that a female mind, especially if restrained within the limits of chastity and modest obedience, could ever possess attractions at all worthy to fix the regard, much less exhaust the capacities of this highest and purest manly love.

\* \* \*

# ALFRED TENNYSON†

## To ———

I

All good things have not kept aloof,
    Nor wandered into other ways:
I have not lacked thy mild reproof,
    Nor golden largess of thy praise,
5        But life is full of weary days.

---

5. In this passage from an essay written in 1831 at Cambridge (printed 1832), Hallam defies prevailing opinion by defending Plato's exaltation of love between men in *Symposium* and *Phaedrus*, the ancient Greek philosopher's two principal dialogues about love.
6. "The beautiful," applied by Greek philosophers to both physical and moral beauty.
†  The following two pieces are reprinted from Tennyson's *Poems* (London: Moxon, 1833), pp. 2–4, 151. Both poems were understood by Hallam (as well as by other friends of Tennyson's) to be addressed to him. The first piece was much revised in later printings and retitled "My life is full of weary days."

## II

Shake hands, my friend, across the brink
  Of that deep grave to which I go.
Shake hands once more: I cannot sink
  So far—far down, but I shall know
10    Thy voice, and answer from below.

## III

When, in the darkness over me,
  The fourhanded mole shall scrape,
Plant thou no dusky cypresstree,
  Nor wreathe thy cap with doleful crape,
15    But pledge me in the flowing grape.

## IV

And when the sappy field and wood
  Grow green beneath the showery gray,
And rugged barks begin to bud,
  And through damp holts, newflushed with May,
20    Ring sudden laughters of the Jay;

## V

Then let wise Nature work her will
  And on my clay her darnels grow.
Come only, when the days are still,
  And at my headstone whisper low,
25    And tell me if the woodbines blow,

## VI

If thou art blest, my mother's smile
  Undimmed, if bees are on the wing:
Then cease, my friend, a little while,
  That I may hear the throstle sing
30    His bridal song, the boast of spring.

## VII

Sweet as the noise in parchèd plains
  Of bubbling wells that fret the stones,
(If any sense in me remains)
  Thy words will be; thy cheerful tones
35    As welcome to my crumbling bones.

## Sonnet [As when with downcast eyes]

As when with downcast eyes we muse and brood,
And ebb into a former life, or seem
To lapse far back in a confusèd dream
To states of mystical similitude;
5   If one but speaks or hems or stirs his chair,
Ever the wonder waxeth more and more,
So that we say, "All this hath been before,
All this *hath* been, I know not when or where."
So, friend, when first I looked upon your face,
10  Our thought gave answer, each to each, so true,
Opposèd mirrors each reflecting each—
Altho' I knew not in what time or place,
Methought that I had often met with you,
And each had lived in the other's mind and speech.

# Literary Contexts

## CATULLUS

### [Elegy for his brother][†]

Brother, I come o'er many seas and lands
    To the sad rite which pious love ordains,
To pay thee the last gift that death demands;
    And oft, though vain, invoke thy mute remains:
5   Since death has ravish'd half myself in thee,
    Oh wretched brother, sadly torn from me!

And now ere fate our souls shall re-unite,
    To give me back all it hath snatch'd away,
Receive the gifts, our fathers' ancient rite
10    To shades departed still was wont to pay;
Gifts wet with tears of heartfelt grief that tell,
    And ever, brother, bless thee, and farewell!

## WILLIAM SHAKESPEARE

### *From* Sonnets[‡]

### XXVII

Weary with toil, I haste me to my bed,
The dear repose for limbs with travel tired;

---

† Reprinted from *The Poems of Caius Valerius Catullus*, trans. George Lamb, 2 vols.
(London: Murray, 1820), 2.94. Tennyson greatly admired this brief elegy by the Roman
poet Catullus (1st century B.C.E.) and in section 57 of *In Memoriam* echoes its famous
final words, *"ave atque vale"* ("hail and farewell"). Although this particular translation
mentions a possible reunion in the afterlife (lines 7–8), no such possibility is present in
the original, as Tennyson observed in an 1880 letter to Gladstone: "neither I nor any
other 'can surpass the beauty' [of Catullus' poem]: nor can any modern elegy, so long as
men retain the least hope in the after-life of those whom they loved, equal in pathos the
desolation of that everlasting farewell" (*Memoir* 2.239).

‡ From *The Poems of William Shakespeare*, ed. Edward Capell (London, 1804), pp. 134–35,
178–79, with slight emendations. Early reviews of *In Memoriam* frequently compared
Tennyson's poem to Shakespeare's *Sonnets* (1609). The resemblance lies less in local

123

But then begins a journey in my head,
To work my mind, when body's work's expired:
5　For then my thoughts (from far where I abide)
Intend a zealous pilgrimage to thee,
And keep my drooping eyelids open wide,
Looking on darkness which the blind do see.
Save that my soul's imaginary sight
10　Presents thy shadow to my sightless view,
Which, like a jewel hung in ghastly night,
Makes black night beauteous, and her old face new.
　Lo thus by day my limbs, by night my mind,
　For thee, and for myself, no quiet find.

## XXX

When to the sessions of sweet silent thought
I summon up remembrance of things past,
I sigh the lack of many a thing I sought,
And with old woes new wail my dear time's waste:
5　Then can I drown an eye, unused to flow,
For precious friends hid in death's dateless night,
And weep afresh love's long-since canceled woe,
And moan the expense of many a vanished sight.
Then can I grieve at grievances foregone,
10　And heavily from woe to woe tell o'er
The sad account of fore-bemoaned moan,
Which I new pay as if not paid before.
　But if the while I think on thee, dear friend,
　All losses are restored, and sorrows end.

## CXV

Those lines that I before have writ, do lie,
Even those that said I could not love you dearer;
Yet then my judgment knew no reason why
My most full flame should afterwards burn clearer.
5　But reckoning time, whose million'd accidents
Creep in 'twixt vows, and change decrees of kings,
Tan sacred beauty, blunt the sharp'st intents,
Divert strong minds to the course of altering things—
Alas! why, fearing of time's tyranny,
10　Might I not then say, *now I love you best*,
When I was certain o'er incertainty,

---

allusions and influences than in the general structure and subject matter: both are long
poetic works made up of shorter lyric sections and addressed to a beloved male friend.
This selection offers a small sampling from Shakespeare's sequence, which includes
154 sonnets, the first 126 of which are addressed to a young man, while the remainder
address a woman.

Crowning the present, doubting of the rest?
  Love is a babe; then might I not say so,
  To give full growth to that which still doth grow.

### CXVI

Let me not to the marriage of true minds
Admit impediments. Love is not love
Which alters when it alteration finds,
Or bends with the remover to remove:
5   O no! it is an ever-fixèd mark,
That looks on tempests, and is never shaken;
It is the star to every wandering bark,
Whose worth's unknown, although his height be taken.
Love's not Time's fool, though rosy lips and cheeks
10   Within his bending sickle's compass come;
Love alters not with his brief hours and weeks,
But bears it out even to the edge of doom.
  If this be error, and upon me proved,
  I never writ, nor no man ever loved.

## JOHN MILTON†

### *From* Lycidas

Yet once more, O ye laurels, and once more
Ye myrtles brown, with ivy never-sere,
I come to pluck your berries harsh and crude,
And, with forced fingers rude,
5   Shatter your leaves before the mellowing year.
Bitter constraint, and sad occasion dear,
Compels me to disturb your season due:
For Lycidas is dead, dead ere his prime,
Young Lycidas, and hath not left his peer.
10   Who would not sing for Lycidas? He knew
Himself to sing, and build the lofty rhyme.
He must not float upon his watery bier
Unwept, and welter to the parching wind,
Without the meed of some melodious tear.

---

† The following two selections are reprinted from *The Poetical Works of John Milton*, ed.
Henry John Todd, 4 vols. (London: Johnson, 1808), 4.71–79, 107, with slight emendations.
"Lycidas" (1638), perhaps the best known elegy in English, exerted a pervasive influence
on Tennyson's poem. It laments the death of Edward King (called Lycidas in the poem, in
accordance with pastoral convention), a classmate and friend of Milton's at Cambridge,
who died in a shipwreck at the age of twenty-five. The ship sections of *In Memoriam* (sec-
tions 9–18) recall the pervasive water imagery of "Lycidas," as does Tennyson's occasional
use of pastoral imagery (as in sections 21, 23, and 89).

15     Begin then, Sisters of the sacred well,[1]
       That from beneath the seat of Jove doth spring,
       Begin, and somewhat loudly sweep the string.
       Hence with denial vain, and coy excuse:
       So may some gentle Muse[2]
20    With lucky words favour my destined urn,
       And, as he passes, turn,
       And bid fair peace be to my sable shroud.
       For we were nurst upon the self-same hill,
       Fed the same flock by fountain, shade, and rill.
25    Together both, ere the high lawns appeared
       Under the opening eye-lids of the morn,
       We drove afield, and both together heard
       What time the gray-fly winds her sultry horn,
       Battening our flocks with the fresh dews of night,
30    Oft till the star that rose, at evening, bright,
       Toward Heaven's descent had sloped his westering wheel.

*  *  *

165   Weep no more, woeful Shepherds, weep no more,
       For Lycidas, your sorrow, is not dead,
       Sunk though he be beneath the watery floor;
       So sinks the day-star in the ocean bed,
       And yet anon repairs his drooping head,
170   And tricks his beams, and with new spangled ore
       Flames in the forehead of the morning sky:
       So Lycidas sunk low, but mounted high,
       Through the dear might of him that walked the waves;[3]
       Where, other groves and other streams along,
175   With nectar pure his oozy locks he laves,
       And hears the unexpressive[4] nuptial song,
       In the blest kingdoms meek of joy and love.
       There entertain him all the saints above,
       In solemn troops, and sweet societies,
180   That sing, and, singing, in their glory move,
       And wipe the tears for ever from his eyes.
       Now, Lycidas, the shepherds weep no more;
       Henceforth thou art the genius[5] of the shore,
       In thy large recompence, and shalt be good
185   To all that wander in that perilous flood.

*  *  *

1. I.e., the Muses.
2. In this case, referring to a future poet.
3. Jesus.
4. Inexpressible.
5. Guardian divinity.

## [Methought I saw]⁶

Methought I saw my late espoused saint
   Brought to me, like Alcestis, from the grave,
   Whom Jove's great son to her glad husband gave,
   Rescued from death by force, though pale and faint.⁷
5  Mine, as whom washed from spot of child-bed taint
   Purification in the old Law did save,⁸
   And such as yet once more I trust to have
   Full sight of her in Heaven without restraint,
Came vested all in white, pure as her mind:
10   Her face was veiled; yet to my fancied sight
   Love, sweetness, goodness, in her person shined
So clear, as in no face with more delight.
   But O, as to embrace me she inclined,
   I waked, she fled, and day brought back my night.

## PERCY SHELLEY

### *From* Adonais†

\* \* \*

Ah woe is me! Winter is come and gone,
155  But grief returns with the revolving year;
The airs and streams renew their joyous tone;
The ants, the bees, the swallows reappear;
Fresh leaves and flowers deck the dead Season's bier;
The amorous birds now pair in every brake,
160  And build their mossy homes in field and brere,
And the green lizard, and the golden snake,
Like unimprisoned flames, out of their trance awake.

Through wood and stream and field and hill and ocean
A quickening life from the Earth's heart has burst

---

6. A sonnet to Milton's second wife, Katherine, who died not long after the birth of their daughter; Milton was already blind when they married and thus had never seen her. The influence of his sonnet-elegy on *In Memoriam* can be felt particularly at the start of section 13, as well as more generally in the sections dealing with dreams of the deceased (such as 69–71) or those in which the speaker is figured as a spouse or widow (such as 9, 60, 85, and 97).
7. In classical mythology the hero Hercules ("Jove's great son") descended to the underworld to rescue Alcestis after her death and return her to her husband, Admetus.
8. A reference to Leviticus 12, which details rites for purification after childbirth.
† From *The Beauties of Percy Bysshe Shelley* (London: Hunt, 1830), pp. 213–14, 220–21. *Adonais* (1821) is Shelley's elegy for his fellow poet John Keats, who died in 1821 at the age of twenty-five. Tennyson would have associated the poem with Arthur Hallam, who enthusiastically championed both Keats and Shelley and who in 1829 helped arrange for the first publication of *Adonais* in England.

165 As it has ever done, with change and motion,
From the great morning of the world when first
God dawned on Chaos; in its stream immersed
The lamps of Heaven flash with a softer light;
All baser things pant with life's sacred thirst;
170 Diffuse themselves; and spend in love's delight
The beauty and the joy of their renewed might.

The leprous corpse touched by this spirit tender
Exhales itself in flowers of gentle breath;
Like incarnations of the stars, when splendour
175 Is changed to fragrance, they illumine death
And mock the merry worm that wakes beneath;
Nought we know, dies. Shall that alone which knows
Be as a sword consumed before the sheath
By sightless lightning?—th'intense atom glows
180 A moment, then is quenched in a most cold repose.

Alas! that all we loved of him should be,
But for our grief, as if it had not been,
And grief itself be mortal! Woe is me!
Whence are we, and why are we? of what scene
185 The actors or spectators? Great and mean
Meet massed in death, who lends what life must borrow.
As long as skies are blue, and fields are green,
Evening must usher night, night urge the morrow,
Month follow month with woe, and year wake year to sorrow.

              *   *   *

He lives, he wakes—'tis Death is dead, not he;
Mourn not for Adonais.—Thou young Dawn
Turn all thy dew to splendour, for from thee
The spirit thou lamentest is not gone;
365 Ye caverns and ye forests, cease to moan!
Cease ye faint flowers and fountains, and thou Air
Which like a mourning veil thy scarf hadst thrown
O'er the abandoned Earth, now leave it bare
Even to the joyous stars which smile on its despair!

370 He is made one with Nature: there is heard
His voice in all her music, from the moan
Of thunder, to the song of night's sweet bird;
He is a presence to be felt and known
In darkness and in light, from herb and stone,
375 Spreading itself where'er that Power may move
Which has withdrawn his being to its own;

Which wields the world with never-wearied love,
Sustains it from beneath, and kindles it above.

He is a portion of the loveliness
380 Which once he made more lovely: he doth bear
His part, while the one Spirit's plastic[1] stress
Sweeps through the dull dense world, compelling there
All new successions to the forms they wear;
Torturing th'unwilling dross that checks its flight
385 To its own likeness, as each mass may bear;
And bursting in its beauty and its might
From trees and beasts and men into the Heaven's light.

*   *   *

1. Shaping or formative.

# Scientific Contexts

## CHARLES LYELL

### *From* Principles of Geology[†]

\* \* \*

We may now conclude our remarks on deltas, observing that, imperfect as is our information of the changes which they have undergone within the last three thousand years, they are sufficient to show how constant an interchange of sea and land is taking place on the face of our globe. In the Mediterranean alone, many flourishing inland towns, and a still greater number of ports, now stand where the sea rolled its waves since the era when civilized nations first grew up in Europe. If we could compare with equal accuracy the ancient and actual state of all the islands and continents, we should probably discover that millions of our race are now supported by lands situated where deep seas prevailed in earlier ages. In many districts not yet occupied by man, land animals and forests now abound where the anchor once sank into the oozy bottom. We shall find, on inquiry, that inroads of the ocean have been no less considerable; and when to these revolutions produced by aqueous causes, we add analogous changes wrought by igneous agency, we shall, perhaps, acknowledge the justice of the conclusion of a great philosopher of antiquity,[1] when he declared that the whole land and sea on our globe periodically changed places.

\* \* \*

† From *Principles of Geology; Being an Attempt to Explain the Former Changes of the Earth's Surface, by Reference to Causes Now in Operation*, 3 vols. (London: John Murray, 1830–33), 1.255; 2.166–69; 3.384–85. Lyell's book, which Tennyson read with close attention in 1837, caused a sensation among contemporary readers; it argued that the earth's form was not fixed but constantly, gradually shifting. Lyell's conclusions significantly influenced the language, imagery, and form of *In Memoriam*, as critics have noted (see for instance the selections by Mattes, Rowlinson, and Geric herein). In the passages reprinted here, Lyell argues—among other things—that land and sea are constantly changing places and that such changes have inevitably led to mass extinctions (compare sections 35, 56, and 123 of *In Memoriam*). The final passage, from the conclusion to Lyell's work, foreshadows the language of progress and of religious justification found in the Epilogue to Tennyson's poem.

1. I.e., Aristotle.

If we attribute the origin of a great part of the desert of Africa to the gradual progress of moving sands, driven eastward by the westerly winds, we may safely infer that a variety of species must have been annihilated by this cause alone. The sand-flood has been inundating, from time immemorial, the rich lands on the west of the Nile, and we have only to multiply this effect a sufficient number of times, in order to understand how, in the lapse of ages, a whole group of terrestrial animals and plants may become extinct.

This desert, without including Bornou and Darfour, extends, according to the calculation of Humboldt, over one hundred and ninety-four thousand square leagues, an area far more than double that of the Mediterranean, which occupies only seventy-nine thousand eight hundred square leagues. In a small portion of so vast a space, we may infer, from analogy, that there were many peculiar species of plants and animals which must have been banished by the sand, and their habitations invaded by the camel and by birds and insects formed for the arid sands.

There is evidently nothing in the nature of the catastrophe to favour the escape of the former inhabitants to some adjoining province; nothing to weaken, in the bordering lands, that powerful barrier against emigration—pre-occupancy. Nor, even if the exclusion of a certain group of species from a given tract were compensated by an extension of their range over a new country, would that circumstance tend to the conservation of species in general; for the extirpation would merely then be transferred to the region so invaded. If it be imagined, for example, that the aboriginal quadrupeds, birds, and other animals of Africa emigrated in consequence of the advance of drift-sand, and colonized Arabia, then the indigenous Arabian species must have given way before them, and have been reduced in number or destroyed.

※    ※    ※

To pursue this chain of reasoning farther is unnecessary; the reader has only to reflect on what we have said of the habitations and the stations of organic beings in general, and to consider them in relation to those effects which we have contemplated in our first volume as resulting from the igneous and aqueous causes now in action, and he will immediately perceive that, amidst the vicissitudes of the earth's surface, species cannot be immortal, but must perish one after the other, like the individuals which compose them. There is no possibility of escaping from this conclusion, without resorting to some hypothesis as violent as that of Lamarck,[2] who imagined, as we have

2. In 1809 the French naturalist Jean-Baptiste Lamarck had proposed that organisms can transmit to their offspring physical modifications that they themselves have acquired in response to environmental pressures.

before seen, that species are each of them endowed with indefinite powers of modifying their organization, in conformity to the endless changes of circumstances to which they are exposed.

*　　*　　*

It has been argued, that as the different states of the earth's surface, and the different species by which it has been inhabited, have had each their origin, and many of them their termination, so the entire series may have commenced at a certain period. It has also been urged, that as we admit the creation of man to have occurred at a comparatively modern epoch—as we concede the astonishing fact of the first introduction of a moral and intellectual being, so also we may conceive the first creation of the planet itself.

We are far from denying the weight of this reasoning from analogy; but although it may strengthen our conviction, that the present system of change has not gone on from eternity, it cannot warrant us in presuming that we shall be permitted to behold the signs of the earth's origin, or the evidences of the first introduction into it of organic beings.

In vain do we aspire to assign limits to the works of creation in *space*, whether we examine the starry heavens, or that world of minute animalcules which is revealed to us by the microscope. We are prepared, therefore, to find that in *time* also, the confines of the universe lie beyond the reach of mortal ken. But in whatever direction we pursue our researches, whether in time or space, we discover everywhere the clear proofs of a Creative Intelligence, and of His foresight, wisdom, and power.

As geologists, we learn that it is not only the present condition of the globe that has been suited to the accommodation of myriads of living creatures, but that many former states also have been equally adapted to the organization and habits of prior races of beings. The disposition of the seas, continents, and islands, and the climates have varied; so it appears that the species have changed, and yet they have all been so modelled, on types analogous to those of existing plants and animals, as to indicate throughout a perfect harmony of design and unity of purpose. To assume that the evidence of the beginning or end of so vast a scheme lies within the reach of our philosophical inquiries, or even of our speculations, appears to us inconsistent with a just estimate of the relations which subsists between the finite powers of man and the attributes of an Infinite and Eternal Being.

# WILLIAM WHEWELL

## The Nebular Hypothesis[†]

\* \* \*

We have referred to Laplace,[1] as a profound mathematician, who has strongly expressed the opinion, that the arrangement by which the stability of the solar system is secured is not the result of chance; that "*a primitive cause* has directed the planetary motions." This author, however, having arrived, as we have done, at this conviction, does not draw from it the conclusion which has appeared to us so irresistible, that "the admirable arrangement of the solar system cannot but be the work of an intelligent and most powerful being." He quotes these expressions, which are those of Newton,[2] and points at them as instances where that great philosopher had deviated from the method of true philosophy. He himself proposes an hypothesis concerning the nature of the *primitive cause* of which he conceives the existence to be thus probable: and this hypothesis, on account of the facts which it attempts to combine, the view of the universe which it presents, and the eminence of the person by whom it is propounded, deserves our notice.

Laplace conjectures that in the original condition of the solar system, the sun revolved upon his axis, surrounded by an atmosphere which, in virtue of an excessive heat, extended far beyond the orbits of all the planets, the planets as yet having no existence. The heat gradually diminished, and as the solar atmosphere contracted by cooling, the rapidity of its rotation increased by the laws of rotatory motion, and an exterior zone of vapour was detached from the rest, the central attraction being no longer able to overcome the increased centrifugal force. This zone of vapour might in some cases retain its form, as we see it in Saturn's ring; but more usually the ring of vapour would break into several masses, and these would generally coalesce into one mass, which would revolve

† From *Astronomy and General Physics Considered with Reference to Natural Theology* (London: Pickering, 1833), pp. 143–44, 156–59. Whewell's treatise introduced the term *nebular hypothesis* to describe recent theories that claimed that stars and planets, including the earth, were not created all at once but formed gradually, by natural processes, out of gaseous matter. It goes on to consider the likelihood that the heavens, like the earth, are constantly changing and will eventually come to an end and to try reconciling this eventuality with religious belief. Whewell was Tennyson's tutor at Cambridge, and Tennyson owned a copy of his book. Tennyson's lifelong interest in astronomy is evident throughout *In Memoriam*; one can see the influence of Whewell, among others, in sections 3, 76, 89, and 118.
1. The great French mathematician and theorist Pierre-Simon Laplace (1749–1827) was one of the first to develop the nebular hypothesis, at the end of the 18th century. Laplace's theory, unlike Whewell's, did not assign a divine origin to the universe.
2. Sir Isaac Newton (1642–1727), English mathematician and astronomer.

about the sun. Such portions of the solar atmosphere, abandoned successively at different distances, would form "planets in the state of vapour." The planets, it appears from mechanical considerations, would have each its rotatory motion, and as the cooling of the vapour still went on, would each produce a planet, which might have satellites and rings, formed from the planet in the same manner as the planets were formed from the atmosphere of the sun.

*       *       *

The vast periods which are brought under our consideration * * * harmonize with all that we learn of the constitution of the universe from other sources. Millions, and millions of millions of years are expressions that at first sight appear fitted only to overwhelm and confound all our powers of thought; and such numbers are no doubt beyond the limits of any thing which we distinctly conceive. But our powers of conception are suited rather to the wants and uses of common life, than to a complete survey of the universe. It is in no way unlikely that the whole duration of the solar system should be a period immeasurably great in our eyes, though demonstrably finite. Such enormous numbers have been brought under our notice by all the advances we have made in our knowledge of nature. The smallness of the objects detected by the microscope and of their parts;—the multitude of the stars which the best telescopes of modern times have discovered in the sky;—the duration assigned to the globe of the earth by geological investigation;—all these results require for their probable expression, numbers, which so far as we see, are on the same gigantic scale as the number of years in which the solar system will become entirely deranged. Such calculations depend in some degree on our relation to the vast aggregate of the works of our Creator; and no person who is accustomed to meditate on these subjects will be surprised that the numbers which such an occasion requires should oppress our comprehension. No one who has dwelt on the thought of a universal Creator and Preserver, will be surprised to find the conviction forced upon the mind by every new train of speculation, that viewed in reference to Him, our space is a point, our time a moment, our millions a handful, our permanence a quick decay.

Our knowledge of the vast periods, both geological and astronomical, of which we have spoken, is most slight. It is in fact little more than that such periods exist; that the surface of the earth has, at wide intervals of time, undergone great changes in the disposition of land and water, and in the forms of animal life; and that the motions of the heavenly bodies round the sun are affected, though with inconceivable slowness, by a force which must end by deranging them altogether. It would therefore be rash to endeavour to establish any analogy between the periods thus disclosed; but we may observe that they *agree* in this, that they reduce all things to the general rule of *finite duration*. As all the geological states of which we find evidence in the present state of the earth, have had their termination, so also the astronomical conditions under which the revolutions of the earth itself proceed, involve the necessity of a future cessation of these revolutions.

The contemplative person may well be struck by this universal law of the creation. We are in the habit sometimes of contrasting the transient destiny of man with the permanence of the forests, the mountains, the ocean,—with the unwearied circuit of the sun. But this contrast is a delusion of our own imagination; the difference is after all but one of degree. The forest tree endures for its centuries and then decays; the mountains crumble and change, and perhaps subside in some convulsion of nature; the sea retires, and the shore ceases to resound with the "everlasting" voice of the ocean: such reflections have already crowded upon the mind of the geologist; and it now appears that the courses of the heavens themselves are not exempt from the universal law of decay; that not only the rocks and the mountains, but the sun and the moon have the sentence "to end" stamped upon their foreheads. They enjoy no privilege beyond man except a longer respite. The ephemeron perishes in an hour; man endures for his three score years and ten;[3] an empire, a nation, numbers its centuries, it may be its thousands of years; the continents and islands which its dominion includes have perhaps their date, as those which preceded them have had; and the very revolutions of the sky by which centuries are numbered will at last languish and stand still.

To dwell on the moral and religious reflections suggested by this train of thought is not to our present purpose; but we may observe that it introduces a *homogeneity*, so to speak, into the government of the universe. Perpetual change, perpetual progression, increase and diminution, appear to be the rules of the material world, and to prevail without exception. The smaller portions of matter which we have near us, and the larger, which appear as luminaries at a vast distance, different as they are in our mode of conceiving them, obey the same laws of motion; and these laws produce the same results; in both cases motion is perpetually destroyed, except it be repaired by some living power; in both cases the relative rest of the parts of a material system is the conclusion to which its motion tends.

\* \* \*

---

3. The biblical phrase for the typical length of a human life (Psalms 90:10). "Ephemeron": a creature that lives for a single day.

# [ROBERT CHAMBERS]

## *From* Vestiges of the Natural History of Creation[†]

\* \* \*

While the external forms of all these various animals are so different, it is very remarkable that the whole are, after all, variations of a fundamental plan, which can be traced as a basis throughout the whole, the variations being merely modifications of that plan to suit the particular conditions in which each particular animal has been designed to live. Starting from the primeval germ,[1] which, as we have seen, is the representative of a particular order of full-grown animals, we find all others to be merely advances from that type, with the extension of endowments and modification of forms which are required in each particular case; each form, also, retaining a strong affinity to that which precedes it, and tending to impress its own features on that which succeeds. This unity of structure, as it is called, becomes the more remarkable, when we observe that the organs, while preserving a resemblance, are often put to different uses. For example: the ribs become, in the serpent, organs of locomotion, and the snout is extended, in the elephant, into a prehensile instrument.

\* \* \*

These facts clearly shew how all the various organic forms of our world are bound up in one—how a fundamental unity pervades and embraces them all, collecting them, from the humblest lichen up to the highest mammifer,[2] in one system, the whole creation of which must have depended upon one law or decree of the Almighty, though it did not all come forth at one time. After what we have seen, the idea of a separate exertion for each must appear totally

---

[†] From *Vestiges of the Natural History of Creation* (London: John Churchill, 1844), pp. 192–93, 197–99, 202–5, 210–11, 275–76, 377, 383–86, with a note omitted. Published anonymously, Chambers's book offers a theory of the origin and development of life on earth; notably, it postulates that all life forms, including humans, have evolved (or "developed") from simpler ones. Chambers claimed primarily to be synthesizing the research and theories of others; he was not himself a professional scientist, and his work was dismissed by those who were. But it was an immediate best seller and did much to popularize and disseminate a notion of evolution well before Charles Darwin published his theory of natural selection in 1859. Tennyson read Chambers's book the year it was published. Although by then many of the sections of *In Memoriam* concerning evolution had already been written, as Hallam Tennyson notes in his *Memoir* (1.223), some of the later-written sections, especially the Epilogue, seem to reveal the influence of Chambers's ideas, as critics have noted (see for instance the selection from Eleanor Bustin Mattes, p. 170 below).

1. I.e., the original single cell from which an animal develops.
2. Mammal.

inadmissible. The single fact of abortive or rudimentary organs condemns it; for these, on such a supposition, could be regarded in no other light than as blemishes or blunders—the thing of all others most irreconcilable with that idea of Almighty Perfection which a general view of nature so irresistibly conveys. On the other hand, when the organic creation is admitted to have been effected by a general law, we see nothing in these abortive parts but harmless peculiarities of development, and interesting evidences of the manner in which the Divine Author has been pleased to work.

We have yet to advert to the most interesting class of facts connected with the laws of organic development. It is only in recent times that physiologists have observed that each animal passes, in the course of its germinal history, through a series of changes resembling the *permanent forms* of the various orders of animals inferior to it in the scale. Thus, for instance, an insect, standing at the head of the articulated animals, is, in the larva state, a true annelid, or worm, the annelida being the lowest in the same class. The embryo of a crab resembles the perfect animal of the inferior order myriapoda, and passes through all the forms of transition which characterize the intermediate tribes of crustacea. The frog, for some time after its birth, is a fish with external gills, and other organs fitting it for an aquatic life, all of which are changed as it advances to maturity, and becomes a land animal. The mammifer only passes through still more stages, according to its higher place in the scale. Nor is man himself exempt from this law. His first form is that which is permanent in the animalcule. His organization gradually passes through conditions generally resembling a fish, a reptile, a bird, and the lower mammalia, before it attains its specific maturity. At one of the last stages of his foetal career, he exhibits an intermaxillary bone, which is characteristic of the perfect ape; this is suppressed, and he may then be said to take leave of the simial type, and become a true human creature.

＊　＊　＊

The tendency of all these illustrations is to make us look to *development* as the principle which has been immediately concerned in the peopling of this globe, a process extending over a vast space of time, but which is nevertheless connected in character with the briefer process by which an individual being is evoked from a simple germ. What mystery is there here—and how shall I proceed to enunciate the conception which I have ventured to form of what may prove to be its proper solution! It is an idea by no means calculated to impress by its greatness, or to puzzle by its profoundness. It is an idea more marked by simplicity than perhaps any other of those which have explained the great secrets of nature. But in this lies, perhaps, one of its strongest claims to the faith of mankind.

The whole train of animated beings, from the simplest and oldest up to the highest and most recent, are, then, to be regarded as a series of *advances of the principle of development*, which have depended upon external physical circumstances, to which the resulting animals are appropriate. I contemplate the whole phenomena as having been in the first place arranged in the counsels of Divine Wisdom, to take place, not only upon this sphere, but upon all the others in space, under necessary modifications, and as being carried on, from first to last, here and elsewhere, under immediate favour of the creative will or energy. The nucleated vesicle,[3] the fundamental form of all organization, we must regard as the meeting-point between the inorganic and the organic—the end of the mineral and the beginning of the vegetable and animal kingdoms, which thence start in different directions, but in perfect parallelism and analogy. We have already seen that this nucleated vesicle is itself a type of mature and independent being in the infusory animalcules, as well as the starting point of the foetal progress of every higher individual in creation, both animal and vegetable. We have seen that it is a form of being which electric agency will produce—though not perhaps usher into full life—in albumen, one of those compound elements of animal bodies, of which another (urea) has been made by artificial means. Remembering these things, we are drawn on to the supposition, that the first step in the creation of life upon this planet was *a chemico-electric operation, by which simple germinal vesicles were produced.* This is so much, but what were the next steps? Let a common vegetable infusion help us to an answer. There, as we have seen, simple forms are produced at first, but afterwards they become more complicated, until at length the life-producing powers of the infusion are exhausted. Are we to presume that, in this case, the simple engender the complicated? Undoubtedly, this would not be more wonderful as a natural process than one which we never think of wondering at, because familiar to us—namely, that in the gestation of mammals, the animalcule-like ovum of a few days is the parent, in a sense, of the chick-like form of a few weeks, and that in all the subsequent stages—fish, reptile, &c.—the one may, with scarcely a metaphor, be said to be the progenitor of the other. I suggest then, as an hypothesis already countenanced by much that is ascertained, and likely to be further sanctioned by much that remains to be known, that the first step was *an advance under favour of peculiar conditions,*

3. I.e., what is now called a cell.

*from the simplest forms of being, to the next more complicated, and this through the medium of the ordinary process of generation.*

\* \* \*

Suppose that an ephemeron,[4] hovering over a pool for its one April day of life, were capable of observing the fry of the frog in the water below. In its aged afternoon, having seen no change upon them for such a long time, it would be little qualified to conceive that the external branchiae[5] of these creatures were to decay, and be replaced by internal lungs, that feet were to be developed, the tail erased, and the animal then to become a denizen of the land. Precisely such may be our difficulty in conceiving that any of the species which people our earth is capable of advancing by generation to a higher type of being. During the whole time which we call the historical era, the limits of species have been, to ordinary observation, rigidly adhered to. But the historical era is, we know, only a small portion of the entire age of our globe. We do not know what may have happened during the ages which preceded its commencement, as we do not know what may happen in ages yet in the distant future. All, therefore, that we can properly infer from the apparently invariable production of like by like is, that such is the ordinary procedure of nature in the time immediately passing before our eyes.

\* \* \*

It may be asked,—Is the existing human race the only species designed to occupy the grade to which it is here referred? Such a question evidently ought not to be answered rashly; and I shall therefore confine myself to the admission that, judging by analogy, we might expect to see several varieties of the being, homo. There is no other family approaching to this in importance, which presents but one species. The corvidae,[6] our parallel in the aves, consist of several distinct genera and sub-genres. It is startling to find such an appearance of imperfection in the circle to which man belongs, and the ideas which rise in consequence are not less startling. Is our race but the initial of grand crowning type? Are there yet to be species superior to us in organization, purer in feeling, more powerful in device and act, and who shall take a rule over us! There is in this nothing improbable on other grounds. The present race, rude and impulsive as it is, is perhaps the best adapted to the present state of things in the world; but the external world goes through

4. General term for an insect that lives for a single day.
5. Gills.
6. Family of birds (Aves) that includes ravens and crows and that Chambers considers to be the most advanced of all types of bird.

slow and gradual changes, which may leave it in time a much serener field of existence. There may then be occasion for a nobler type of humanity, which shall complete the zoological circle on this planet, and realize some of the dreams of the purest spirits of the present race.

\* \* \*

It is clear, moreover, from the whole scope of the natural laws, that the individual, as far as the present sphere of being is concerned, is to the Author of Nature a consideration of inferior moment. Everywhere we see the arrangements for the species perfect; the individual is left, as it were, to take his chance amidst the *mêlée* of the various laws affecting him. If he be found inferiorly endowed, or ill befalls him, there was at least no partiality against him. The system has the fairness of a lottery, in which every one has the like chance of drawing the prize.

\* \* \*

It will occur to every one, that the system here unfolded does not imply the most perfect conceivable love or regard on the part of the Deity towards his creatures. Constituted as we are, feeling how vain our efforts often are to attain happiness or avoid calamity, and knowing that much evil does unavoidably befall us from no fault of ours, we are apt to feel that this is a dreary view of the Divine economy; and before we have looked farther, we might be tempted to say, Far rather let us cling to the idea, so long received, that the Deity acts continually for special occasions, and gives such directions to the fate of each individual as he thinks meet; so that, when sorrow comes to us, we shall have at least the consolation of believing that it is imposed by a Father who loves us, and who seeks by these means to accomplish our ultimate good. Now, in the first place, if this be an untrue notion of the Deity and his ways, it can be of no real benefit to us; and in the second, it is proper to inquire if there be necessarily in the doctrine of natural law any peculiarity calculated materially to affect our hitherto supposed relation to the Deity. It may be that, while we are committed to take our chance in a natural system of undeviating operation, and are left with apparent ruthlessness to endure the consequences of every collision into which we knowingly or unknowingly come with each law of the system, there is a system of Mercy and Grace behind the screen of nature, which is to make up for all casualties endured here, and the very largeness of which is what makes these casualties a matter of indifference to God. For the existence of such a system, the actual constitution of nature is itself an argument. The reasoning may proceed thus: The system of nature assures us that benevolence is a leading principle in the divine mind. But that system is at the same time deficient in a means of making this benevolence of invariable operation. To reconcile this to the recognised character of the Deity, it is necessary to suppose that the present system is but a part of a whole, a stage in a Great Progress, and that the Redress is in reserve. Another argument here occurs—the economy of nature, beautifully arranged and vast in its extent as it is, does not satisfy even man's idea of what might be; he feels that, if this multiplicity of theatres for the exemplification of such phenomena as we see on earth were to go on for ever unchanged, it would not be worthy of the Being capable of creating it. An endless monotony of human generations, with their humble thinkings and doings, seems an object beneath that august Being. But the mundane economy might be very well as a portion of some greater phenomenon, the rest of which was yet to be evolved. It therefore appears that our system, though it may at first appear at issue with other doctrines in esteem amongst mankind, tends to come into harmony with them, and even to give them support. I would say, in conclusion, that, even where the two above arguments may fail of effect, there may yet be a faith derived from this view of nature sufficient to sustain us under all sense of the imperfect happiness, the calamities, the woes, and pains of this sphere of being. For let us but fully and truly consider what a system is here laid open to view, and we cannot well doubt that we are in the hands of One who is both able and willing to do us the most entire justice. And in this faith we may well rest at ease, even though life should have been to us but a protracted disease, or though every hope we had built on the secular materials within our reach were felt to be melting from our grasp. Thinking of all the contingencies of this world as to be in time melted into or lost in the greater system, to which the present is only subsidiary, let us wait the end with patience, and be of good cheer.

# CRITICISM

# Reviews

Despite Hallam Tennyson's assertion that the earliest reviews of *In Memoriam* "were not on the whole sympathetic," the poem seems to have received nearly universal acclaim from the start. For a useful overview of its initial reception, see the chapter from Edgar F. Shannon's *Tennyson and the Reviewers* reprinted below (p. 183). The following excerpts exemplify the terms in which *In Memoriam* was praised and occasionally criticized by its first readers. Reviews at this time were always anonymous, but the authors of many of these pieces have been identified; the attributions here are those given either by Shannon or by Walter Houghton in the *Wellesley Index to Victorian Periodicals*.

## [JOHN FORSTER]

### *The Examiner* (June 8, 1850)[†]

\* \* \*

The volume contains one hundred and twenty-nine poems, entirely different in the structure of the verse from the sonnet, yet resembling it very often in length, and always in the completeness of each poem within itself. These several poems are at the same time fused into a whole by the unity of the pervading sentiment, and by the common topic which suggests them all. They are excursions into almost every region into which fancy ventures; but they all proceed from, and they all return to, one and the same starting point. There is subjoined to them a kind of hymn upon a marriage day, bringing into subtle relation with the subject of the poems another once possible marriage festival; and prefixed to them is a simply grand expansion of the sentiment, "Thy Will Be Done." The sonnets or *canzoni* (if we may so designate them) are the scattered blossoms shed from a series of years—some the utterance of early and poignant grief, which seems capable of no consolation, some the expression of that

† From "The Literary Examiner," *The Examiner* 2210 (June 8, 1850): 356–57.

dignified and lasting sorrow, which is not incompatible with, but rather adds a sober dignity to, the true enjoyment of life. Intermingled with them are reflections evidently the suggestion of a later time, and embodying allusions to more recent events. The prefatory poem—a vivid picture of the mood in which the author reviews after the lapse of some few years the voice of past emotions—serves as a keystone in the arch he has thus piled up, rendering it substantial and enduring.

\*    \*    \*

To such as have not seen this volume we may appear to have quoted sufficiently. Yet our extracts convey but the faintest idea of the variety of beauties contained in it. We might compare it to one of the master-pieces of gothic architecture, in its blending the most delicate ornaments with the most enduring strength—in the subtlety of reflection and nobleness of thought which inform its fresh and graceful imagery. While it fills the mind by its grandeur as a whole, it supplies numberless images of various beauty. All the changing phenomena of the year are mirrored in it; almost every chord of the human heart is touched in turn; the infinite diversity of human character is reproduced; the most complicated relations of society indicated. It is not a poem to become immediately popular; the nature of the subject, the unavoidable monotony, and as it were weariness of sorrow, in whatever changing forms of beauty presented, would itself prevent this; but, addressed alike to the imagination, the reason, and the faith, it seizes upon them all with a powerful grasp, and will retain its hold.

## [G. H. LEWES]

### *The Leader* (June 22, 1850)†

\* \* \* On first announcing the volume we stated our belief that it was unique in the annals of literature. The only poems that occurred to us as resembling it were the *Lament of Bion,* by Moschus; *Lycidas,* by Milton; and *Adonais,* by Shelley;[1] but these are all distinguished from it both by structural peculiarities, and by the spirit which animates them. They may fitly be compared with each other, because they are all rather the products of sorrowing Fancy than of genuine sorrow. Herein note a fundamental difference from *In Memoriam,* which is the iterated chant of a bereaved soul always uttering one plaint, through all the varying moods of sorrow. \* \* \* Tennyson

---

†  From "Tennyson's New Poem," *The Leader* 1.13 (June 22, 1850): 303–4.
1.  For extracts from Milton's and Shelley's elegies, see above, pp. 125 and 127. Moschus's *Lament of Bion* is a Greek pastoral elegy of the 2nd century B.C.E.

does not, like Moschus, Milton, and Shelley, call upon the woods and streams, the nymphs and men, to weep for his lost Arthur; he weeps himself. He does not call upon his fancy for images of woe; he lets his own desolate heart break forth in sobs of music. The three great poets are superior to him in what the world vulgarly calls poetry, in the graceful arabesque of fancy, when the mind at ease plays with a grief that is just strong enough to stimulate it, not strong enough to sombre it; but they are all three immeasurably below him in strength, depth, and passion, consequently in the effect produced upon the minds of others. * * *

## *Sharpe's London Journal* (July 1850)[†]

* * *

Our readers cannot have failed to remark that the metre in which these elegies are composed, has been most happily selected by Mr. Tennyson. In the charm of versification, and in the due apprecia-tion of the properties of style and minute niceties of expression, no modern poet can be said to have surpassed him. His least impor-tant poems abound with musical and mellifluous lines, and no Englishman has had the good fortune to make our language appear more flexible and harmonious. In the present volume there are many rhythmical peculiarities which prove to us that its author is a con-summate master of the art of poetical composition. One of the earlier elegies, for instance, concludes with the following stanza; and we call the attention of our readers to the artistic introduction of an apparent harshness in the last line, to embody the idea of dreariness and discomfort:—

> "He is not here; but far away
>   The noise of life begins again,
>   And ghastly through the drizzling rain
> *On the bald street breaks the blank day.*"    [7.9–12]

We could multiply examples of mere felicities of style; but we turn from these minor excellences to take a final view of the per-vading spirit of these matchless elegies. In many of the author's former compositions we have lamented the apparent absence of any direct or intelligible aim; whilst his poetry appeared to breathe a spirit of refined philosophy, we could not discover in it that genuine sympathy with the influences which assist the cause of human pro-gress generally found in the highest order of poetry. But the present volume abounds with noble aspirations and generous sentiments

† From "Reviews: 'In Memoriam,'" *Sharpe's London Journal* 12 (July 1850): 119–21.

which reflect equal glory on the philanthropist and the poet, and which prove to us that we have not been wrong in classing Alfred Tennyson among the great and moving spirits of the age. \* \* \*

## Westminster and Foreign Quarterly Review (July 1850)†

Of a surety there is but one known poet, now living, who could have produced this exquisite volume. David and Jonathan, Damon and Pythias[1]—all that old tradition has given us of devoted, loving friendship between man and man—high-souled man—is here embodied. No mere sense of attachment, which may exist amongst the commonest of mankind, but the perfect perception of all that is highest and finest—all that is true, and beautiful, and religious, in the noblest sense, linked these two great hearts together. Alas, that they should have been separated!

> "Death put our lives so far apart
> We cannot hear each other speak."[2]

Not now can this volume be dwelt on, for it is not of the *ephemerae*. Suggestive of all high and holy thoughts, we leave its sympathetic appreciation to be dealt with in a future number. Meanwhile, we bid all weary-laden spirits receive it for a hymn-book, that cheers even in its mournfulness—the poet-breathings of a heart whose sorrow seventeen years' lapse has served only to chasten, not to extinguish. May some kindred spirit one day be found to wed them to fitting music.

## [T. H. GILL]

## Prospective Review (July 1850)‡

\*   \*   \*

When grief seeks the expression of poetry, it has ceased to be a cry out of the anguished heart. While the fancy, imagination, and

†  From "Miscellaneous Notices," *Westminster and Foreign Quarterly Review* 53.2 (July 1850): 572. This is the complete text of the initial notice in the *Westminster*, an important quarterly journal. For selections from the fuller review that appeared in the following issue, see p. 157 below.
1.  Biblical and classical examples of male friendship. The story of Jonathan, son of the king of Israel, and David, the future king, is told in the first book of Samuel. Damon and Pythias were legendarily loyal Greek friends whose story was retold by Cicero, among others.
2.  *In Memoriam* 82.15–16, with "Death" substituted for "He."
‡  From "*In Memoriam*," *Prospective Review* 23 (July 1850): 306–31.

invention are dealing with such themes, and mechanic skill adapt-
ing the forms of unpliant words, the diverted affections must have
stopped their bleeding. Time at least must have lent its healing, and
the Sorrow, no more an agony of bereavement or passion, have
passed into the perhaps holier form of a spiritual influence, a senti-
ment, a worship. Its object is translated, the sense of daily loss has
been gradually softened, the memories of earth have become the
hopes of heaven, and wear only spiritual looks, and speak only spir-
itual words. It is the soul that now communes with grief, and no
longer the unshielded heart. It is necessary to remember this in our
perusal of 'In Memoriam,' else a sensitive mind may be in danger of
revolt and disgust at its appearance of fondling and making much
of sorrow. * * * It is difficult to conceive that the heart could so
soon bear to give itself to the contemplation of the images which
the fancy so exquisitely supplies:—

[Quotes 9.1–16.]

There are no less than eight poems addressed to this ship, and
most of them of a wonderful beauty, yet so full of the untroubled sug-
gestions of fancy, and of the finest observation of external nature,
and so elaborately wrought by the poetic art, that one is induced to
believe, indeed to hope, that the chronology of the events is not the
same with the chronology of the compositions; and that though now
arranged in the order of time, the poems are not the records of the
very feelings of the first anguished hours.[1] We confess to a start of
repulsion, and a wonder how any man's heart could dwell upon the
image or offer it to another, when in the opening of the volume the
old Yew over the tombstone is introduced for no higher purpose, for
what follows is but a gloomy unspiritual dirge, than to show us the
fibres netting the dreamless head, and the roots wrapped about the
bones.[2] This surely is an untender abuse of power, a needless wound
to the heart. In the same way we cannot all at once sympathize
with the poet's contemplation of the wreck of the vessel that carries
the corpse, and of the sea-change on the body of his friend buried
beneath the waves, nor with his ascription of it at that moment to a
foolish, home-bred fancy, that it would be sweeter to our hearts that
it should rest beneath the clover-sod.[3] Yet what a living mind, what a
variety of thought, sympathy, and power, is in this short poem!—

[Quotes section 10 in its entirety.]

1. In fact section 9 was one of the first to be written, drafted within a week of Tennyson's
   learning the news of Hallam's death.
2. Refers to section 2.
3. Refers to section 10, which the reviewer then quotes in full just below.

# [COVENTRY PATMORE]

## *North British Review* (August 1850)[†]

\* \* \*

[P]robably the most striking instance of thorough knowledge and pure feeling for metre which has been displayed by a modern poet, is shewn in the choice of the metre of "In Memoriam." We introduce our account of this metre by an example of its use, in one of the most musical poems in the volume.

[Quotes section 86 in its entirety.]

This seems to us to be one of the most perfect rhymed measures for continuous verse ever invented. The divisions are scarcely to be regarded as stanzas, for the beauty of the measure mainly depends upon its adaptation to lengthy phrases. A stanza ought to contain a completed phrase: stanzas of any but the shortest lengths should terminate in a full stop; and no good metrist would separate even the brief ballad-stanzas, unless for some rare and striking effect, with less than the semicolon. The punctuation in the above metre, however, takes no cognizance of the termination of the rhymed compartments; the continuity between them being even more entire than that between couplets or quatrains printed in succession. In these the last rhyme always carries the principal weight; but in the metre of "In Memoriam," the rhyme which concludes the division is so far from its fellow, that the additional importance thus acquired by it, although marked by a typographical space, is more than balanced by the intervening couplet. \* \* \* The adaptation of this, not only most un-epigrammatical, but anti-epigrammatical metre, to the mournful tenor of the poem, is admirable; and not less praiseworthy is the strictness with which the author has adhered all through the work to the simple laws of his measure. \* \* \*

\* \* \*

A fact that is vividly suggested by this book is, that the great elementary truths of life, which have constituted the A B C of Christian philosophy in all ages, up to the last century, were in that period so far forgotten in their vitality, and permitted to die into the most impotent truisms, that they now require to be resuscitated with a labour like that of discovery. \* \* \* The practical oblivion of which we have been speaking, of course, has not confined itself to elementary truth; the

† From *North British Review* 13.26 (August 1850): 532–55.

whole fabric of Christianity has been alike affected. The consequence
is that thousands now make their whole religion, if it deserves to be
so called, of the rediscovered *ground-work* of the Christian faith.
\* \* \* Another and a far more lamentable fact is, that, with the gen-
eral resuscitation of deep truths familiar to ancient practice, there is
also taking place a revival in far greater proportion, of obsolete and
exploded heresies. Now the great philosophical worth of the poem
before us, and the element of its merit, which makes it peculiarly
what all great poems have been, a work addressing itself especially to
its own time, is to be found in the fact that while it proclaims primary
truths with an astonishing force of conviction and persuasion, it roots
up, with equal zeal and efficacy, the poisonous weeds that are germi-
nating in all directions, and choking the good crop. \* \* \*

# [FRANKLIN LUSHINGTON]

## *Tait's Edinburgh Magazine* (August 1850)[†]

\*   \*   \*

The touching and graceful modesty of all the comparisons drawn
between the writer's self and the "nobler tone" of the soul which
has passed away, reminds us again of the sonnets of Shakespeare.
Whether he sighs in solitude, like the

> "Poor girl, whose heart is set
> "On one whose rank exceeds her own,"

or, like the old playmate of "some divinely-gifted man," who had
risen from the "simple village gren" to be "the pillar of a people's
hope, the centre of a world's desire," stands musing in the furrow of
the field of his childhood, within which the fate of his own man-
hood is as firmly bound,

> "Does my old friend remember me?"

or whether he looks upward in happy trust, like the simple wife of
some great philosopher, who, while her husband's weight of learn-
ing and abstraction of thought rarely condescend to the expression
of playful tenderness, still preserves a fixed faith in the depth of his
attachment, and "darkly feels him great and wise;" we cannot but
feel that, however dwarfed the living may appear to the dead, how-
ever small a point our own planet occupies in the realms of space,
the earnestness of such love is a warrant for its being reciprocated
on equal terms.

[†]  From *Tait's Edinburgh Magazine* 17.200 (August 1850): 499–505.

"I loved thee Spirit, and love, nor can
The soul of Shakspeare love thee more."[1]

\*    \*    \*

# [CHARLES KINGSLEY]

## *Fraser's Magazine* (September 1850)[†]

\*    \*    \*

[T]his last work of our only living great poet seems to us at once the culmination of all his efforts and the key to many difficulties in his former writings. Heaven forbid that we should say that it completes the circle of his powers. On the contrary, it gives us hope of vaster effort in new fields of thought and forms of art. But it brings the development of his Muse and of his Creed to a positive and definite point. It enables us to claim one who has been hitherto regarded as belonging to a merely speculative and peirastic[1] school as the willing and deliberate champion of vital Christianity, and of an orthodoxy the more sincere because it has worked upward through the abyss of doubt; the more mighty for good because it justifies and consecrates the aesthetics and the philosophy of the present age. We are sure, moreover, that the author, whatever right reasons he may have had for concealing his own name, would have no quarrel against us for alluding to it, were he aware of the absolute idolatry with which every utterance of his is regarded by the cultivated young men of our day, especially at the universities, and of the infinite service of which this *In Memoriam* may be to them, if they are taught by it that their superiors are not ashamed of Faith, and that they will rise instead of falling, fulfil instead of denying the cravings of their hearts and intellects, if they will pass upwards with their teacher from the vague though noble expectations of *Locksley Hall*, to the assured and everlasting facts of the proem[2] to *In Memoriam*,—in our eyes, the noblest Christian poem which England has produced for two centuries.

\*    \*    \*

And in this volume, the record of seventeen years, we have the result of those spiritual experiences in a form calculated, as we

1. See 60.1–4; 64.1–4, 15–16, 27–28; 97.34; 61.11–12.
† From "Tennyson," *Fraser's Magazine* 42.249 (September 1850): 245–55.
1. I.e., tentative, experimental.
2. Refers to what is now called the Prologue of *In Memoriam*. "Locksley Hall" was a popular dramatic monologue by Tennyson (1842).

believe, to be a priceless benefit to many an earnest seeker in this generation, and perhaps to stir up some who are priding themselves on a cold dilettantism and barren epicurism, into something like a living faith and hope. Blessed and delightful it is to find, that even in these new ages the creeds which so many fancy to be at their last gasp, are still the final and highest succour, not merely of the peasant and the outcast, but of the subtle artist and the daring speculator! Blessed it is to find the most cunning poet of our day able to combine the complicated rhythm and melody of modern times with the old truths which gave heart to martyrs at the stake, to see in the science and the history of the nineteenth century new and living fulfilments of the words which we learnt at our mothers' knee! Blessed, thrice blessed, to find that hero-worship is not yet passed away; that the heart of man still beats young and fresh; that the old tales of David and Jonathan, Damon and Pythias, Socrates and Alcibiades, Shakespeare and his nameless friend,[3] of 'love passing the love of woman,' ennobled by its own humility, deeper than death, and mightier than the grave, can still blossom out if it be but in one heart here and there to show men still how sooner or later 'he that loveth knoweth God, for God is Love!'[4]

## *English Review* (September 1850)[†]

* * *

Never has friendship been placed in a loftier and more ideal point of view: we have no doubt, by the bye, that hundreds of rhymers will begin to discover from this time forward, that they are all possessed of the dearest bosom-friends in the world! It might be presumed that such a work, extending to pages 210, upon the same simple theme, would be monotonous: but this is scarcely the case. At least, if there be any monotony here, the monotony of sorrow, it is so eminently beautiful, that we could not wish it other than it is: but, in truth, the hopes and fears of the poet, as to a Providence and a life beyond the grave, and his general views of human life, are all embodied in this most exquisite collection; an heirloom bequeathed to our nation, and to be treasured by it, as long as the English tongue endures. This, we say, speaking generally, and recording our broad impression; but

---

3. On David and Jonathan and Damon and Pythias, see n. 1, p. 148 above. In Plato's *Symposium*, Alcibiades declares his passionate love for Socrates. The majority of Shakespeare's love sonnets are addressed to an unnamed young man.
4. See 2 Samuel 1:26 and 1 John 4:8, respectively; the standard translation of the latter reads "He that loveth not knoweth not God; for God is love."
† From "New Poetry: Tennyson, Browning, and Taylor," *English Review* 14.28 (September 1850): 65–92.

by no means implying that we imagine this work to be free from faults. Even literary faults, we think, can be discovered in it; philosophical and religious deficiencies are, alas! only too patent.

\*    \*    \*

We can scarcely conceive more dangerous language than *this* of his,—more flattering to the small vanity of a very numerous class already existing among us, and more calculated to lead thousands more astray:—

> "O thou, that after toil and storm,
>     Mayst *seem* to have reach'd a purer air,

("*Seem*" indeed!—but let us go on!)—

>     "Whose *faith has centre every where*,

(that is, *no where*,)—

>     "Nor *cares to fix itself to form*,—

>     "Leave thou thy sister, when she prays,
>         Her early heaven, her happy views:

(How condescending!)—

>         Nor thou *with shadow'd hint* confuse
>         A life that leads melodious days."

Really, we could find it in our hearts to whip this self-conceited rhymester. But we will give the last two mischievous verses without any comment:—

>     "Her faith, thro' form is pure *as thine*,
>         Her hands are quicker unto good.
>         Oh, sacred be the flesh and blood
>     To which *she* links a truth divine!

>     "See, thou that countest *reason ripe*
>         In holding by the *truth within*,
>         Thou fail not in a world of sin,
>     And even for want of such a type."[1]

Rather ten thousand-fold give us the insolent denunciations and open assaults of a Froude,[2] than such insulting commiseration as this! Honestly, Mr. Tennyson, what is it justifies *you* in employing

---

1. Section 33; as throughout, all italics in the quoted sections are the reviewer's. Compare the very different response to this section by the theologically liberal *Westminster Review* that follows.
2. J. A. Froude published *The Nemesis of Faith*, a novel that questioned Christian beliefs, in 1849.

such language? Is it your own firm possession of "faith—void of form?" *This*, at all events, does not look very much like it!:—

> "*So runs my dream: but what am I?—*
> *An infant crying in the night;*
> *An infant crying for the light:*
> *And with no language but a cry!*"     [53.17–20]

This does not *seem* the plenitude of self-contented faith and reason!

We are sorry to appear cruel, but "we are only cruel to be kind;" and we are bound to consider the interests of many thousands of the poet's readers. *Has Mr. Tennyson any perception of truth at all? Does he care for truth? Is he not an exclusive worshipper of the beautiful?* We very much suspect it! He appears to us to have faith or no faith, according to the poetic effect such quality, or the absence of such quality, may have upon his poetry; not consciously, perhaps, (we do not charge him with baseness,) but *really*, and as a matter of fact. Sometimes he questions there being any life beyond the grave; *questions only*, but obviously with a doubt.

\* \* \*

> "*There lives more faith in honest doubt,*
> *Believe me, than in half the creeds.*"     [96.11–12]

Now, we repeat, that such language as this is infinitely mischievous. Such things are caught up as the catchwords of unbelievers, and go very far towards justifying them in their own esteem in their vanity and folly. No doubt there *may* be honest doubters, and there *are* hypocritical believers; but the assumption here seems to be that doubt is almost of necessity a more honest thing than faith! Another very mischievous poem is that on p. 56, commencing.—

> "Tho' truths in manhood darkly join,
> Deep-seated in our mystic frame,
> We yield all blessing to the name
> Of him that made them current coin."     [36.1–4]

That is, of course, of Christ our Lord. This is simply and purely blasphemy! \* \* \* We might quote more to the same effect, but refrain. In other passages the dreams of the author of "Vestiges of Creation"[3] seem to be realized and accepted by the poet, who says, addressing humanity, with reference to its earliest age:—

> "Arise and fly
> The reeling [Faun], the sensual feast:

---

3. Robert Chambers; for extracts from his anonymously published *Vestiges of the Natural History of Creation* (1844), see p. 137 above.

> Move upward, *working out the beast,*
> *And let the ape and tiger die.*"          [118.25–28]

But now let us leave this painful theme. We remain undecided as to Mr. Tennyson's faith, though we opine, that, strictly speaking, *he has none*, whether negative or affirmative, and advise him, for his soul's good, to try to get one!

＊　＊　＊

The epilogue, respecting the marriage of a younger sister of the poet, a child at the period of his friend's decease, is very exquisite, and will be felt by many, perhaps, as much if not more than any thing else in the volume: it is full of a happy, and we might almost say, a holy pathos, which melts on the heart like dew. And so we bid this work farewell. Much, much, remains to say concerning it; but we have no space for further comments. We must add, however, that it is scarcely possible not to think, that the existence of "Shakespeare's Sonnets" in some measure prompted the poet to the composition of his work: he has furnished them with a full worthy counterpart. One magnificent strain we have omitted to notice, on the bells ringing *out* the old, and *in* the new year: we are sorry to find it conclude with an expression, which *may* be interpreted as an endeavour to swell the cry of Carlyle, and Emerson, and "George Sand,"[4] and so many others for the future Antichrist; namely, "Ring in *the Christ that is to be;*" but one verse should be cited for the sake of its mournful modesty:—

> "Ring out the want, the care, the sin,
>     The faithless coldness of the times:
>     *Ring out, ring out, my mournful rhymes,*
> But ring the fuller minstrel in."     [106.17–20]

He may long delay his coming: yet such a minstrel there no doubt *may be*; for, as we observed before, despite the really exquisite beauty of much of his writing, Mr. Tennyson will always be a *class poet*; he will never be *very generally popular*. Then, too, he *teaches* us nothing; he needs teaching himself; he is rather an exponent of his age's wants, than one who can in any measure undertake to satisfy them. And yet, with all this, we repeat, he is a great poet; and great he for ever will remain.

＊　＊　＊

4. The British historian Thomas Carlyle, the American essayist Ralph Waldo Emerson, and the French novelist George Sand (the pen name of Aurore Dupin) in different ways all endorsed a progressive vision of Christianity.

## Westminster and Foreign
## Quarterly Review (October 1850)[†]

\* \* \*

The poem immediately following the one last given, enforces in an earnest, persuasive spirit, a truth that is too often kept out of sight. Its beauty must find it a place among our selections, though that plea cannot often be admitted, or our article would be enriched with the whole volume.

[Quotes section 33 in its entirety.][1]

The time is surely drawing nearer when we shall ask nothing else of each other than

"A life that leads melodious days."

And when, on the grounds of possessing clearer perceptions of Truth than those do who use the aid of forms to keep the light of Truth shining on their lives, we pity or warn such, do we not condemn ourselves, and show our religion to be more intellectual than living? To a heaven of infinite blessedness, must be an infinite variety of ways. There is need of all—room for all. For him who fasts, as for him who does not; for him who makes a special sabbath once in the week, as for him who reckons every day a sabbath; for him who is conscientiously guided by laws imposed by others, as for him who is a law unto himself, recognising no interposition between his conscience and his God. The wise in heart that occupy diametrically opposite points on questions of doctrine, could more fully sympathize and rejoice with each other, than either could with those who, like to them in their doctrinal belief, live without God in their life. They do not know this as they will do; they do not open their eyes that they may see how one spirit in different garbs equally animates them; how from one source is derived their power to wrestle with evil, and to overcome it with good; how like they are to each other in all inner-soul experience, leaning on one rock, led onward through a world of change by one promise. Who that reverences truth has not been touched to fine issues[2] by the earnest voice of a humble follower in the steps of his great Master, even when his mind has been at variance with the doctrinal conclusions of the

---

† From "Tennyson's *In Memoriam*," *Westminster and Foreign Quarterly Review* 54.1 (October 1850): 85–103.
1. For a very different response to section 33, see the preceding excerpt from the *English Review*.
2. See Shakespeare, *Measure for Measure* 1.1.35–36: "Spirits are not finely touched / But to fine issues."

preacher?—and who has not walked wearied away from hearing that which his mind entirely approved, but which, coming from no heart alive with holiness, has failed to kindle the conscience?

\*    \*    \*

# [MANLEY HOPKINS]

## *The Times* (November 28, 1851)[†]

\*    \*    \*

In turning to consider these verses we will mention on the threshold two leading defects likely, in our opinion, to largely lessen the satisfaction of a reflective and tasteful reader. One is the enormous exaggeration of the grief. We seem to hear of a person unlike ourselves in failings and virtues. The real fades into the legendary. Instead of a memorial we have a myth. Hence the subject suffers loss even from its magnitude. The hero is beyond our sympathy. \* \* \* The disproportion of phrase is sometimes ludicrous. Can the writer satisfy his own conscience with respect to these verses?

> "But, brooding on the dear one dead,
>     "And all he said of things divine,
>     "(*And dear as sacramental wine*
> "*To dying lips, is all he said.*)"                    [37.17–20]

For our part, we should consider no confession of regret too strong for the hardihood that indicted[1] them.

\*    \*    \*

A second defect, which has painfully come out as often as we take up the volume, is the tone of—may we say so?—amatory tenderness. Surely this is a strange manner of address to a man, even though he be dead:—

> "So, dearest, now thy brows are cold,
>     "I see thee what thou art, and know
>     "Thy likeness to the wise below,
> "Thy kindred with the great of old.

---

† From *The Times* (November 28, 1851): 8. Manley Hopkins, the probable author of this review, was the father of the poet Gerard Manley Hopkins and one of the very few contemporary reviewers to object to the perceived homoeroticism of *In Memoriam*. For different responses among early reviewers to this aspect of the poem, and to its resemblance to Shakespeare's sonnets, see the initial notice in the *Westminster Review* (p. 148 above), Lushington's review in *Tait's* (p. 151 above), and Kingsley's in *Fraser's* (p. 152 above).
1. The word intended is *indite*, meaning "to write." The form "indict" here is either an archaism or, more probably, a mistake, though a suggestive one.

"But there is more than I can see,
"And what I see I leave unsaid,
"Nor speak it, knowing death has made
"His darkness beautiful with thee."[2]     [74.5–12]

Very sweet and plaintive these verses are; but who would not give them a feminine application? Shakspeare may be considered the founder of this style in English. In classical and Oriental poetry it is unpleasantly familiar. His mysterious sonnets present the startling peculiarity of transferring every epithet of womanly endearment to a masculine friend,—his master-mistress, as he calls him by a compound epithet, harsh as it is disagreeable.[3] * * * We really think that floating remembrances of Shakspeare's sonnets have beguiled Mr. Tennyson. * * *

# [GEORGE ELIOT]

## *Westminster Review* (October 1855)[†]

If we were asked who among contemporary authors is likely to live in the next century, the name that would first and most unhesitatingly rise to our lips is that of Alfred Tennyson. He, at least, while belonging emphatically to his own age, while giving a voice to the struggles and the far-reaching thoughts of this nineteenth century, has those supreme artistic qualities which must make him a poet for all ages. As long as the English language is spoken, the word-music of Tennyson must charm the ear; and when English has become a dead language, his wonderful concentration of thought into luminous speech, the exquisite pictures in which he has blended all the hues of reflection, feeling, and fancy, will cause him to be read as we read Homer, Pindar, and Horace. Thought and feeling, like carbon, will always be finding new forms for themselves, but once condense them into the diamonds of poetry, and the form, as well as the element, will be lasting. * * * But the time would fail us to tell of all we owe to Tennyson, for, with two or three exceptions, every poem in

---

2. For Tennyson's response to these comments (or others very like them), see n. 7, p. 54 above.
3. See Shakespeare, Sonnet 20.1–2: "A woman's face, with Nature's own hand painted, / Hast thou, the master-mistress of my passion." Other 19th-century writers, including Henry Hallam (Arthur's father), also wrote disapprovingly of the homoeroticism of Shakespeare's sonnets.
† From "Belles Lettres," *Westminster Review* 64 (October 1855): 596–615. Before she began publishing the novels that would make her famous under the pen name George Eliot, Mary Ann Evans was an editor and frequent contributor to the *Westminster Review*. This excerpt comes from the beginning of a generally negative review of Tennyson's *Maud* (1855).

his two volumes is a favourite. The "Princess,"[1] too, with all that criticism has to say against it, has passages of inspiration and lyrical gems imbedded in it, which make it a fresh claim on our gratitude. But, last and greatest, came "In Memoriam," which to us enshrines the highest tendency of this age, as the Apollo Belvedere[2] expressed the presence of a free and vigorous human spirit amidst a decaying civilization. Whatever was the immediate prompting of "In Memoriam," whatever the form under which the author represented his aim to himself, the deepest significance of the poem is the sanctification of human love as a religion. If, then, the voice that sang all these undying strains had remained for ever after mute, we should have had no reason to reproach Tennyson with gifts inadequately used. * * *

1. Book-length poem by Tennyson (1847) that received mixed reviews.
2. Classical statue in the collection of the Vatican.

# Critical Readings

## A. C. BRADLEY

### The Structure of *In Memoriam*†

I. The most obvious sign of definite structure in *In Memoriam* consists in the internal chronology, and it will be well to begin by making this clear.

Tennyson[1] himself tells us (*Memoir*, I. 305) that the divisions of the poem are made by the Christmas-tide sections (XXVIII., LXXVIII., CIV.). That the first of these refers to the first Christmas after the death of the friend in autumn is evident from XXX., 14–16:

> We sung, tho' every eye was dim,
>   A merry song we sang with him
> *Last year:*[2]

and we certainly receive the impression from the other Christmas poems that the second refers to the Christmas of the next year, and the third to that of the next again. Thus, when we have reached section CIV., we are distant from the death of the friend about two years and a quarter; and there is nothing in the sections after CIV. to make us think that they are supposed to cover any length of time. Accordingly, the time imagined to elapse in the poem may be set down as rather less than three years.

These results are confirmed by other facts. Between the Christmas poems there come occasional sections indicating the progress of time by reference to the seasons and to the anniversaries of the death of the friend; and between two Christmas poems we never find a hint that more than one spring or one summer has passed, or

---

† From *A Commentary on Tennyson's* In Memoriam (London: Macmillan, 1901), pp. 20–30. Notes are the author's unless otherwise indicated.

1. It will be understood that generally, both in this Introduction and in the Notes, when I speak of 'the poet' I mean the poet who speaks *in* the poem. I refer to the author who composed the poem as 'Tennyson' or 'the author.'

2. These lines are decisive, and their evidence is not weakened by the fact that some poems referring to the burial precede this first Christmas section, whereas the burial of Arthur Hallam did not really take place until after Christmas, 1833. The author did not choose to make the internal chronology coincide with the actual order of events.

that more than one anniversary has come round. After the third Christmas we have a spring poem (cxv.), but after this no sign of summer or of the return of the anniversary of the friend's death.

The unmistakable indications of the internal chronology are shown in the following table:

| Section XI. | Early Autumn. |
|---|---|
| XV. | Later. |
| XXVIII.–XXX. | Christmastide. |
| XXXVIII.–IX. | Spring. |
| LXXII. | Anniversary. |
| LXXVIII. | Christmastide. |
| LXXXIII. | Delaying spring. |
| LXXXVI., LXXXVIII. | Spring. |
| LXXXIX., XCV., XCVIII. | Summer. |
| XCIX. | Anniversary. |
| CIV.–CV. | Christmastide. |
| CVI. | New Year's Day. |
| CVII. | Winter. |
| CXV., CXVI. | Spring. |

Against all these indications there seems nothing to be set except the few passages, already noted, where a phrase or the tone of a section appears to be not quite in harmony with this internal chronology. That these passages are so few is a proof of the care taken by the author to preserve the clearness and consistency of the scheme. And it is undoubtedly of use in giving the outlines of a structure to the poem, and of still greater use in providing beautiful contrasts between the sections which deal with the recurring seasons and anniversaries; though it is somewhat unfortunate that the contents of some of the final sections imply a greater distance of time from the opening of the series than is suggested by the chronological scheme.

II. If we describe in the most general terms the movement of thought and feeling in *In Memoriam*, the description will be found to apply also to *Lycidas* or *Adonais*.[3] In each case the grief of the opening has passed at the close into triumph: at first the singer thinks only of loss and death, and at last his eyes are fixed upon the vision of a new and greater life. But in *Lycidas* and *Adonais* this change is expressed in one continuous strain and is therefore felt by the reader to occupy but a few hours of concentrated experience; and in *Adonais* especially the impression of passionate rapidity in the transition from gloom to glory is essential to the effect. In *In Memoriam* a similar

---

3. Elegies by John Milton (1638) and Percy Shelley (1821), respectively; see above, pp. 125 and 127 [*Editor*].

change is supposed to fill a period of some years, and the impression of a very gradual and difficult advance is no less essential. It is conveyed, of course, not only by the indications of time which have just been considered, but by the mere fact that each of the 131 sections is, in a sense, a poem complete in itself and accordingly felt to be the expression of the thought of one particular time.

In many cases, however, we soon observe that a single section is not really thus independent of its predecessor and successor. On the contrary, some are scarcely intelligible if taken in isolation; and again and again we discover groups which have one subject, and in which the single sections are devoted to various aspects of this one subject. The poet in his progress has come upon a certain thought, which occupies him for a time and is developed through a series of stages or contrasted with a number of other thoughts. And even in cases where we cannot trace such a close connection in thought we often find that several consecutive sections are bound together, and separated from the poems that surround them, by a common tone of feeling. These groups or clusters correspond with single paragraphs of *Lycidas*, or with single stanzas or groups of stanzas in *Adonais*; and their presence forms a second means by which a certain amount of structure is given to the poem.

There are many readers of *In Memoriam* who have never read the poem through, but probably everyone who has done so has recognised to some extent the existence of groups. Everyone remarks, for instance, that near the beginning there are a number of sections referring to the coming of the ship, and that there are other consecutive poems which deal with Christmastide. But perhaps few readers are aware of the large part played by these groups. The fact is that, taken together, they account for considerably more than one-half of the poem; and in this estimate no notice has been taken of mere pairs of connected sections, such as XIX., XX.; XLVIII., XLIX.; LVII., LVIII.; CXV., CXVI.; or of parts of the poem where the sections, though not so closely connected as to form a distinct group, are yet manifestly united in a looser way. If these additions are made to our estimate, it will be found to include nearly 100 poems out of the total of 131.

Of the remaining sections (*a*) a small number may properly be called occasional poems, though the positions which they occupy in the whole are always more or less significant. Such are LXXXVII., which describes the visit to Cambridge; XCVIII., on the brother's tour to Vienna; the long retrospective poem, LXXXV.; or the poem on Hallam's birthday, CVII. (*b*) Others at once remind us of preceding sections suggested by a like occasion, and in this way bring home to us the change which has taken place in the poet's mind during the interval. The Christmas poems are the most prominent instance; the later spring poems recall the earlier; the second 'Risest thou thus' brings back the first; the two sections beginning, 'Dark house,' and the two poems on the Yew-tree, form similar pairs. (*c*) Lastly, we find that the sections which immediately follow connected groups are often of one and the same kind. The subject which has occupied the poet's thoughts being dismissed, there follows a kind of reaction. He looks inward, and becomes more keenly conscious of the feeling from which his attention had been for the time diverted (*e.g.* XXXVIII.), or of the feeling in which his thoughts have culminated (*e.g.* LVII.). Not seldom this feeling suggests to him some reflection on his own songs: his singing comforts him on his dreary way, or he feels that it is of no avail, or that it expresses nothing of his deepest grief. And not only thus at the close of groups, but at various other points throughout *In Memoriam* there occur sections in which the poet's songs form the subject, pointing backwards and forwards to one another, and showing the change which passes over his mind as time goes on (*e.g.* V., XXI., LVIII., CXXV.). In these various ways, as well as by the presence of definite groups, some kind of connection is established between section and section almost throughout the whole of the poem.

III. We are now in a position to observe the structure of this whole, reserving for the Commentary the fuller characterisation of particular parts.

The 'Way of the Soul' we find to be a journey from the first stupor and confusion of grief, through a growing acquiescence often disturbed by the recurrence of pain, to an almost unclouded peace and joy. The anguish of wounded love passes into the triumph of love over sorrow, time and death. The soul, at first almost sunk in the feeling of loss, finds itself at last freed from regret and yet strengthened in affection. It pines no longer for the vanished hand and silent voice; it is filled with the consciousness of union with the spirit. The world which once seemed to it a mere echo of its sorrow, has become the abode of that immortal Love, at once divine and human, which includes the living and the dead.

Is it possible to find in this 'Way' any turning-point where grief begins to yield to joy,—such a turning-point as occurs in *Adonais* when indignation rouses the poet from his sorrow and the strain suddenly rises into the solemn affirmation,

'Peace, peace! he is not dead, he doth not sleep'?

If so, *In Memoriam* may be considered to fall into two fairly distinct parts, though the dividing-line would not necessarily come, any more than in *Adonais*, at the centre of the poem.

It might seem natural to take the long section LXXXV. as marking such a line of division, for here the poet himself looks back over the way he has traversed, and when he renews his journey the bitterness of grief seems to have left him. But the passing away of this bitterness has been already clearly observable before section LXXXV. is reached, and the change of tone after that section does not seem sufficiently decided to justify us in regarding it as a central point in the whole.

More tempting would be a proposal to consider section LVII. as marking the centre of *In Memoriam*. In these verses the most troubled and passionate part of the poem reaches the acme of a climax, while after them there is, on the whole, a steady advance towards acquiescence. But in reality the distress which culminates in section LVII. is characteristic only of the group which closes with that section; it is not a distress which has deepened from the outset of the poem; indeed, many tokens of advance have been visible before that group is reached, and the main direction of the movement towards it is definitely upward.[4]

If a turning-point in the general feeling of *In Memoriam* is to be sought at all, it must certainly be found not in section LVII., nor in section LXXXV., but in the second Christmas poem, LXXVIII. It seems true that, in spite of gradual change, the tone of the poem so far is, on the whole, melancholy, while after LXXVIII. the predominant tone can scarcely be called even sad; it is rather the feeling of spring emerging slowly and with difficulty from the gloom of winter. And it is probable that Tennyson himself intended this change to be associated with the second coming of Christmas, since the first and the third coming also announce a definite change, and since he says that the divisions of *In Memoriam* are made by the Christmas sections. At the same time it is questionable whether the transition at section LXXVIII. is so marked as to strike a reader who was not looking for signs of transition; and, this being so, it would seem to be a mistake to regard *In Memoriam* as a poem which, like *Adonais*, shows a dividing line clearly separating one part of the whole from the other. Its main movement is really one of advance almost from the first, though the advance is for a long time very slow.

✳    ✳    ✳

4. I am not converted, therefore, by Mr. Beeching's words, which have appeared since the above was written: 'Here the poem, as at first designed, seems to have ended. The 57th elegy [58th in the copyright text] represents the Muse as urging the poet to a new beginning; and the 58th [59th] was added in the fourth edition, as though to account for the difference in tone between the earlier and later elegies' (Introduction, p. x). Apart from the objection urged above, the first sentence here seems to be scarcely consistent with Tennyson's own account of the composition of *In Memoriam*, nor can I believe that he ever thought of ending his poem in tones of despair. But it is certainly true that there is a more marked *break* at Section LVII. than at LXXVIII. or LXXXV.

# T. S. ELIOT

## *From* In Memoriam[†]

Tennyson is a great poet, for reasons that are perfectly clear. He has three qualities which are seldom found together except in the greatest poets: abundance, variety, and complete competence. We therefore cannot appreciate his work unless we read a good deal of it. We may not admire his aims: but whatever he sets out to do, he succeeds in doing, with a mastery which gives us the sense of confidence that is one of the major pleasures of poetry.

✻   ✻   ✻

It is, in my opinion, in *In Memoriam*, that Tennyson finds full expression. Its technical merit alone is enough to ensure its perpetuity. While Tennyson's technical competence is everywhere masterly and satisfying, *In Memoriam* is the most unapproachable of all his poems. Here are one hundred and thirty-two passages, each of several quatrains in the same form, and never monotony or repetition. And the poem has to be comprehended as a whole. We may not memorize a few passages, we cannot find a 'fair sample'; we have to comprehend the whole of a poem which is essentially the length that it is. We may choose to remember:

> *Dark house, by which once more I stand*
>    *Here in the long unlovely street,*
>    *Doors, where my heart was used to beat*
> *So quickly, waiting for a hand,*
>
> *A hand that can be clasp'd no more—*
>    *Behold me, for I cannot sleep,*
>    *And like a guilty thing I creep*
> *At earliest morning to the door.*
>
> *He is not here; but far away*
>    *The noise of life begins again,*
>    *And ghastly thro' the drizzling rain*
> *On the bald street breaks the blank day.*    [7]

This is great poetry, economical of words, a universal emotion related to a particular place; and it gives me the shudder that I fail to get

† From *Selected Essays* (London: Faber & Faber, 1972), pp. 328–38. Originally published in *Essays Ancient and Modern* (Faber, 1936). Copyright © 1975 by Valerie Eliot. Reprinted by permission of Faber & Faber, Ltd. and Houghton Mifflin Harcourt Publishing Company. Eliot's footnotes have been omitted; all notes are the editor's.

from anything in *Maud*.[1] But such a passage, by itself, is not *In Memoriam: In Memoriam* is the whole poem. It is unique: it is a long poem made by putting together lyrics, which have only the unity and continuity of a diary, the concentrated diary of a man confessing himself. It is a diary of which we have to read every word.

Apparently Tennyson's contemporaries, once they had accepted *In Memoriam*, regarded it as a message of hope and reassurance to their rather fading Christian faith. It happens now and then that a poet by some strange accident expresses the mood of his generation, at the same time that he is expressing a mood of his own which is quite remote from that of his generation. This is not a question of insincerity: there is an amalgam of yielding and opposition below the level of consciousness. Tennyson himself, on the conscious level of the man who talks to reporters and poses for photographers, to judge from remarks made in conversation and recorded in his son's Memoir, consistently asserted a convinced, if somewhat sketchy, Christian belief. And he was a friend of Frederick Denison Maurice[2]—nothing seems odder about that age than the respect which its eminent people felt for each other. Nevertheless, I get a very different impression from *In Memoriam* from that which Tennyson's contemporaries seem to have got. It is of a very much more interesting and tragic Tennyson. His biographers have not failed to remark that he had a good deal of the temperament of the mystic— certainly not at all the mind of the theologian. He was desperately anxious to hold the faith of the believer, without being very clear about what he wanted to believe: he was capable of illumination which he was incapable of understanding. The 'Strong Son of God, immortal Love,' with an invocation of whom the poem opens, has only a hazy connexion with the Logos, or the Incarnate God. Tennyson is distressed by the idea of a mechanical universe; he is naturally, in lamenting his friend, teased by the hope of immortality and reunion beyond death. Yet the renewal craved for seems at best but a continuance, or a substitute for the joys of friendship upon earth. His desire for immortality never is quite the desire for Eternal Life; his concern is for the loss of man rather than for the gain of God.

> *shall he,*
>
> *Man, her last work, who seem'd so fair,*
> *Such splendid purpose in his eyes,*
> *Who roll'd the psalm to wintry skies,*
> *Who built him fanes of fruitless prayer,*

1. Tennyson's next major poem (1855).
2. The Reverend F. D. Maurice was a prominent writer on theology whose unorthodox views led to his dismissal from his position at King's College, London, in 1853; he was godfather to Tennyson's son Hallam.

> *Who trusted God was love indeed,*
>   *And love Creation's final law—*
>   *Tho' Nature, red in tooth and claw*
> *With ravine, shriek'd against his creed—*
>
> *Who loved, who suffer'd countless ills.*
>   *Who battled for the True, the Just,*
>   *Be blown about the desert dust,*
> *Or seal'd within the iron hills?*       [56.8–20]

That strange abstraction, 'Nature,' becomes a real god or goddess, perhaps more real, at moments, to Tennyson than God (*'Are God and Nature then at strife?'*). The hope of immortality is confused (typically of the period) with the hope of the gradual and steady improvement of this world. Much has been said of Tennyson's interest in contemporary science, and of the impression of Darwin. *In Memoriam*, in any case, antedates *The Origin of Species* by several years,[3] and the belief in social progress by democracy antedates it by many more; and I suspect that the faith of Tennyson's age in human progress would have been quite as strong even had the discoveries of Darwin been postponed by fifty years. And after all, there is no logical connexion: the belief in progress being current already, the discoveries of Darwin were harnessed to it:

> *No longer half-akin to brute,*
>   *For all we thought, and loved and did*
>   *And hoped, and suffer'd, is but seed*
> *Of what in them is flower and fruit;*
>
> *Whereof the man, that with me trod*
>   *This planet, was a noble type*
>   *Appearing ere the times were ripe,*
> *That friend of mine who lives in God,*
>
> *That God, which ever lives and loves,*
>   *One God, one law, one element,*
>   *And one far-off divine event,*
> *To which the whole creation moves.*
>        [Epilogue, 133–44]

These lines show an interesting compromise between the religious attitude and, what is quite a different thing, the belief in human perfectibility; but the contrast was not so apparent to Tennyson's contemporaries. They may have been taken in by it, but I don't think that Tennyson himself was, quite: his feelings were more honest

---

3. Charles Darwin's *On the Origin of Species by Means of Natural Selection* was published in 1859.

than his mind. There is evidence elsewhere—even in an early poem, *Locksley Hall*, for example—that Tennyson by no means regarded with complacency all the changes that were going on about him in the progress of industrialism and the rise of the mercantile and manufacturing and banking classes; and he may have contemplated the future of England, as his years drew out, with increasing gloom. Temperamentally, he was opposed to the doctrine that he was moved to accept and to praise.

Tennyson's feelings, I have said, were honest; but they were usually a good way below the surface. *In Memoriam* can, I think, justly be called a religious poem, but for another reason than that which made it seem religious to his contemporaries. It is not religious because of the quality of its faith, but because of the quality of its doubt. Its faith is a poor thing, but its doubt is a very intense experience. *In Memoriam* is a poem of despair, but of despair of a religious kind. And to qualify its despair with the adjective 'religious' is to elevate it above most of its derivatives. For *The City of Dreadful Night*, and *A Shropshire Lad*,[4] and the poems of Thomas Hardy, are small work in comparison with *In Memoriam:* It is greater than they and comprehends them.

In ending we must go back to the beginning and remember that *In Memoriam* would not be a great poem, or Tennyson a great poet, without the technical accomplishment. Tennyson is the great master of metric as well as of melancholia; I do not think any poet in English has ever had a finer ear for vowel sound, as well as a subtler feeling for some moods of anguish:

> *Dear as remember'd kisses after death,*
> *And sweet as those by hopeless fancy feign'd*
> *On lips that are for others; deep as love*
> *Deep as first love, and wild with all regret.*[5]

And this technical gift of Tennyson's is no slight thing. Tennyson lived in a time which was already acutely time-conscious: a great many things seemed to be happening, railways were being built, discoveries were being made, the face of the world was changing. That was a time busy in keeping up to date. It had, for the most part, no hold on permanent things, on permanent truths about man and God and life and death. The surface of Tennyson stirred about with his time; and he had nothing to which to hold fast except his unique and unerring feeling for the sounds of words. But in this he had something that no one else had. Tennyson's surface, his technical accomplishment, is intimate with his depths: what we most

4. By James Thomson (1874) and A. E. Housman (1896), respectively.
5. From "Tears, Idle Tears," one of the lyrics in Tennyson's long poem *The Princess* (1847).

quickly see about Tennyson is that which moves between the sur-
face and the depths, that which is of slight importance. By looking
innocently at the surface we are most likely to come to the depths,
to the abyss of sorrow. Tennyson is not only a minor Virgil, he is
also with Virgil as Dante saw him, a Virgil among the Shades, the
saddest of all English poets, among the Great in Limbo, the most
instinctive rebel against the society in which he was the most perfect
conformist.

Tennyson seems to have reached the end of his spiritual develop-
ment with *In Memoriam;* there followed no reconciliation, no
resolution.

> *And now no sacred staff shall break in blossom,*
>   *No choral salutation lure to light*
>   *A spirit sick with perfume and sweet night,*[6]

or rather with twilight, for Tennyson faced neither the darkness nor
the light in his later years. The genius, the technical power, persisted
to the end, but the spirit had surrendered. A gloomier end than that
of Baudelaire: Tennyson had no *singulier avertissement.*[7] And having
turned aside from the journey through the dark night, to become
the surface flatterer of his own time, he has been rewarded with the
despite of an age that succeeds his own in shallowness.

# ELEANOR BUSTIN MATTES

## [Scientific Challenges to Faith and Reassurances][†]

### I

As far as "the way of the soul" was concerned, the year 1837 brought
Tennyson an experience more crucial to the further development of
*In Memoriam* than either the moment of mystical union with Hal-
lam or the departure from Somersby; for "during some months" of
that year he was "deeply immersed in . . . Lyell's *Geology.*"[1]

Charles Lyell's *Principles of Geology,* which appeared in three vol-
umes from 1830–1833, proved revolutionary not only to the geologic
theories of the period but to religious thought as well. On the basis

---

6. From Algernon Charles Swinburne's "Ave Atque Vale: In Memory of Charles Baude-
laire" (1867), lines 166–68.
7. In 1862 the French poet Charles Baudelaire (1821–1867) had a *singulier avertissement*
or "sudden warning" that his poetic ability was passing from him.
†  From *In Memoriam: The Way of a Soul* (New York: Exposition Press, 1951), pp. 55–63,
76–85. Reprinted by permission of the executor of the author's estate. The author's
notes have been abridged, and some section numbers have been adjusted.
1. *Memoir,* I, 162.

of studies made by his predecessors and his own geologic observations over a number of years, Lyell sought to demonstrate that the present state of the earth is wholly the result of natural forces like wind and water erosion, rock faulting, and sedimentation, operating over long periods of time. This hypothesis challenged Cuvier's theory that various catastrophic disturbances were responsible for the present configurations of the earth. In his second volume Lyell then proceeded to explain that the continual physical changes which geology revealed pointed to the certain extinction of species after species throughout the earth's history, as they found themselves unable to cope with the new conditions they encountered.

None of Lyell's conclusions were actually new. James Hutton, in his *Theory of the Earth*, published in 1795, had asserted that one can account for all the past changes of the earth's surface by reference to natural forces still in operation. And the French naturalist Buffon had insisted upon the inevitable extinction of man and all his works.

But Hutton's *Theory of the Earth* had no popular sale like that of Lyell's *Geology*, and Buffon had few English readers. The whole situation in England was, moreover, markedly different from that in France, where the astronomer Laplace is said to have brushed aside Napoleon's question as to where the Creator figured in his nebular theory, with the reply, "Sire, I have no need of that hypothesis." In England, in the early 1830's, the official Church of England theology was predominantly rationalist, and the outstanding scientists were also religious men, so that there had been no serious questioning of the eighteenth-century assumption that science is the handmaid of religion, since it leads men to appreciate "the Power, Wisdom, and Goodness of God as manifested in the Creation." And as late as 1837, when the distinguished geologist Adam Sedgwick was Chairman of the British Association (for the advancement of scientific research), he concluded its annual meeting by declaring that if he found his science "interfere in any of its tenets with the representations of doctrines of Scripture, he would dash it to the ground."[2]

Lyell, although he by no means shared Sedgwick's sentiments, was no iconoclast, and he therefore did everything possible to conceal the disturbing religious implications of his theories. He found that most churchmen were willing to accept almost any description of the *manner* of God's activity in the universe, so long as the *fact* of such divine activity was affirmed. He accordingly cloaked and minimized the revolutionary nature of his conclusions, as he disclosed in a confidential statement of his strategy:

2. Caroline Fox, *Memories of Old Friends, Being Extracts from the Journals and Letters of Caroline Fox from 1835 to 1871* (Philadelphia, J. B. Lippincott and Co., 1882), p. 25.

> If you don't triumph over them, but compliment the liberality and candour of the present age, the bishops and enlightened saints will join us in despising both the ancient and modern physico-theologians . . . I give you my word that full *half* of my history and comments was cut out, and even many facts, because . . . I . . . felt that it was anticipating twenty or thirty years of the march of honest feeling to declare it undisguisedly.[3]

And those who read to the end of the *Principles of Geology* might well have any uncomfortable doubts allayed by its eloquent, pious conclusion:

> In vain do we aspire to assign limits to the works of creation in *space*, whether we examine the starry heavens, or that world of minute animalcules which is revealed to us by the microscope. We are prepared, therefore, to find that in *time* also, the confines of the universe lie beyond the reach of mortal ken. But in whatever direction we pursue our researches, whether in time or space, we discover everywhere the clear proofs of a Creative Intelligence, and of His foresight, wisdom, and power.[4]

For Tennyson, however, such a conclusion—if he read it—did not gloss over the shocking implications that he sensed in Lyell's descriptions of geologic process. He had never been interested in the deist's Master Mind, nor convinced that His existence and wisdom could be demonstrated from the wonders of nature. When the Apostles at Cambridge had asked: "Is an intelligible First Cause deducible from the phenomena of the Universe?" he had voted "no."[5] And when he looked through a microscope at the minute life it revealed he said: "Strange that these wonders should draw some men to God and repel others. No more reason in one than in the other."[6] But in the early sections of *In Memoriam* he had assumed, with Wordsworth, that nature does testify to immortality, and had repeatedly affirmed the eternal quality of love. Lyell's conclusions challenged both these premises, the first directly, the second implicitly; and the next phase of *In Memoriam* was the recording of Tennyson's reaction to this shock.

3. Mrs. (Katherine) Lyell, ed., *Life, Letters and Journals of Sir Charles Lyell* (London, J. Murray, 1881), I, 271.
4. Charles Lyell, *Principles of Geology, Being an Attempt to Explain the Former Changes of the Earth's Surface, by Reference to Causes Now in Operation* (1st ed.; London, 1830–33), III, 384.
5. *Memoir*, I, 44, n. 1.
6. *Ibid.*, I, 102.

## II

Writing a hundred years earlier than Lyell, Joseph Butler had challenged the supposed "reasonableness" of natural religion by pointing out that nature by no means shares the solicitous concern for every creature which the New Testament ascribes to God, since "of the numerous Seeds of Vegetables and Bodies of Animals, which are adapted and put in the Way, to improve to such a Point or State of natural Maturity and Perfection, we do not see perhaps that one in a million actually does."[7] And Tennyson, who must have read Butler's *Analogy of Religion* at Cambridge if not before, may have been indebted to this thought in section 55 of *In Memoriam*:

> Are God and Nature then at strife,
>     That Nature lends such evil dreams?
>     So careful of the type she seems,
> So careless of the single life;
>
> That I, considering everywhere
>     Her secret meaning in her deeds,
>     And finding that of fifty seeds
> She often brings but one to bear,
>
> I falter where I firmly trod.
>
> (55:5–13)

But it was almost certainly his reading in the *Principles of Geology* that led Tennyson to write section 56.

Lyell's second volume has this disconcerting quotation[8] on its title page: "The inhabitants of the globe, like all the other parts of it, are subject to change. It is not only the individual that perishes, but whole species."[9] The volume then presents an accumulation of evidence which leads relentlessly to the conclusion that

> . . . the reader has only to reflect on what we have said of the habitations and the stations of organic beings in general, and to consider them in relation to those effects . . . resulting from the igneous and aqueous causes now in action, and he will immediately perceive that, amidst the vicissitudes of the earth's surface, species cannot be immortal, but must perish one after the other, like the individuals which compose them.[1]

---

7. Joseph Butler, *The Analogy of Religion, Natural and Revealed, to the Constitution and Course of Nature* (London, 1881), p. 146.
8. From John Playfair's *Illustrations of the Huttonian Theory*.
9. Charles Lyell, *op. cit.*, II, title page.
1. *Ibid.*, II, 168–69.

Section 56 of *In Memoriam* takes up the assumption of section 55 and gives it the drastic revision required by Lyell's findings:

> "So careful of the type?" but no.
>    From scarped cliff and quarried stone
>    She cries, "A thousand types are gone;
> I care for nothing, all shall go.
>
> "Thou makest thine appeal to me:
>    I bring to life, I bring to death:
>    The spirit does but mean the breath:
> I know no more."
>
>                              (56:1–8)

It states in specific and personal terms what these findings imply for man's hope of immortality:

>                  And he, shall he,
>
> Man, her last work, who seem'd so fair,
>    Such splendid purpose in his eyes,
>                         (56:8–10)
>
>       . . . . . . . . . . . . . . . . . . . . . .
>    Be blown about the desert dust,
> Or seal'd within the iron hills?
>
> No more? . . .
>                         (56:19–21)

and the lines echo Lyell's conclusion "'that none of the works of a mortal being can be eternal.' . . . And even when they have been included in rocky strata, . . . they must nevertheless eventually perish, for every year some portion of the earth's crust is shattered by earthquakes or melted by volcanic fire, or ground to dust by the moving waters on the surface."[2] It recognizes that Lyell's theory of natural laws operating ruthlessly throughout the earth's history is incompatible with belief that God is love and love is the law of creation (56:13–14). And it suggests that a horrible mockery and self-delusion permeates the entire structure of Western civilization, in which men build churches to worship a God of love whom nature disproves, and fight for supposedly eternal values like truth and justice, which die with the species that cherishes them.

It is easy to see how the whole fabric of assurance that Tennyson had woven in the earlier-written sections seemed destroyed by his reading of Lyell. The arguments for immortality he found in

2. *Ibid.*, II, 271.

Wordsworth, and Isaac Taylor's confident assertions that the departed retain their affections for their earthly friends in their new spheres of life, took for granted a benevolent Nature and a loving God, which all Lyell's evidence seemed to deny. And, although Tennyson could long for his dead friend's "voice to soothe and bless" (56:26), as it had always done while Hallam lived, he could find no actual rebuttal to Lyell in what he remembered of Hallam's religious views or in the *Remains.*

Tennyson could not, however, accept such a dismal conception of man as a transient phenomenon on the earth's surface, who vainly believes in an immortality and a God of love that ruthless nature belies. So he closed this disturbed section 56 by asserting that the questions raised by Lyell's findings must remain unanswered until he could penetrate "behind the veil" (56:28). One cannot state the exact meaning or certain source of this allusive phrase. But Tennyson was seeking refuge in the position that the so-called realities of the physical world hide as much as they reveal of the truth, which man can have full access to only at death, when the "veil" of finite mortal limitations is withdrawn.

## III

When Tennyson came to write section 123, Lyell's findings were still vivid in his mind, and the first stanza,

> There rolls the deep where grew the tree.
>     O earth, what changes hast thou seen!
>     There where the long street roars hath been
> The stillness of the central sea.
>
> (123:1–4)

is a poetic summary of descriptions like the following:

> . . . seas and lakes have since been filled up, the lands whereon the forests grew have disappeared or changed their form, the rivers and currents which floated the vegetable masses can no longer be traced . . . [3]

> . . . how constant an interchange of sea and land is taking place on the face of our globe. In the Mediterranean alone, many flourishing inland towns, and a still greater number of ports, now stand where the sea rolled its waves since the era when civilized nations first grew up in Europe. If we could compare with equal accuracy the ancient and actual state of all the islands and continents, we should probably discover that millions

3. *Ibid.,* I, 2.

of our race are now supported by lands situated where deep
seas prevailed in earlier ages.[4]

At this time, however, Tennyson could borrow word pictures from
Lyell without being distressed by his theories, and he concluded 123
on a note very different from that of 56.—But this is anticipating a
later phase of his spiritual journey.

*       *       *

## IV

Although Tennyson in certain moods responded to Wordsworth's
and Shelley's romanticist view of nature, yet Lyell's *Geology* had too
vividly depicted a nature "red in tooth and claw" for him to embrace
pantheism consistently at this time. And, although he grasped at
Carlyle's assertions that man's intuitive belief in God and immortal-
ity is more valid than the scientific evidence which challenges it, he
was not prepared wholly to dismiss this evidence. For he himself had
a lively interest in science, and he also appreciated its hold upon his
contemporaries. It is therefore easy to see why he would be receptive
to answers to his questionings which found religious meaning in,
rather than in spite of, the natural processes science described, and
especially receptive if he met with such answers in the writings of
scientists and of their popularisers, as he apparently did in 1843 and
1844 or 1845.

Tennyson seems to have come into possession of J. F. W. Herschel's
*A Preliminary Discourse on the Study of Natural Philosophy* in Octo-
ber, 1843, although it first appeared in 1830. And in November, 1844,
he asked his friend and publisher Moxon to obtain for him *Vestiges
of the Natural History of Creation,* which the *Examiner* had enthusi-
astically reviewed.[5] Herschel's book, the first of a series of discourses
on the "objects and advantages of the study of the principal depart-
ments of human knowledge,"[6] presented clearly and simply the rea-
sons for studying the physical sciences, the basic principles and
methods involved in such study, and the chief subject matter included.
Robert Chambers' *Vestiges of Creation,* published anonymously,[7]
professed to be "the first attempt to connect the natural sciences
into a history of creation," beginning with the formation of the
solar systems, and tracing the mutations of the earth's surface and
the development of life revealed by geologic evidence, up to the

4. *Ibid.*, I, 255.
5. *Memoir,* I, 222–23.
6. Quoted from the "Advertisement" appended to the 1832 edition.
7. For fear its divergence from currently accepted, orthodox views of Creation would
   injure Chambers' literary reputation or bring his publishing firm into disrepute.

appearance of the "adult Caucasian"—the present highest form of organic life.

In these popular treatises Tennyson could and apparently did find a religious interpretation of the scientific findings they describe. For, although Herschel's volume preceded the *Principles of Geology,* both it and *Vestiges of Creation* refer to "development" and interpret it as an aspect of progress.

The *Discourse on Natural Philosophy* has a section on geology which mentions the wearing away of old continents and the building up of new ones, but for Herschel this cast no doubt upon man's immortality, which he wrote of confidently in the opening pages of his book, asking:

> Is it wonderful that a being so constituted should first encourage a hope, and by degrees acknowledge an assurance, that his intellectual existence will not terminate with the dissolution of his corporeal frame but rather that, in a future state of being . . . endowed with acuter senses, and higher faculties, he shall drink deep at that fountain of beneficent wisdom for which the slight taste obtained on earth has given him so keen a relish?[8]

The development revealed in the history of the human species seemed to him equally valid ground for optimism, leading him to comment:

> . . . we cannot fail to be struck with the rapid *rate of dilatation* which every degree upward of the scale, so to speak, exhibits, and which, in an estimate of averages, gives an immense preponderance to the present over every former condition of mankind, and, for aught we can see to the contrary, will place succeeding generations in the same degree of superior relation to the present that this holds to those passed away.[9]

The whole outlook of the volume would, in fact, be reassuring to Tennyson. For Herschel denied emphatically that the study of science leads men "to doubt the immortality of the soul," insisting that instead it leaves the mind "open and free to every impression of a higher nature which it is susceptible of receiving, . . . encouraging, rather than suppressing, every thing that can offer a prospect or a hope beyond the present obscure and unsatisfactory state."[1] And he concluded his introductory apologia with a thought which to Tennyson must immediately have suggested Hallam and their relations: namely, that

8. J. F. W. Herschel, *A Preliminary Discourse on the Study of Natural Philosophy* (Vol. I in the Rev. Dionysius Lardner's "The Cabinet of Natural Philosophy," London, Longman, Rees, Orme, Brown & Green, 1831), p. 7.
9. *Ibid.,* pp. 67–68.
1. *Ibid.,* pp. 7–8.

the observation of the calm, energetic regularity of nature, the immense scale of her operations, and the certainty with which her ends are attained, tends, irresistibly, to tranquillise and re-assure the mind. . . . And this it does . . . by calling upon us for the exercise of those powers and faculties by which we are sus-ceptible of the comprehension of so much greatness, and which forms, as it were, a link between ourselves and the best and noblest benefactors of our species, with whom we hold communion in thoughts and participate in discoveries which have raised them above their fellow-mortals, and brought them nearer to their Creator.[2]

*Vestiges of Creation* was not so simply reassuring to religious faith as Herschel's *Discourse on Natural Philosophy.* For, while it affirmed, very early in the exposition, "that there is a First Cause to which all others are secondary and ministrative, a primitive almighty will, of which these [physical] laws are merely the mandates,"[3] it premised that "the organic creation is . . . the result of natural laws"[4] rather than of any direct act of God. Secondly, it represented man as a part of "the animal scale"[5]—the paragon of animals—and so a part of the vast process of organic development which geologic evidence reveals. Thirdly, it pointed out that "the individual, as far as the present sphere of Being is concerned, is to the Author of Nature a consideration of inferior moment. Everywhere we see the arrangements for the species perfect; the individual is left, as it were, to take his chance amidst the mêlée of the various laws affecting him."[6] This conception of the mutual relation of God, man, and nature was clearly at variance with Christian teaching. It repudiated the biblical account of a Divine creative act: it was incompatible with the doctrine of man's fall from an originally per-fect state: most serious of all, it ran counter to the Gospels' message of a loving God who marks the fall of every sparrow and watches over each of His children with tender care.

Many readers, therefore, found *Vestiges of Creation* disturbing and irreligious. Edward FitzGerald asked his friend Bernard Bar-ton: "How do you like Vestiges of Creation?—Are you all turned infidels—or Atheists, as Mrs. Turly was minded to become?"[7] And Fanny Kemble, while she was reading it in 1847, reported a very unfa-vorable first reaction: "The book is extremely disagreeable to me, though my ignorance and desire for knowledge combined give it,

2. *Ibid.,* pp. 16–17.
3. [Robert Chambers], *Vestiges of the Natural History of Creation* (New York, Wiley and Putnam, 1845), p. 25.
4. *Ibid.,* p. 117.
5. *Ibid.,* p. 151.
6. *Ibid.,* p. 281.
7. In a letter of December 29, 1844.

when treating of facts, a thousand times more interest than the best of novels for me; but its conclusions are utterly revolting to me. . . ."[8]

There was nothing in the *Vestiges of Creation* to shock Tennyson, however. He had never been a biblicist. As early as in his college days he had been attracted by the theory "that the 'development of the human body might possibly be traced from the radiated, vermicular, molluscous and vertebrate organisms.'"[9] Furthermore, in reading Lyell he had already confronted the geologic indications that man, not only as individual but also as species, is subject to the processes of extinction which the onward and upward surge of nature makes inevitable.

The disturbing features in *Vestiges of Creation* were, therefore, already familiar to Tennyson, and it contained counter-reassurances, and suggested a meaning and purpose underlying the seemingly ruthless sweep of development, which were not to be found in Lyell's presentation. For it proposed that the very vastness of space and time which astronomy and geology disclose points to the fragmentary character of whatever natural processes man can see, and warrants his confidence that the seeming injustices within this segment are a necessary part of a larger, perfect plan:

> It may be that, while we are committed to take our chance in a natural system of undeviating operation . . . there is a system of Mercy and Grace behind the screen of nature, which is to make up for all casualties endured here, and the very largeness of which is what makes these casualties a matter of indifference to God. . . . To reconcile this [discrepancy between God's loving intention and its realization] to the recognized character of the Deity, it is necessary to suppose that the present system is but a part of the whole, a stage in a Great Progress, and that the Redress is in reserve. . . . The mundane economy might be very well as a portion of some greater phenomenon, the rest of which was yet to be evolved. . . . Let us but fully and truly consider what a system is here laid open to view, and we cannot well doubt that we are in the hands of One who is both able and willing to do us the most entire justice. . . . Thinking of all the contingencies of this world as to be in time melted into or lost in the greater system, to which the present is only subsidiary, let us wait the end with patience, and be of good cheer.[1]

And it suggested that even the supplanting of man as he now is by some more highly developed form of humanity will mean the

---

8. Letter of November 14, 1847, in Frances Ann Kemble, *Records of Later Life* (London, Richard Bentley & Son, 1882), III, 242. Fanny Kemble was the sister of John Kemble, one of Tennyson's Cambridge contemporaries and close friends.
9. *Memoir*, I, 44.
1. Chambers, *op. cit.*, p. 286.

fulfillment rather than the frustration of his highest aspirations and hopes. For the prospect of future organic development led the author to speculate:

> Is our race but the initial of the grand crowning type? Are there yet to be species superior to us in organization, purer in feeling, more powerful in device and act, and who shall take a rule over us! . . . There may then be occasion for a nobler type of humanity, which shall complete the zoological circle on this planet, and realize some of the dreams of the purest spirits of the present race.[2]

Fanny Kemble justly observed: ". . . the hypothesis . . . that other and higher destinies, developments, may, and probably do, await humanity than anything it has yet attained here . . . though most agreeable to the love of life and desire of perfection of most human creatures, in no sort hinges logically on to his [Chambers'] *absolute chain of material progression* and development."[3] But Tennyson apparently did not share this criticism, for, whatever his debt to the *Vestiges of Creation,*[4] section 118 and the Epilogue of *In Memoriam* draw from the evidence of organic development conclusions that were essentially Herschel's and Chambers'.

V

Section 118 is generally regarded as a key statement of the philosophy or "message" of *In Memoriam*, and quite understandably so. For it is Tennyson's most explicit attempt to present some reassuring word on the relation of development to man's beliefs and hopes, probably the most disturbing religious problem of the 1840's to the Victorian public as well as to Tennyson personally.

In the opening stanza Tennyson repudiated the depressing thoughts which he had voiced in section 56—the view "of human love and truth, As dying Nature's earth and lime" (118:3–4). For, as he re-examined the evidence of the past, apparently with the eyes of Chambers rather than of Lyell, he found that it pointed not so much to extinction as to progress. Man must therefore think of himself, not as a prospective fossil—Tennyson's nightmare of section 56—but as "The herald of a higher race" (118:14).

---

2. *Ibid.,* pp. 207–8.
3. Kemble, *op. cit.,* III, 245.
4. In a note to the account of Tennyson's request for *Vestiges of Creation* from Moxon, his son stated: "The sections of 'In Memoriam' about Evolution had been read by his friends some years before the publication of the *Vestiges of Creation* in 1844" (*Memoir,* I, 233, n. 1). This note is ambiguous, however, since it does not state *which* sections. And the evidence for the date of the Epilogue (see Appendix, p. 124) indicates that it, at least, was not written "some years before" Tennyson saw Chambers' book.

This hopeful prospect for the humanity of the future did not, of course, meet the primary religious demand of the elegies—the demand for personal immortality; nor was it a necessarily reassuring prospect, as Chambers discovered from the reactions to his book. But Tennyson, possibly encouraged by Herschel's optimism in the *Discourse on Natural Philosophy,* also affirmed the progress of the individual to higher spheres and endeavors after death:

> But trust that those we call the dead
> Are breathers of an ampler day
> For ever nobler ends. . . .            (118:5–7)

There is even less scientific basis for predicting man's onward and upward advance in the after-world than for Chambers' vision of a "nobler type of humanity," despite Isaac Taylor's pretension of presenting a "*physical* theory of another life." There is, furthermore, no natural connection between the two kinds of progression. Tennyson avoided the first difficulty by appealing to faith rather than to reason, urging his readers to "trust" in the expanding life of "those we call the dead." He overcame the other difficulty by asserting that the advance of both the individual and the species is dependent upon a third kind of development: namely, moral; that man is to be

> The herald of a higher race,
> And of himself in higher place,
> *If* so he type this work of time
>
> Within himself, from more to more.
>                       (118:14–17)[5]

Thus Tennyson, in section 118, drew from development not only a religious meaning but also a moral message, giving the elegies a homiletic note worthy of his Apostolic mission:

> . . . Arise and fly
> The reeling Faun, the sensual feast;
> Move upward, working out the beast,
> And let the ape and tiger die.            (118:25–28)

* * *

## VI

The Epilogue of *In Memoriam* is even more certainly indebted to *Vestiges of Creation* than is section 118.[6] When Tennyson wrote the Epi-

---

5. Italics are mine.
6. Since the Epilogue was written late in 1844 or early in 1845, when Tennyson had almost surely obtained *Vestiges of Creation.*

logue he apparently already had in mind for the elegies the formal, artifical structure of "a kind of *Divina Commedia*, ending with happiness."[7] For in the Epilogue he wrote of the marriage of his youngest sister, Cecilia, with his friend Edmund Lushington, and anticipated the arrival of their child, thus bringing the memorial poems from their early preoccupation with death to the expectation of birth. This promise of birth, in turn, led him to reiterate what is essentially Chambers' optimistic view of the religious meaning of organic development.

As he pictured Cecilia and Edmund Lushington on their wedding journey, Tennyson imagined:

> A soul shall draw from out the vast
> And strike his being into bounds,
>
> And, moved thro' life of lower phase,
>     Result in man, be born and think,
>     And act and love. . . .
>                                          (Epi. 123–127)

He was familiar with the theory of foetal development referred to in lines 125–126 long before he read *Vestiges of Creation*, for a stanza in the 1832 version of "The Palace of Art" specifically refers to this theory.[8] But Chambers' statement that man's "organization gradually passes through conditions generally resembling a fish, a reptile, a bird, and the lower mammalian, before it attains its specific maturity"[9] may have brought the theory to the foreground of his thought. Tennyson was, in any case, surely indebted to Chambers' speculation: "Is our race but the initial of the grand crowning type? Are there yet to be species superior to us in organization, purer in feeling, more powerful in device and act, and who shall take a rule over us!"[1] when he pictured the Lushingtons' child as

> . . . a closer link
> Betwixt us and the crowning race
>
> Of those that, eye to eye, shall look
>     On knowledge; under whose command
>     Is Earth and Earth's, and in their hand
> Is Nature like an open book;

7. *Memoir*, I, 304.
8. "From change to change four times within the womb
      The brain is moulded," she began,
   "So through all phases of all thought I come
      Into the perfect man."
   This stanza was altered in the revised version of "The Palace of Art" included in the *Poems* of 1842, and was replaced by another in the 1853 edition of the *Poems*.
9. Chambers, *op. cit.*, pp. 150–51.
1. *Ibid.*, p. 207.

No longer half-akin to brute,
> For all we thought and loved and did,
> And hoped, and suffer'd, is but seed
Of what in them is flower and fruit.   (Epi. 127–136)

And he was almost certainly also indebted to Chambers for the following suggestion that Hallam's rare gifts and virtues had a special relation to the greater man of the future:

> Whereof the man, that with me trod
> This planet, was a noble type
> Appearing ere the times were ripe.
> (Epi. 137–139)

For Chambers predicted that the "*nobler type* of humanity" he anticipated would "realize some of the dreams of the purest spirits of the present race."[2]

By thus relating Hallam to his interpretation of development Tennyson brought together the original and later concerns of the elegies. And in the closing lines of the Epilogue he brought together the religious reasurrances he had offered piecemeal in various earlier sections, by reaffirming the relation of both Hallam and development to God:

> That friend of mine who lives in God,

> That God, which ever lives and loves,
> One God, one law, one element,
> And one far-off divine event,
> To which the whole creation moves.
> (Epi. 140–144)

\* \* \*

# EDGAR FINLEY SHANNON, JR.

## The Reception of *In Memoriam*[†]

*In Memoriam*, that monument to the religious questioning of the nineteenth century as well as to the memory of Arthur Henry Hallam, was published by Moxon on June 1, 1850. The product of seventeen years of rumination engendered by the sudden death of Tennyson's

---

2. *Ibid.*, p. 208. The italics are mine.
† From *Tennyson and the Reviewers: A Study of His Literary Reputation and of the Influence of the Critics upon His Poetry, 1827–1851* (Cambridge: Harvard University Press, 1952), pp. 141–54. Copyright © 1952 by the President and Fellows of Harvard College. Reprinted by permission of the publisher. All notes are the editor's. For fuller excerpts from some of the reviews mentioned here, see "Reviews," p. 145 above.

college friend in Vienna on September 15, 1833, the elegy came before the reading public unheralded by publisher's advertisements and without its author's name on the title page.

There was little doubt, however, as to the identity of the pen from which the unusual work emanated. On Wednesday, May 29, Mudie's Select Library advertised in the London daily papers that fifty copies of Tennyson's new poem would be available on Saturday, the day of publication. And on that day the fifty copies were announced as in circulation. The *Sun* in August complained that the opportunity of revealing the author's name from internal evidence had been cut off by the rumors linking the poem with Tennyson "even prior to the day of its publication." The first periodicals to notice the book, the *Spectator* and the *Examiner*, unhesitatingly informed their readers on June 8 that Tennyson was the writer and Hallam the person to whom the poem was addressed. A week later the *Atlas* pretended to be vexed that speculations and learned disquisitions had thus been anticipated by the "outspokenness of our periodical critics, who blurt out the secret before the volume is a week old. . . . the whole truth even now stands revealed to the world. There is no mystery about it." Only the *Literary Gazette* distinguished itself by welcoming on June 15 "a female hand" to "the Muses' banquet," after it had already listed *In Memoriam* as by Tennyson in its column of new books on June 1.

The reception of *In Memoriam* by the periodicals during the year of its publication was in general extremely laudatory. The weekly journals printed in London, as usual the first to notice a new work, responded with no fewer than nine reviews during the month of June. The *Leader*, the newly established republican paper captained by George Henry Lewes and Thornton Hunt, and the faithful *Examiner* were fervid in their commendation. Lewes, who wrote the encomium in the *Leader*, called Tennyson the "greatest living poet" and judged *In Memoriam* superior to "Lycidas."[1] "The comparison," he said, "is not here of genius, but of feeling. Tennyson sings a deeper sorrow, utters a more truthful passion, and singing truly, gains the predominance of passion over mere sentiment." He concluded with a prophetic opinion of the poem, "We shall be surprised if it does not become the solace and delight of every house where poetry is loved. A true and hopeful spirit breathes from its pages. . . . All who have sorrowed will listen with delight to the chastened strains here poured forth *In Memoriam*." The *Examiner*, in an article presumably by Forster, was no less eulogistic. *In Memoriam* was not unworthy of comparison to Milton's "Lycidas," Petrarch's and Shakespeare's sonnets, and Dante's "Purgatorio" and "Paradiso." Tennyson's poem, the writer said,

1. Major elegy by John Milton (1638); see above, p. 125.

is a pathetic tale of real human sorrow, suggested rather than told. It exhibits the influence of a sudden and appalling shock, and lasting bereavement, in the formation of character and opinion. It is the record of a healthy and vigorous mind working its way, through suffering, up to settled equipoise and hopeful resignation. The effect of the poem, as a whole, is to soften yet to strengthen the heart; while every separate part is instinct with intense beauty, and with varied and profound reflections on individual man, on society, and on their mutual relations. It is perhaps the author's greatest achievement. A passion, deep-felt throughout it, has informed his ever subtle thoughts and delicate imagery with a massive grandeur and a substantial interest.

The *Guardian*, which had approved of *The Princess*,[2] was as appreciative of *In Memoriam*. Although it was not so enthusiastic as the *Leader* and the *Examiner*, it declared, "Judged even by the standard of Shakespeare and Spenser, Mr. Tennyson will not be found wanting."

Even the weeklies that had handled *The Princess* severely had overcome their aversion for Tennyson to a remarkable degree. The *Spectator* quoted approvingly sections LXXXIX ("Witch-elms that counterchange the floor") and CVI ("Ring out, wild bells") and said, "The volume is pervaded by a religious feeling, and an ardent aspiration for the advancement of society. . . . These two sentiments impart elevation, faith, and resignation; so that memory, thought, and a chastened tenderness, generally predominate over deep grief." The *Spectator* found fewer of the eccentricities of style against which it had been protesting for twenty years and felt that the scheme of the poem was "favourable to those pictures of common landscape and daily life, redeemed from triviality by genial feeling and a perception of the lurking beautiful, which are the author's distinguishing characteristic." If the reviewer in the *Literary Gazette*, possibly Jerdan, whose long editorship was just coming to an end, mistook the identity of the author, he had only the warmest praise for the poem. The *Atlas* had been completely won over, though the critic doubted that the poem would "find as large a circle of readers as other emanations of Tennyson's muse." The series of poems which make up the whole work "are entirely worthy of the poet," he said. "They overflow with plaintive beauty. They are the touching heart-utterances of a genuine and noble sorrow. There is a homeliness and simplicity about them which bear ample testimony to their truth. There is nothing ornate or elaborate in them; they are thoughtful, chastened, and subdued." The *Britannia*, which had looked upon *The Princess* as despicable, conceded that in the new poem, amidst some repetition of the poet's old faults, there were beauties "which take their place at once and for

---

2. Tennyson's last major poem (1847) before *In Memoriam*.

ever in the poetry of England." The *Athenaeum*, in another review by
J. Westland Marston, firmly endorsed the volume:

> It belongs to those deepest forms of poetic expression which
> grow out of the heart and stand distinguished from those which
> have their origin in the imagination. . . . In its moral scope the
> book will endear itself to all who suffer, both by its vivid appre-
> ciation of their grief and by its transmutation of that grief into
> patience and hope. No worthier or more affecting tribute could
> be rendered to the dead than one which like this, converts the
> influence of their memory into solace for the living.

Reviewing Tennyson for the first time, the Unitarian *Inquirer*
alone found more to blame than to praise; but its attitude cannot be
called hostile. It was "grateful for the purity and elegance that
breathe throughout the volume" and desisted from quoting examples
of the "mellow fruit" shining out amid the "weeds" in order not to
overthrow "our critical objections to the poem as a whole." The objec-
tions of this sectarian journal, whose reviews were devoted almost
entirely to religious works, could not have had much effect upon the
literary world in the face of the approval of the *Athenaeum*, the *Exam-
iner*, the *Spectator*, and the *Atlas*, not to mention the other weeklies.

It was somewhat curious that Forster in the *Examiner*, sharing the
view of the critic for the *Atlas*, should think that *In Memoriam* would
not "become immediately popular." Henry Taylor privately expressed
the same opinion. On July 1, 1850, he wrote to Miss Isabella Fen-
wick, "Have you read Tennyson's 'In Memoriam'? It is a wonderful
little volume. Few—very few—words of such power have come out of
the depths of this country's poetic heart. They might do much, one
would think, to lay the dust in its highways and silence its market
towns. But it will not be felt for a while, I suppose; and just now
people are talking of the division of last Friday."

But Lewes' forecast was the correct one, and the prophets of gloom
had reckoned without the people and without the praise of the
press. Besides the notices in the London weeklies, favorable
reviews and excerpts from *In Memoriam* were printed by various
newspapers throughout the United Kingdom during the month of
June. In July additional complimentary articles appeared. Encomi-
ums of the poem flowered in the periodicals for August. The *North
British Review*, in the first elaborate critique of *In Memoriam*,
sounded the note that succeeding critics echoed: "There are cer-
tain great epochs in the history of poetry. The publication of 'Para-
dise Lost'[3] was one of these. The next, which was at all similar
in importance, was the appearance of the 'Excursion.'[4] . . . Our

3. By Milton (1667).
4. By William Wordsworth (1814).

immediate impression upon the perusal of 'In Memoriam' was that it claimed a place in the very highest rank, and that it was the first poem of historical importance which has appeared since the 'Excursion.'" Franklin Lushington, one of the family to whom Tennyson was so closely bound by ties of affection and marriage, proclaimed in *Tait's Edinburgh Magazine* that *In Memoriam* was "the finest poem the world has seen for very many years." "Its title," he said, "has already become a household word among us. Its deep feeling, its wide sympathies, its exquisite pictures, its true religion, will soon be not less so. The sooner the better." Patmore, writing in the *Palladium*, a newly established Edinburgh magazine, was practically breathless with adulation. Tennyson's new work contained "the best religious poetry that has ever been written in our language—if we except a very few of the lovely and too seldom appreciated effusions of George Herbert." After quoting section CIII ("On that last night"), Patmore remarked, "In our opinion, there is nothing nearly equal to the above, in splendour of language and imagination, depth and classicality of thought and feeling, perfection of form, and completeness in every way, in the whole scope of modern English poetry." *Sharpe's London Journal* exclaimed,

> All the qualifications which have rendered him [Tennyson] so acceptable to the critical readers and discreet lovers of poetry, are here displayed in their matured excellence:—the graceful diction and exquisite harmony of versification; the subtle flights of thought and fancy; the delicate sense of beauty and keen appreciation of the beautiful; the power of condensation, and of presenting the commonest objects in a new and unexpected light;—these and many more characteristics of his genius are observable in the pages of *"In Memoriam."*

*Hogg's Instructor* found "high merit" in the poem's "general tone of lofty spiritualism. . . . The thoughts awakened by reflections on life and death—on the reality life and the reality death—give to this work that vitality which outlives mere beauty of description and mere pathos of sentiment." The *Court Journal* cried, "Never yet did fairer wreath deck the tomb where lies the loved and lost; chisel never yet fashioned monumental marble more graceful, more expressive of the homage paid by the living to the dead, than in this tribute of a sorrowing heart to the memory of one so beloved."

At the end of August, two of the London daily newspapers added their voices to these paeans. The *Sun* called *In Memoriam* a "masterpiece of poetic composition" and asserted, "Of the exquisite simplicity of the whole effusion we cannot speak in terms of too earnest admiration." The ever-loyal *Morning Post* maintained, "Only a poet would have conceived the idea; and Wordsworth himself, in his happiest moments, would not have produced a more touching or beautiful composition." Concerning the sections which make up the poem, the *Post* remarked, "It is not merely the intensity of feeling which they manifest nor the musical power and simplicity of the language which gives so great a charm and so absorbing an interest to these stanzas; it is the harmony and depth of thought, illustrated and adorned with the riches of a fertile fancy and a well-stored intellect, which form their chief excellence and repay with the disclosure of new beauties every fresh perusal."

By the beginning of September *In Memoriam* had reached a second edition and probably a third. Sir Charles Tennyson says that there were 5,000 copies in the first edition; and it is likely that a larger number was printed for the second and third editions. The book was selling at a phenomenal rate, setting at naught all predictions to the contrary.

Three articles in the magazines and reviews for September, which appeared about the first of the month, continued the flood of panegyric. For the *Eclectic Review* the chief importance of the poem lay in "the revealment of greatness in the spirit of the artist." And "the second great value of the book" was said to be its "expression of a cycle of experience common to thoughtful humanity." Charles Kingsley in *Fraser's Magazine* thought *In Memoriam* "the noblest English Christian poem which several centuries have seen." The *English Review*, while mercilessly exposing Tennyson's lack of faith (to which I shall return presently), described the poem as "an heirloom bequeathed to our nation, and to be treasured by it, as long as the English tongue endures."

The October number of the *Westminster Review* devoted nineteen pages to an article which was in no sense critical and can only be described as a fulsome eulogy of both author and work.

In the criticism of *In Memoriam* during the first four months after its publication, the reviewers had a good deal to say concerning the poem's technical or literary qualities—its unity, diction, meter, and monotony. They generally agreed that the sometimes almost unconnected sections of the work did not destroy its total effect. *Hogg's Instructor* felt that though the poem was "thus made up of a series of detached parts, yet is the unity of the whole unbroken, because there is ever a recurrence to one and the same melancholy event." The *Morning Post* said, "Not only is the unity of design and of subject apparent throughout, but the thoughts follow each other in a natural sequence, the continuity of which renders it necessary to contemplate the work as a whole in order fully to appreciate its beauties." The *Eclectic* declared, "An organic unity informs the whole; unity of feeling and of interest." And Lushington in *Tait's* asserted that the poem was "perfect and unique as a whole, to a degree and in a style very rarely reached."

The diction, always one of the focal points of attack on Tennyson, met with more approval than censure. Some critics, such as those in the *Inquirer*, the *Britannia*, and the *Court Journal*, repeated the old charges of quaint and obscure phraseology. Marston and Lushington, in the *Athenaeum* and *Tait's*, respectively, were more directly concerned with the poet's problem of expressing succinctly metaphysical conceptions and objected that the language did not always represent with sufficient clarity abstract ideas. More representative of the prevailing opinion was that of the *Eclectic*: "As regards words merely, Tennyson is undeniably one of the greatest of *Expressers*. His is the master's facility. His are the 'aptest words to things.' In expert 'fitting' of the one to the other, his present practice far exceeds even his original gift. Unerring is his speech, as opulent. It is ever *adequate* to the thought. The balance of the two brings about lucidness, unexampled, in thought so large, feeling so deep, poetry so subtle."

The stanza in which the poem was written provoked extensive comment, but the weight of critical opinion was strongly in its favor. The *Leader* remarked, "How exquisitely adapted the music of the poem is to its burden; the stanza chosen, with its mingling rhymes, and its slow, yet not imposing march, seems to us the very perfection of stanza for the purpose." The *Eclectic* called the stanza a "happy one"; *Sharpe's London Journal* said that it was "most happily selected"; and Kingsley in *Fraser's* pronounced it "exquisitely chosen." The *North British Review* went so far as to say, "This seems to us to be one of the most perfect rhymed measures for continuous verse ever invented."

There were, however, a few dissenting voices. The *Inquirer*, for instance, complained, "The measure is of too obvious facility, and, in a less masterly hand, might break into the very false gallop of verses. Even in spite of the division into short canzonets or sonnets, which breaks the continuity of the air, there is a poverty and sameness in it which produces weariness and fatigue, so that there is danger of losing the full appreciation of the burden for want of greater variety and strength in the verse." The *Christian Reformer*, also wishing for more variety, regretted that Tennyson had confined himself to one meter. The *Sun* thought the stanza "at the first somewhat unpalatable from its monotony," yet confessed in the end to being overcome by its "irresistible fascination." The *Westminster*, charmed by the rhyme scheme of the stanzas, maintained that "the sweetness of the notes, the earnest truth of the thought, the comprehensiveness of the love, relieve them of all monotony."

The question of the monotony of the poem was also raised by other reviewers. The *Spectator* felt that there was "inevitably something of sameness in the work" and that the subject was "unequal to its long expansion." The *Atlas* believed that the sections were "too mournfully monotonous," and even Forster in the *Examiner* conceded an "unavoidable monotony." But this point of view did not go unchallenged. *Hogg's Instructor* said that, although the poem might appear to be monotonous, "to many this very monotony will be its chief beauty." And the *English Review* asserted, "It might be presumed, that such a work, extending to pages 210, upon the same simple theme, would be monotonous: but this is scarcely the case. At least, if there be any monotony here, the monotony of sorrow, it is so eminently beautiful, that we could not wish it other than it is."

Among the general features of the poem, the portrayal of English landscape and of domestic scenes and affections elicited unanimous approbation. But probably the most interesting aspect of the criticism of *In Memoriam* is the attitude of the reviewers toward its religious doctrine. A vast majority commended this element of the work and, with a somewhat human tendency to read more into the meaning than the poet had actually expressed, found the theology sound and the faith inspiring. Kingsley rejoiced as follows: "Blessed it is to find the most cunning poet of our day able to combine the complicated rhythm and melody of modern times with the old truths which gave heart to the martyrs at the stake, to see in the science and history of the nineteenth century new and living fulfilments of the words which we learnt at our mothers' knee!" Patmore maintained that the reader was exalted by the strains in which "sorrow is gradually shown to be the teacher of a pure, or rather the only pure philosophy" and "secular knowledge is humbled before loving faith." The *Guardian* and the *Spectator* said that the volume was "full of religious feeling." The *Morning Post*, in a notice of *Fraser's Magazine* for September, spoke of "the pure Christianity" of *In Memoriam*. The *North British Review* asserted that the poem uttered primary Christian truths, which the age, having lost, was in the process of recovering; and *Tait's* mentioned the volume's "true religion." For the *Sun* the "philosophy" of the poem was "ever pure and lofty." The *Westminster* thought the poem was thoroughly devout, and the *Prospective Review* cherished the poet's declaration for faith over knowledge.

In this overwhelming tide of laudation, only three instances of protest have come to light. The *Britannia* noticed "an almost total absence of those higher consolations which religion should suggest." "We miss," the reviewer said, "those hues of cheerfulness and manly resignation with which Christianity invests the outpourings of her stricken children." Yet he was moved to comment on section CVI ("Ring out, wild bells"), "It is suggestive, healthy, full of generous aspirations, poetical, sympathetic, Christian." The *Court Journal* feared that Tennyson did "not always seek his consolation at the one sufficing source," but hoped that the passages which compelled

such a remark had been misconstrued. The critic for the High
Church *English Review* alone examined in detail Tennyson's theo-
logical position. Although some of his views were extreme, he
anticipated by some eighty-six years Mr. T. S. Eliot's dictum that *In
Memoriam* is more conspicuous for the doubt than for the faith
which it expresses.[5] In the first place, he took the poet to task for not
capitalizing in the proem the pronouns referring to the Divinity.
Concerning the lines,

> O thou that after toil and storm
>     Mayst seem to have reach'd a purer air,
>     Whose faith has centre everywhere,
> Nor cares to fix itself to form,
>
> Leave thou thy sister when she prays,
>     Her early Heaven, her happy views;
>     Nor thou with shadow'd hint confuse
> A life that leads melodious days,
>
>                        (XXXIII, 1–8)

he charged, "It is most falsely, and, we may add, offensively assumed,
that the unbeliever in Christianity can possess a faith of his own,
quite as real and as stable as that of the believer!" He suspected
Tennyson of being *"an exclusive worshipper of the beautiful."* The
lines,

> There lives more faith in honest doubt,
> Believe me, than in half the creeds,
>
>                        (XCVI, 11–12)

he pronounced "infinitely mischievous." The stanza,

> Tho' truths in manhood darkly join,
>     Deep seated in our mystic frame,
>     We yield all blessing to the name
> Of Him that made them current coin,
>
>                        (XXXVI, 1–4)

he declared to be "simply and purely blasphemy." He viewed with
distrust Tennyson's apparent acceptance of the principles of evolu-
tion and concluded, "We remain undecided as to Mr. Tennyson's
faith, though we opine, that, strictly speaking, *he has none*, whether
negative or affirmative, and advise him, for his soul's good, to try to
get one!"

But in spite of this attack upon the poet's theology, the critic pre-
served an adulatory respect for his work. For the first time in the
contemporary criticism of Tennyson, aesthetic qualities outweighed

5. See T. S. Eliot's essay on p. 166 above.

moral values. Tennyson, he said, "*teaches* us nothing; he needs teaching himself; he is rather an exponent of this age's wants, than one who can in any measure undertake to satisfy them. And yet, with all this, we repeat, he is a great poet; and great he for ever will remain."

It was now generally agreed that Tennyson was not only the leading poet of the day but a poet of commanding genius. The *Leader* had already proclaimed him the "greatest living poet." The *Eclectic* had found his "greatness" revealed by *In Memoriam*. The *Standard of Freedom*, noticing *Fraser's* for September, called him "that great poet." As one reviewer put it, he had become "the rage," and the *Globe* said on September 4, 1850, "For one genuine reader of Wordsworth there are thousands who relish Tennyson."

At last Tennyson was thought to have fulfilled his promise and to have accepted the mission that had been envisaged for him. *Sharpe's London Journal* had felt it necessary to lament "the apparent absence of any direct or intelligible aim" in his previous poetry and had been unable to "discover in it that genuine sympathy . . . with . . . human progress generally found in the highest order of poetry." "But the present volume," the critic said, "abounds with noble aspirations and generous sentiments which reflect equal glory on the philanthropist and the poet, and which prove to us that we have not been wrong in classing Alfred Tennyson among the great and moving spirits of the age." The *Eclectic* also testified to the poet's achievement. *Poems*, 1842, and *The Princess* had shown that Tennyson's nature was "eminently elevated, pure . . . sympathizing, genuine, refined," but also that it was "a reserved and fastidious one." His skill and artistry had made him seem "removed and distant. Rarely was a direct sentiment or sympathy, the central influence of a poem." With *In Memoriam*, however, "All wants are now amply compensated by one continuous revealment of our poet in his spiritual individuality; one exclusive outlet of personal feeling and sympathies. Their expression is enlarged into relevance with universal humanity." The poem contains "the poetic solution of every-day problems of thought." In addition, "More than once, a penetrating poet's glance is turned on this age itself. A calmly attuned voice is raised in testimony to 'The mighty hopes that make us men:' a voice of large trust, of deep-seated faith, of long prophecy; singing of that 'crowning race,' the 'flower and fruit' of that, in us the seed.'"

Thus *In Memoriam* was believed to embody all the qualities which the age expected of poetry. The poem awakened chords of universal human sympathy. It played upon and ministered to emotions experienced by all men at one time or another. It was eminently of the day and concerned itself with the solution of current problems; it was complete with prophecy and the doctrine of progress; it inculcated the moral of faith and hope derived from the catharsis of suffering. Tennyson had finally produced an elevated, sustained, and unified poem of a philosophical nature and had convinced most of his contemporaries that he was a vigorous and profound thinker.

It was the consensus of the reviewers that *In Memoriam* was the great work which had been awaited from Tennyson's pen. The poem was neither an epic nor a drama, as had been prescribed, but it was a work to stand beside *Paradise Lost* and *The Excursion*, beside the "Purgatorio" and "Paradiso" of Dante, and the sonnets of Petrarch and Shakespeare. Of the periodicals that made the comparison, only the *Inquirer*, admittedly reactionary in matters of literary taste, thought *In Memoriam* inferior to "Lycidas."

A work of such eminence was naturally thought to be of timeless significance. Through his mastery of poetic technique, Tennyson was said to have embalmed his "great thoughts" and "elevated feeling" "for the ages." *In Memoriam* contained "joys, in which our children and our children's children will participate as largely as ourselves." The thoughts of the poet "who revolves the problems of free-will and fate, and gives utterance to his feelings of awe and hope . . . [are] not 'such perishable stuff as dreams are made of,' but they 'wander through eternity.'" And to the memory of Arthur Hallam, the poem was "a monument 'more lasting than brass,'" "a memorial more lasting than bronze."

## The Laureateship

Wordsworth had died on April 23, 1850; and, while the praise of *In Memoriam* was steadily mounting, the office of poet laureate, left vacant by his death, remained unfilled. The discussion prevalent in literary circles about an appropriate successor was echoed in the press. Although Chorley assiduously advanced Mrs. Browning's claims in the *Athenaeum*, the most likely candidates were conceded to be Tennyson and Leigh Hunt. The Queen had acted promptly in offering the post on May 8 to Samuel Rogers, the literary veteran, famous as a host and connoisseur as well as a poet. But Rogers, then eighty-seven, declined the honor because of his age, and the laureateship went unoccupied until the autumn.

On September 7, 1850, the Prime Minister wrote to the Queen: "Lord John Russell has had the honour of receiving at Taymouth a letter from the Prince. He agrees that the office of Poet Laureate ought to be filled up. There are three or four authors of nearly equal merit, such as Henry Taylor, Sheridan Knowles, Professor Wilson, and Mr Tennyson, who are qualified for the office." On October 3 Russell wrote to Rogers, "H. M. is inclined to bestow it on Mr Tennyson, but I should wish, before the offer is made, to know something of his character, as well as of his literary merits." The old poet having vouched for Tennyson's respectability, Russell informed Prince Albert on October 21, "Mr Tennyson is a fit person to be Poet Laureate"; and on November 5 Sir Charles Phipps, Keeper of the Privy Purse, wrote to Tennyson for the Queen, offering him the post "as a mark of Her Majesty's appreciation of your literary distinction." Tennyson, after a day's hesitation, accepted; and the appointment was officially made on November 19, 1850. It seems to have been received with general satisfaction by the public, though Chorley, who admitted there was no question of Tennyson's merit, grumbled about the "multiplication of . . . benefices to a single subject." The *Leader* reported the appointment with pleasure, saying that "the name of ALFRED TENNYSON is so beloved that any good fortune befalling him will delight the public." Hunt like a good loser, wrote in his new periodical, *Leigh Hunt's Journal*,

> If the Office in future is really to be bestowed on the highest degree of poetical merit, and on that only (as being a solitary office, it unquestionably ought to be, though such has not hitherto been the case), then Mr. Alfred Tennyson is entitled to it above any other man in the kingdom; since of all living poets he is the most gifted with the sovereign poetical faculty, Imagination. May he live to wear his laurel to a green old age; singing congratulations to good Queen Victoria and human advancement, long after the writer of these words shall have ceased to hear him with mortal ears.

Wordsworth had raised the dignity of the laureateship to a new level in public esteem; and if the Queen's intention was to preserve this high standing, Tennyson was the obvious, and actually the only, choice. *In Memoriam* had elevated him to an unassailable pinnacle. His appointment as poet laureate was the accolade for twenty years of poetic endeavor.

※　※　※

# PETER HINCHCLIFFE

## Elegy and Epithalamium in *In Memoriam*[†]

### I

If literature is a map, then scholars and critics are surveyors and cartographers. Our task is to take new bearings and to draw new contours, not just to complete the work of our predecessors, but to

† From *University of Toronto Quarterly* 52.3 (Spring 1983): 241–62. © University of Toronto Press. Reprinted with permission from University of Toronto Press.

determine where we have moved from those predecessors in rela-
tion to the landmarks that we study. As literary works recede into
the past, some perspectives—immediacy of response and personal
recollection, for example—become closed to us, but new perspec-
tives open out. Critical studies of *In Memoriam* written during the
last twenty-five years show us a poem more complex and serious
than readers of the two previous generations would have been
willing to accept, and a different kind of poem from the one that
Tennyson's Victorian readers acclaimed. Yet despite the increasing
sophistication of our map-making skills *In Memoriam* remains
stubbornly puzzling, and the questions that puzzle its readers can
be reduced to two: 'Is it possible to apprehend the *In Memoriam*
sequence as a whole poem?' and 'What kind of poem is it?' In other
words, the central issues are structural and generic, and if we could
give assured answers to those two questions, we would know better
how to read *In Memoriam*.

The difficulties of apprehending the structure of *In Memoriam*
are obvious and formidable. The 133 individual poems were written
from time to time over seventeen years, and not in continuous order.
Though scholars have been able to date the composition of many
sections, we know very little about Tennyson's act of arranging or
how he made his final choice of inclusion. (Not all the sections that
Tennyson wrote made their way into the final version of *In Memo-
riam*. See Appendix A to Christopher Ricks's *Poems of Tennyson*.)
Within the published text we find an encyclopedic variety of subject-
matter and many different signs of organization—recurring anniver-
saries, repeated metaphors, patterns of syntax, etc—yet each of these
signs just misses becoming definitive. The ending of *In Memoriam*
is problematic in a way that some readers find gravely disturbing.
Tennyson's own comments about the structure of *In Memoriam* are
tantalizing gems of reticence and indirection, worthy of the Ancient
Sage or of Merlin himself. The common element in all these diffi-
culties is that author and poem are always saying both too much
and too little, but Tennyson seems to have found this a necessary
condition of writing *In Memoriam*: 'words, like Nature, half reveal /
And half conceal the Soul within' (5.3–4). Finally, of all the long
poems in English, *In Memoriam* insists most strongly on the singu-
larity of its parts. Sorrow

> holds it sin and shame to draw
> The deepest measure from the chords:
>
> Nor dare she trust a larger lay,
>     But rather loosens from the lip
>     Short swallow-flights of song, that dip
> Their wings in tears, and skim away.          (48.11–16)

When we consider the genre of *In Memoriam*, we encounter again this same difficulty of too much and too little. *In Memoriam* appears too long to be read with assurance as an elegy, too short to be taken for anything else. Several recent critics have been troubled by what seems to be its displacement or rejection of the pastoral motifs that are conventional in elegy. Others, aware that the use of traditional genres by nineteenth-century English writers has itself become a critical problem, look to other forms than elegy to explain what kind of poem it is. As it does with its indications of structure, *In Memoriam* provides the reader with a bewildering variety of generic signals. Epic, drama, novel, confessional autobiography, sonnet sequence, collection of aphorisms—all have been claimed as formal models for *In Memoriam*, and epic and sonnet sequence, at least, are hinted at by Tennyson himself. These generic claims are competing, not complementary; I do not see how any poetic sequence could fulfil more than a couple of them. Moreover, just to list the possible genres is to realize that my two initial questions are inextricably related. The judgment that any reader makes about the wholeness of the poem will affect his or her perceptions of genre, and vice versa.

Fortunately, some of these difficulties resolve themselves in the reading. Despite the self-deprecating insistence upon singularity that recurs throughout the sequence, most people who reach the end of *In Memoriam* believe that they have read a complete poem and not an anthology—though many do not seem to have read the same poem. Similarly, as we read we do not juggle all the generic possibilities but choose one as our dominant assumption and read in the light of that.

What happens, I believe, as we read *In Memoriam* is this. The whole sequence is coherent (at this point I will not say 'unified'), and its coherence is rhetorical rather than argumentative or thematic. Tennyson made an initial choice of stanza and metre, and as he wrote he developed patterns of trope and syntax, such as sustained comparisons of higher and lower, and the repeated subjunctive and optative verbs that make so many of the *In Memoriam* lyrics hypothetical. Devices like these gave Tennyson the shape and proportions with which he worked, and they help to create the intuitive sense of coherence that most readers feel.[1]

However, rhetoric does not determine the contents of the poem or their order. After many years of reading and teaching *In Memo-*

---

1. This assertion needs to be argued in detail, and other people have done this better than I could do, though in piecemeal fashion. See Alan Sinfield, *The Language of In Memoriam* (Oxford: Blackwell 1971), and the pertinent chapters of F.E.L. Priestley, *Language and Structure in Tennyson's Poetry* (London: André Deutsch 1973), W. David Shaw, *Tennyson's Style* (Ithaca: Cornell University Press 1976), and Robert Pattison, *Tennyson and Tradition* (Cambridge, Mass.: Harvard University Press 1979). For the most recent survey of critical writing on *In Memoriam* the reader is directed to Joseph Sendry, '*In Memoriam*: Twentieth-Century Criticism,' *Victorian Poetry*, 18 (1980), 105–18.

*riam* I can find no single argument that unites all the sections, yet I would call none of it random. My understanding is of separate patterns of argument and image that are related to each other in ways that enable us to speak of a plurality where all the parts are homologous. Moreover, although the order of the particular sections is not inevitable, their placing is guided by a powerful sense of direction which is provided, I believe, by Tennyson's acceptance of the requirements of elegy—for that is *my* dominant assumption.

To illustrate and clarify these statements I propose to write a discussion of genre in *In Memoriam* in which I shall concentrate upon the trope of the bride leaving home as a metaphor for the death of Arthur Hallam. This trope is introduced in section 40, and it undergoes expansions and changes in the rest of the sequence until it reappears in its original form in the Epilogue. By itself the bride-leaving-home trope constitutes a minor pattern in the whole poem, but it is related to larger actions. Specifically, it forms a necessary part of defining the elegiac consolation that Tennyson hopes to achieve. This achievement of consolation is only partial, in my view, and I contend that because Tennyson is completely faithful to his genre he reaches an impasse at the end of *In Memoriam*. Elegy requires the apotheosis of Arthur Hallam and his transformation into a type; but Tennyson wants to retain Hallam as his personal and private friend. Tennyson's attempts to be true to both these demands result in what Barbara Herrnstein Smith has called 'failures of closure' at the end of the sequence.[2] Tennyson retrieves his failures as best he can in the Epilogue, which replaces elegy by its complementary genre, epithalamium.

The necessary prelude to this argument is a brief poetics of elegy and epithalamium, and to that we now turn.

## II

From its first appearance in our culture, in the Greek eclogues of Alexandria, the elegy has exhibited an extraordinary variety and flexibility of subject-matter, conventions, and poetic action. However, one can abstract a typical poetic action that is performed by elegies written in English, at least since the seventeenth century. This typical action involves acknowledging an absence. The absence may consist of a lost time or place, as in elegies whose subject is exile. It may even take the form of an anticipated presence, as in erotic elegies like John Donne's Elegy XIX 'To His Mistress, Going to Bed.' Most poems that we call elegy, however, acknowledge an absence caused by the death of a beloved person. In the related forms of dirge and complaint,

---

2. Barbara Herrnstein Smith, *Poetic Closure: A Study of How Poems End* (Chicago: University of Chicago Press 1968), pp 210–34.

acknowledging an absence and lamenting it are the whole action of the poem. Elegy differs from these simpler forms in moving beyond lament to some recovery of what has been lost. The exile can create a new homeland in his place of banishment; the lover in Donne's elegy can anticipate the pleasures of sexual union; the mourner can assert that his beloved has transcended death: 'Weep no more, woeful shepherds, weep no more, / For Lycidas your sorrow is not dead.'

This achievement requires a double ritual action, which is both fast and slow. Elegies move as swiftly as they can to the announcement that death has been transcended, a catastrophic change from woe to joy, as Dwight Culler calls it in his book on Tennyson.[3] Yet the advance to this joyful catastrophe is delayed by another action, a meditative probing of alternatives that appear to lead the elegist towards dead ends—false consolations and false endings—from which he must retreat and begin his journey again (e.g., the 'Fame is the spur' passage and St Peter's speech in 'Lycidas,' or the Lost Angel in 'Adonais,' who mistakes her own tear for one of his). The meditative aspect of elegy is not simply a delaying tactic. Meditation is necessary to provide a context in which the catastrophic change can be accepted as valid, for part of the elegist's task is to construct a new emotional and moral order that will replace the chaos of his initial experience of grief, an order in which the beloved's death can be regarded as purposeful and necessary. This act of reconstruction is unavoidably slow and difficult, but when it is complete the elegy achieves an anagnorisis, Aristotle's term in the *Poetics* for recognition or discovery. And, as Aristotle tells us, the most effective anagnorisis is one in which the poet realizes the truth of something that he knew all along.

The joyful catastrophe of elegy manifests itself in some combination of the following actions: the beloved undergoes an apotheosis, like Lycidas 'sunk low, but mounted high,' or the soul of Adonais transformed into a star. Simultaneously with this apotheosis, the beloved returns to earth and is absorbed into the natural cycle—so Lycidas returns as 'Genius of the shore' at the same time as he is being entertained by the saints above, and Adonais 'is made one with Nature . . . / . . . a portion of the loveliness / Which once he made more lovely' (lines 370, 379–80). Finally the beloved is assigned an exemplary or tutelary role that he can fulfil only in death—Genius of the shore or the star beaconing from the abode of the immortals. This new role may be combined either with the apotheosis or with the return to earth, and it is an essential part of the consolation because it goes beyond asserting that the beloved has transcended

---

3. A. Dwight Culler, *The Poetry of Tennyson* (New Haven: Yale University Press 1976), p 150. Culler denies that *In Memoriam* is generically an elegy because he sees the poem's 'gradualist' action as precluding catastrophe.

death to accept this death and to justify it. In other words, when the ritual of elegy is complete, apotheosis and anagnorisis become one.

What is involved in all these different forms of consoling vision is a transformation of the beloved from an individual person into a type. This transformation seems to be a necessary characteristic of elegy. Think, for example, of Gray's poet replaced by his own epitaph at the end of 'Elegy Written in a Country Churchyard,' or of Abraham Lincoln become a type for all the dead of the Civil War in 'When Lilacs Last in the Dooryard Bloom'd,' and of these dead in turn subsumed into 'Lilac and star and bird' (line 205). Even erotic elegies of anticipation tend to transform the beloved into a type: 'O my America! my new-found-land' (Elegy xix.27).

Any description of elegy must consider its relations to pastoral, especially when one is preparing to discuss *In Memoriam*, for it has been maintained that Tennyson's poem uses pastoral motifs so sparsely and in such unorthodox ways that *In Memoriam* cannot be called an elegy at all.[4] Such statements appear to confuse a pattern of action—loss and recovery—with one conventional way of depicting loss, which is the function of pastoral imagery. The main sources of pastoral images in our culture, Greek and Latin lyric poetry and the Bible, associate pastoral life with a state of lost innocence. Since the time of Bion and Moschus elegies have drawn upon pastoral imagery for their depiction of loss, and with the assimilation of biblical pastoral into secular poetry during the Middle Ages and the Renaissance a tradition of great richness has developed. The connection between elegy and pastoral is unbreakably intimate, yet it is not necessarily definitive. As an analogy one might consider the hero's death at the end of a tragedy. Certainly this death is one of the identifying conventions of the genre, yet this particular depiction of loss and defeat is not required by any definition of tragedy, and no one denies that *Œdipus Rex* is tragic. Furthermore, we do not identify every literary death as tragic, nor is every use of pastoral elegiac. Pastoral appears in idyll and in satire, genres which also require recognizable images of innocence, but which have different patterns of action.

*In Memoriam* uses pastoral conventions less obviously than most earlier elegies, or even later ones like 'Thyrsis.' Yet the traditional pastoral motifs are all there: a mourning shepherd playing on his pipes (section 21), Melpomene, the pastoral muse of Spenser's

4. E.g. Robert Langbaum, 'The Dynamic Unity of *In Memoriam*' in *The Modern Spirit* (New York: Oxford University Press 1970), pp 51–75; Kerry McSweeney, 'The Pattern of Natural Consolation in *In Memoriam*,' *Victorian Poetry*, 11 (1973), 87–99; Ian H.C. Kennedy, '*In Memoriam* and the Tradition of Pastoral Elegy,' *Victorian Poetry*, 15 (1977), 351–66. All three of these studies suggest that Tennyson uses pastoral conventions to subvert the elegiac pattern of loss and recovery, thereby transforming *In Memoriam* from a ritual poem to a poem of experience.

*Shepherd's Calendar* (section 37), idyllic memories of the past (e.g., sections 23, 71, and especially 89), a flower passage (section 83), and, many times throughout the sequence, the cycle of the seasons. That the presence of these motifs is not obvious is due, first, to the comparatively great length of *In Memoriam*, which dilutes the effects that other elegies concentrate. Second, it is due to Tennyson's exploiting the less than definitive nature of pastoral conventions, as he does with all the other organizing signs in the sequence. We shall examine this later, with particular attention to section 89.

One more general remark about elegy is necessary before we examine *In Memoriam* itself: elegies are anxious poems. They reach their resolution through justifying the beloved's death, deifying him and asserting that he serves as an example for the poet to follow. This is indeed consoling, yet it points to an inescapable difficulty. No matter how hopeful a poet's personal belief in immortality or how strong the dynamics of elegy, there is something factitious in denying what everyone who has experienced bereavement knows, that we apprehend a beloved person's death as a final and irrevocable separation. Elegy makes this denial, but at the cost of generating anxiety. Successful tragedy reaches an ending in which all the potential energy of the plot has been discharged. Elegy, by comparison, seems to be an inherently unstable form. The suicidal hyperbole with which Shelley concludes 'Adonais' is an eminent example of this instability. Even when an elegy succeeds in resolving its action, as I think 'Lycidas' does, a lingering feeling may remain that the elegist has put something over on his readers.

The characteristics that make elegy a dangerous form for some poets are in fact particularly congenial to Tennyson's imagination, which thrives on anxiety. From early poems like 'The Lady of Shalott' and 'The Palace of Art' to late poems like 'Lucretius' and 'Balin and Balan' anxiety is one of the main sources of his imaginative energy.[5] The anxious poems are the more authentic ones; rarely do we find in Tennyson's serene poems a complete and unforced resolution. 'Audley Court' is a fine example of such a poem, but it is exceptional. More common is a poem like 'The Ancient Sage,' which, to me at least, gives the impression of an anxious poet trying to sound serene against all his instincts and better judgment. Yet if anxiety is to be a source of poetry and not of imaginative paralysis, it must be directed and controlled, for even a poet for whom anxiety is the natural mood can go too far. At the end of *In Memoriam* Tennyson

5. There is room for a full study of Tennyson's 'anxiety of influence,' especially towards Keats (Harold Bloom's chapter in *Poetry and Repression* is only a beginning). However, what I have in mind here is anxiety in its ordinary sense, an intense feeling of distress and expectancy that often has no definite object. The plight of the Lady of Shalott is the most concise example of anxiety in Tennyson's poetry: 'She has heard a whisper say, / A curse is on her if she stay / To look down to Camelot. / She knows not what the curse may be.'

attempts to control anxiety by shifting from elegy to epithalamium. This shift is not arbitrary because their attitude towards anxiety forms one of the main links between the two genres.

If one is willing to accept any hierarchical ranking of genres, then elegy is a minor one, related to the major genre of tragedy as epithalamium is related to the major genre of comedy.[6] Tragedy ends, if not always with death, certainly with loss—loss of power, virtue, and the hero's place in the social order. Comedy usually ends with a marriage, which signifies the re-integration of an order that has been threatened with chaos. Where tragedy and comedy end, elegy and epithalamium begin. They are both retrospective genres, looking back to a prior event, and introspective as well, for the protagonist in these two forms laments someone else's death or celebrates someone else's marriage, then reflects upon its significance for his own life. One could almost relate the four genres in a proportional equation:

$$\text{tragedy/elegy} = \text{comedy/epithalamium}$$

Not quite, however. Marriage (ideally, at least) is a self-justifying event; death is not. We have already seen how elegy's attempt to justify death generates anxiety which can provide most of the emotional energy of the poem. An epithalamium, by contrast, is a poem of stable serenity. Despite its subject-matter, epithalamium is less erotic than its counterpart, because there is no frustrated personal desire in the poet's celebration of the sexual union of bride and groom. As an example, compare Tennyson's address to Hallam in an elegiac lyric like section 129, 'Dear friend, far off, my lost desire,' with the chaste description of his sister's wedding night in the Epilogue.

### III

*In Memoriam* enacts with great fidelity the elegiac patterns that I have traced. The poem begins with meditations upon the loss that Arthur Hallam's death has occasioned for the poet who speaks throughout the sequence. What he has lost is Hallam's personal presence and the significance of present and future time. Present time is a blank, and a real future is unimaginable (though the first two-thirds of *In Memoriam* abounds in hypothetical futures); only the irrecoverable past has meaning. The poet, then, has a double task: he must regain a sense of Hallam's presence, and he must learn how to justify the ways of time to men.

6. Recent discussions of nineteenth-century elegy emphasize its affinities with 'public' genres like ode and prophecy. Later in this paper I offer some remarks on *In Memoriam* and epic, but elegy is flexible enough to move to the minor key as well. See Andrew Fichter, 'Ode and Elegy: Idea and Form in Tennyson's Early Poetry,' *ELH*, 40 (1973), 398–427; Michael Cooke, 'Elegy, Prophecy and Satire in the Romantic Order,' in *Acts of Inclusion* (New Haven: Yale University Press 1979), pp 1–54.

The recovery of Hallam's presence is achieved in a triple apotheosis of dream and vision which culminates in sections 71, 95, and 103. This apotheosis is followed by Hallam's return to the earth, most obviously in section 130, 'Thy voice is on the rolling air,' but implicitly in many others of the last thirty-five sections; and by Hallam's transformation into an exemplary type of public virtue in sections 109–14. The public career that Hallam lost through his death becomes a model for everyone who reads the poem. We readers can realize the unfulfilled possibilities, and so the hypothetical future becomes a real one. These actions constitute *In Memoriam*'s joyful catastrophe, a prolonged one, to be sure, but given the size of the whole poem I do not think that it is too prolonged. The visions and transformations can still strike the reader as sudden.

*In Memoriam*'s anagnorisis, the construction of a new imaginative order in which time's ways are justified, takes longer to achieve, and the approach to it is necessarily indirect. Throughout most of *In Memoriam* the poet perceives time as an adversary, senseless, 'a maniac scattering dust' (50.7), and cruel, 'that remorseless iron hour' (84.14). Section 1 is a meditation upon strategies for outwitting this adversary:

> But who shall so forecast the years
>     And find in loss a gain to match?
>     Or reach a hand through time to catch
> The far-off interest of tears?
>
> Let Love clasp Grief lest both be drowned,
>     Let darkness keep her raven gloss:
>     Ah, sweeter to be drunk with loss,
> To dance with death, to beat the ground,
>
> Than that the victor Hours should scorn
>     The long result of love, and boast,
>     'Behold the man that loved and lost,
> But all he was is overworn.'
>
> (Lines 5–16)

In subsequent sections this adversarial relation is sustained, as the poet tries to coerce random time into teleology. As late as section 85 (two-thirds of the way through *In Memoriam*, though the lines I quote were written by 1834),[7] the poet celebrates a small victory over his enemy:

---

7. The earliest MS versions of section 85 have recently been redated (from 1833) by Joseph Sendry. See his '*In Memoriam*: The Minor Manuscripts,' *Harvard Library Bulletin*, 27 (1979), 45 and n.

> I, the divided half of such
> A friendship as had mastered Time;
>
> Which masters Time indeed, and is
>     Eternal, separate from fears:
>     The all-assuming months and years
> Can take no part away from this:          (Lines 63–8)

Only after the threefold apotheosis is complete, and after the poet has announced the new stage of his life that began with the Tennyson family's move from Somersby to Epping (section 108), can he disengage himself from this unresolvable conflict. Tentatively at first, then with increasing certitude, the poet accepts that time has work to do. Time's duration and delays are necessary if the love of Hallam and the poet is to reach its due fulfillment, and if the human race is to attain its full moral growth (sections 117 and 118). In section 123, 'There rolls the deep where grew the tree,' the poet accepts geological change without fear. He no longer perceives this change as a threat to human love because it too is part of the work of time. Finally, in section 128, the poet, who has laboured so long to erect a monument to his friend, recognizes that time is also an artist, and in time's extended works he can find the reflection of his own achievement: 'I see in part / That all, as in some piece of art, / Is toil cöoperant to an end' (lines 22–4).

Yet this recognition that time is teleological has already been implied in the transformation of Hallam into a type whose future can be fulfilled by the poem's readers, and in the three dreams and visions with their celebration of past, present, and future. The poet's first dream about Hallam in section 71 recovers the past and brings it to life again:

> Sleep, kinsman thou to death and trance
>     And madness, thou has forged at last
>     A night-long Present of the Past
> In which we went through summer France.   (Lines 1–4)

The mystic vision of section 95 restores not just the presence of Hallam but also present time. As Hallam's 'living soul was flashed' on the poet's, the united friends 'came on that which is, and caught / The deep pulsations of the world, / Æonian music measuring out / The steps of Time—the shocks of Chance— / The blows of Death' (lines 36, 39–43). The dream vision of 103, like 'Morte D'Arthur,' which it so much resembles, looks from a dying present to a future of hope. Apotheosis and anagnorisis come together, and the elegiac paradigm that I sketched above is complete.

Here is a more ample version of this account, showing how Tennyson uses metaphor to flesh out the formal paradigm. The earliest sections of *In Memoriam* form a complaint; they recount the loss that the poet must express before the poetic action of recovery can begin. By the time the sequence has reached the stopping-point of the first Christmas, the poet knows that his consolation will be found in enduring the passage of time and asserting the permanence of love:

> Still onwards winds the dreary way;
> I with it; for I long to prove
> No lapse of moons can canker Love,
> Whatever fickle tongues may say. (26.1–4)

His next task is to find a vehicle that will articulate this consolation. In sections 31–6 the poet attempts to construct a theodicy based upon the raising of Lazarus, but no sooner has he stated his argument than Urania intervenes to chide Melpomene, the poet's muse. Melpomene's art is not expounding revelation but 'render[ing] human love his dues' (37.16), and—reluctantly—she turns from divine argument to domestic metaphor.[8]

Section 40 begins with a comparison of 'Spirits breathed away' to a bride who leaves her parents' home to begin her married life:

> parting with a long embrace
> She enters other realms of love;
>
> Her office there to rear, to teach,
> Becoming as is meet and fit
> A link among the days, to knit
> The generations each with each;
>
> And, doubtless, unto thee [Hallam's spirit] is given
> A life that bears immortal fruit
> In those great offices that suit
> The full-grown energies of heaven. (Lines 11–20)

A comparison of marriage with death is one of Tennyson's master-metaphors, used in many ways throughout the whole of his career. (Tennyson's earliest extant poem is a translation of part of Claudian's 'Rape of Proserpine'; 'The Death of Œnone' was completed in

8. A full account of why this theodicy is rejected would require another essay, but here are the main reasons. First, the raising of the dead, even through a divine miracle, is a frightening and repugnant notion to Tennyson (cf section 90—despite its brave disclaimer—'The Lotos Eaters,' and especially 'Enoch Arden'). I think that this is so because Tennyson can only imagine such a resurrection as reversing the forward direction of time, and in Tennyson's poetry reversals of direction are always disastrous. Second, in section 36 the poet boasts that the Bible is written in plain language, but throughout *In Memoriam* scriptural language shares this characteristic with the language of poetry, that its real power lies in its reticence.

1890.) Here the point of the comparison is that the dead friend, like a bride, is entrusted with the mediating office of linking past and future. It has been pointed out before, but it bears repeating, that the speaker in *In Memoriam* never seriously doubts the immortality of the soul, but he fears the nature of that immortality.[9] In particular, he fears that continued friendship between the dead and the living may not be possible, and section 40 throws this fear into high relief. A bride links past and future by sending news and visiting her old home, but this is precisely what the dead cannot do.

Section 41 voices a further fear, that the poet will be permanently separated from his friend because of the different times of their deaths:

> Yet oft when sundown skirts the moor
>   An inner trouble I behold,
>   A spectral doubt which makes me cold,
> That I shall be thy mate no more,
>
> Though following with an upward mind
>   The wonders that have come to thee,
>   Through all the secular to-be,
> But evermore a life behind.    (Lines 17–24)

Baldly put, this is an eccentric scruple, yet it is the true basis of all the poet's doubts. To counter them he constructs a new argument in sections 42–7 which can be paraphrased as follows: Time is teleological because life after death is a more mature version of earthly life, as adulthood is a mature version of infancy. If the buried memories of infancy can influence the course of adult life, then the memories of earthly life may do the same to life after death. Therefore the influence of the poet on Arthur Hallam may continue, at least to the point of mutual recognition after the poet's own death.[1]

In composing this argument Tennyson drew extensively upon the ideas of his age about physiology, natural science—especially astronomy—and philosophical theology to devise what Dwight Culler has called 'a science of immortality.'[2] Yet this argument is a false consolation, like the theodicy before it. No sooner has the poet recounted his version of reunion, 'And we shall sit at endless feast, / Enjoying each the other's good' (47.9–10), than the assurance begins to fade. What if this reunion should be only a moment of farewell?

---

9. See Christopher Ricks's introductory note to 'Tithonus' in *Poems of Tennyson* (London: Longmans 1969), p 1113, and Culler, *Poetry of Tennyson*, pp 174–5.
1. Sections 41, 42, 44, and 45 are among the poems that appear in the fragmentary Huntington MS, which Joseph Sendry dates as 1837–9: 'In Memoriam: The Minor Manuscripts,' pp. 49–51. This almost certainly means that section 40, which first appears in the later Trinity MS, was composed afterwards as a way of focusing an inchoate argument.
2. Culler, *Poetry of Tennyson*, p 175.

This section is followed by two self-deprecating lyrics where the poet questions again the value of his own words. Then come the 'evolution poems' (50–8) which end the first half of *In Memoriam*.

In these poems the consoling formula, already shaky, is subjected to a test of experience, and the analogical argument of sections 40–7 collapses. In section 53, 'How many a father have I seen,' the poet confronts a scandalous paradox. The wages of sin may be virtue; there is no predictable link among the days of an individual human life. When he considers the 'secret meaning' of Nature's deeds (55.10), the only sign of purpose that he finds is prodigal abundance to counterbalance reckless waste. The fossils in 'scarpèd cliff and quarried stone' (56.2) record that this prodigality extends through the whole of history. In the face of such evidence the poet can no longer maintain his assertion that time is teleological, and this realization leads to another, unbearable analogy which is implied throughout this group of poems: 'If time is without significance, then so is my love.' This dismay is compounded by a failure of presence. 'Be near me when my light is low' is the poet's prayer to Hallam in the first line of section 50, but the desired presence never manifests itself. The voice of Nature in section 56 is also a disavowal of presence: 'Thou makest thine appeal to me: / I bring to life, I bring to death: / The spirit does but mean the breath: / I know no more' (lines 5–8). The poet's last cry to Hallam's spirit is a lament for his unanswered prayer, 'O for thy voice to soothe and bless!' (56.26), but Hallam's voice is silent.

After all this there would appear to be nothing left to say, and in section 57 it sounds as though *In Memoriam* were in fact concluding. But in elegies, as well as a convention of false consolations, there is also a convention of false endings, as I pointed out above. Recall again St Peter's speech in 'Lycidas,' or the warning to the philosopher-child in Wordsworth's 'Intimations Ode,' which is close enough to elegy to provide a pertinent example. Both appear to be speeches of dreadful finality, yet those poems are able to renew themselves and move on to true consolation. Something similar happens at this point in *In Memoriam*. Urania, the high Muse, intervenes a second time to chide Melpomene: 'Wherefore grieve / Thy brethren with a fruitless tear? / Abide a little longer here, / And thou shalt take a nobler leave' (57.9–12). The reason for Urania's second rebuke is essentially the same as in section 37. Melpomene has attempted another argument beyond her art, and again the remedy is for her to 'Go down beside thy native rill' (37.5) and meditate on the immediacy of personal experience.

Section 59 sends us back to *In Memoriam*'s beginnings, but not to the beginning of the sequence, and in this respect the address

to Sorrow is misleading. The path that the poet and his muse
retrace is the one that led from section 40 to section 47, and the
argument of the next group of poems, 60–5, requires another ver-
sion of the bride-leaving-home metaphor as its vehicle. The pattern
of this trope is the same as the previous one. Hallam's spirit is the
blessed and favoured person who leaves home, and the poet identi-
fies himself with those who remain behind; but there is a change of
roles, a change of direction in the link among the days, and—most
important—a change in the kind of assurance that the poet seeks.

Instead of a bride, feminine and passive, Hallam's spirit now takes
the role of one whose death is compared to the emergence of a gifted
man from domestic and rural obscurity to public, civic brilliance.
The poet is feminine in two of these poems, passive in all of them,
and entirely at the mercy of Hallam, who can maintain the ties of
friendship or break them, as he pleases. In section 60 the poet is
'Like some poor girl whose heart is set / On one whose rank exceeds
her own' (lines 3–4). In section 62 the poet is 'some unworthy heart'
(line 7), the old flame of a virtuous man who perhaps looks back
upon his youthful folly with condescension. Two other poems in this
group concentrate upon Hallam's exalted state. In section 61 the
poet imagines Hallam consorting in heaven with Shakespeare and
others in 'the circle of the wise' (line 3). The poet sees himself as
'slight,' 'dwarfed,' and 'blanched with darkness' by comparison.
Finally, in section 64, Hallam is depicted as a man of great abilities
but 'low estate' who has broken through the barrier of social class to
embrace a career as a statesman. The poet is his childhood friend,
now a humble country labourer. In all of these lyrics Hallam's spirit
moves in an atmosphere of confidence, but the poet resides in doubt.
'How should he love a thing so low?' the poor girl of section 60 asks
herself (line 16), and the country labourer muses, 'Does my old friend
remember me?' (line 28).

All of these comparisons sound as though they should provoke com-
plicated anxieties that will take a long time to resolve themselves, but
this is not the case. In only twelve lines section 65 transforms all the
poet's fears into a serene assurance that mutual friendship between
the dead and the living may indeed continue. This sudden change
comes about because, either directly or by implication, the poet is able
to solve the problems that were so intractable in the previous attempt
at consolation. In sections 55 and 56 the poet had been appalled at the
random prodigality of Nature, 'finding that of fifty seeds / She often
brings but one to bear' (55.11–12). The answer to that fear is in sec-
tion 65, in the economy of love that wastes nothing: '"Love's too pre-
cious to be lost, / A little grain shall not be spilt"' (lines 3–4). The link
among the days that the poet asserts here is not the joining of a dead

past with an unimaginably distant future, as it was before. Now the
link is one of easy reciprocity, joining present with present:

> Since we deserved the name of friends,
>     And thine effect so lives in me,
>     A part of mine may live in thee
> And move thee on to noble ends.          (Lines 9–12)

Finally, there is an implication throughout this group of poems that
leads to assurance. The questions in the poems demand answers,
and the answers depend upon the poet's judgment of Arthur Hallam's
character. Is Hallam the kind of man who would jilt his lover or cut
his friend just because he has advanced in the social world? No, he
is too much of a gentleman. Like other implications in *In Memoriam*
this one appears both eccentric and a bit banal when we spell it
out—very Victorian, we could say. Yet it is the true response to the
equally eccentric fear of section 40, that the poet would find himself
'evermore a life behind' his dead friend. To overcome that fear the
poet tried to work out the 'science of immortality' which failed him
when he tested it. Now he has replaced that unworkable attempt at
consolation with one that depends upon personal trust rather than
scientific or philosophical demonstration.

In the previous movement of *In Memoriam* the poet had expressed
a need to overtake a friend who kept advancing beyond his reach.
After the act of acceptance in section 65 the poet abandons his stren-
uous attempts at pursuit. Instead, he waits for Hallam's spirit to
reveal itself to him, and this opens the way for the true consolation
of the visionary apotheoses. The dream of sections 68–71, the trance
of section 95, and the second dream in section 103 all occur at Hal-
lam's initiative, after the poet has relaxed his own efforts to conjure
up his friend's spirit. The poet's assurance that these experiences are
valid depends upon personal trust in Arthur Hallam's benevolence
and power rather than upon any scientific demonstration.

The trope of the bride leaving home plays no direct part in these
lyrics of apotheosis, but the 'divinely gifted man' of section 64 is
revived and amplified for the group of poems that present Hallam
as the exemplary type of public virtue (sections 109–14). As in the
group that we have just examined, roles change again, and so does the
nature of the link among the days. In those earlier poems Hallam's
public status pointed back to the poet himself and his private anxiety:
'Does my old friend remember me?' The implied answer to the poet's
question must be yes, and the reason for this affirmation must be
Hallam's possession of exactly the kinds of virtue that are spelled
out in sections 109–11. To all who knew him Hallam was the fount
of 'heart-affluence,' of intelligent judgment, of trustworthiness,
together with power to impress those qualities upon his companions:

'And thus he bore without abuse / The grand old name of gentle-man' (111.21–2). Like the gentleman in John Henry Newman's cel-ebrated definition, 'he is one who never inflicts pain.'

However, Hallam as he appears in these later poems is more than what he was in life. The poet is also concerned with the public role that would certainly have been Hallam's if he had lived:

> A life in civic action warm,
>    A soul on highest mission sent,
>    A potent voice of Parliament,
> A pillar steadfast in the storm,
>
> Should licensed boldness gather force,
>    Becoming, when the time has birth,
>    A lever to uplift the earth
> And roll it in another course.          (113.9–16)

In section 64 Hallam was described as 'The pillar of a people's hope, / The centre of a world's desire' (lines 15–16). Here he is again a pillar, but a pillar of refuge in revolutionary times and an exemplar of moral perfection that the whole world can aspire to. Thus the link among the days changes once again, as *In Memoriam* directs its readers to an immediate future where their responsibility is to live out Hallam's unfulfilled career.

The poet's role also changes in this group from the friend left behind to a companion who 'felt thy triumph was as mine' (110.14), and who is able to impute his own 'imitative will' (line 20) to the whole world:

> I would the great world grew like thee,
>    Who grewest not alone in power
>    And knowledge, but by year and hour
> In reverence and in charity.          (114.25–8)

This last quotation also signifies a consolidation of the earlier turning away from science towards personal trust as the authority for a consoling order. In section 114 Knowledge is praised for her beauty and power but relegated to a position inferior to Wisdom and the affective virtues: 'Let her know her place; / She is the sec-ond, not the first' (lines 15–16). The higher qualities, of course, are the ones characteristic of Arthur Hallam. This does not consti-tute a repudiation of science. It is quite compatible with the poet's maintaining a keen interest in scientific phenomena. Indeed, the number and range of scientific references increase in the last sec-tions of *In Memoriam,* but the poet no longer accepts scientific knowledge as an authority that can direct his will. Trust and affec-tion have that office.

Finally we come to the group of poems that provide the justification of the works of time—not a theodicy but a 'chronodicy.' I have already traced this pattern, culminating in the poet's recognition that time is an artist like himself. The bride/friend-leaving-home-trope has no place here, but just as it lies behind the visions of apotheosis, so the attitudes of trust and affection that have been established through this trope lie behind *In Memoriam*'s chronodicy. There is one final hint of connection, in section 128.10. Like the bride and the dead friend of the previous groups, time has a mediating 'office' that goes beyond appearances.

So far, so good.

What I have written is, I believe, a valid account of how *In Memoriam* functions as an elegy. This account does not interpret the whole poem, of course. In particular, it ignores the encyclopedic discussion that is such a striking feature of *In Memoriam,* and it gives little indication of the part played in the sequence by the constant expression of changing feelings. However, I do not intend my generic description to be exclusive. Cultural concerns and personal feeling in *In Memoriam* can be related to the poem's elegiac action because all are dealt with as aspects of time with which the poet must come to terms, but they point in the direction of other genres as well. For me, they point mostly towards epic, and it is instructive to compare *In Memoriam* with Wordsworth's *Prelude,* the other great English poem of 1850. The two works are reciprocals of each other, for *The Prelude* is a heroic poem whose main action is an account of loss and recovery, 'Imagination and Taste, How Impaired and Restored,' thus pointing the whole work in the direction of elegy. Yet the presence of an elegiac action does not prevent our apprehending *The Prelude* as a poem in which Wordsworth has solved the problem of how to write a post-Miltonic epic by taking his own life as his subject and internalizing the heroic action. Similarly, I can see *In Memoriam* as a poem that leans heavily in the direction of the same kind of Romantic epic as *The Prelude*—in its encyclopedic treatment of early Victorian culture and in its account of the poet's heroic endurance—yet to acknowledge this does not destroy my apprehension of the poem as an elegy.

A more serious objection to my paradigmatic reading of *In Memoriam* is that the sequence does not end at the point where I have located the completion of its elegiac action; it continues through four more sections and 184 more lines. Indeed, section 128 itself is in some measure an afterthought, being absent from the privately printed trial edition and incomplete in two extant manuscripts (see Ricks's textual notes, *Poems of Tennyson,* p 978).

This brings us to a real crux in our reading of *In Memoriam*: can any systematic explanation adequately and consistently account for

the ending of the sequence? Certainly some readers of *In Memoriam*
find the ending eminently satisfying. Others find that it makes them
uneasy, though few can say precisely how or why. My own responses
lie with the uneasy readers, and one purpose of this essay is to suggest
some formal and structural reasons for our sense of dissatisfaction
with the ending of the poem.

In a book that I have already mentioned, Barbara Herrnstein
Smith's *Poetic Closure,* the author explains in general terms how
poems achieve their endings:

> Closure occurs when the concluding portion of a poem creates
> in the reader a sense of appropriate cessation. It announces and
> justifies the absence of further development; it reinforces the
> feeling of finality, completion, and composure which we value
> in all works of art; and it gives ultimate unity and coherence
> to the reader's experience of the poem by providing a point
> from which all the preceding elements may be viewed compre-
> hensively and their relations grasped as part of a significant
> design.[3]

This summary describes an ideal poem. Actual poems have closures
that are relatively strong or weak, and a further remark of Professor
Smith's is useful in understanding how readers can react so differ-
ently to the ending of *In Memoriam*:

> The reader's experience of closure both depends upon and
> affects his interpretation of the poem—not his critical exege-
> sis, but his general impression of, in both senses, its *design*: its
> intention (tones and motives) and its pattern (most significant
> generating principles). Again, when closural effects are fairly
> strong, readers with more or less different interpretations of a
> poem are likely to agree about the adequacy of its conclusion.
> But when the effects are weak, the reader's interpretation may
> become crucial in his experience of closure.[4]

*In Memoriam*'s closural effects are weak ones, I believe. After
the lyrics that present Arthur Hallam as a type of civic virtue, the
sequence begins its final movement with the last change of seasons,
'Now fades the last long streak of snow' (section 115). I have already
abstracted from this movement the justification of time, which cul-
minates in section 128. That is one possible closure for *In Memo-
riam*, but there are others in this same movement. Section 121, the
Hesper-Phosphor poem, also sounds as though it could be an end-
ing; so does the next section; so does section 127. Yet all these possi-
ble conclusions move the reader in different directions. Section 128

3. Smith, *Poetic Closure,* p 36.
4. Ibid, p 212.

is the conclusion of an extended argument. Section 121 is a metonymic poem in which the morning and evening star stands as a 'double name' for the poet's experience persisting through all change. Section 122 is a reprise of the vision in section 95, and it ends with an epiphany of Hallam's presence in the poet, 'enter[ing] in at breast and brow' (line 11), an epiphany that is expressed in striking metaphors of compression and expansion:

> And all the breeze of Fancy blows,
>> And every dew-drop paints a bow,
>> The wizard lightnings deeply glow,
> And every thought breaks out a rose.     (Lines 17–20)

Section 127 is an apocalyptic justification of Hallam's role as a type of civic virtue, and a final apotheosis as well: 'While thou, dear spirit, happy star, / O'erlook'st the tumult from afar, / And smilest, knowing all is well' (lines 18–20). Finally, each of the last three numbered sections is a peroration, yet there seems to be no natural climactic order among them, as is shown by Tennyson's transposing sections 129 and 130 in the trial edition.

Readers who can find complete satisfaction in the ending of the *In Memoriam* sequence are fortunate, their experience is valid, and in a different frame of mind I could share it, but this experience seems to depend upon a heavily thematic reading of the poem.[5] Those readers who emphasize the doctrinal elements in *In Memoriam*— whether those doctrines are theological or scientific—are most likely to find that the ending provides 'a sense of appropriate cessation.' But readers who approach *In Memoriam* in formal terms are apt to find that the rhetorical ambiguity of the final lyrics renders the conclusion less than adequate. In the introduction to this paper I have already suggested my own explanation for the inadequacies of the ending. In developing *In Memoriam* as an elegy Tennyson has transformed Hallam into a type, as the genre demands. Yet surely this is not what Tennyson really wants. He wants Hallam as his personal friend, and he wants his poem to celebrate the retention of friendship. To some extent the final lyrics of *In Memoriam* are assertions of friendship retained, but can we (or the poet) really believe those assertions?

> Dear friend, far off, my lost desire,
>> So far, so near in woe and weal;
>> O loved the most, when most I feel
> There is a lower and a higher;

---

5. For example, a study of the Christology of *In Memoriam* would require that the concept of 'type' be treated much more favourably than I treat it here, and surely that would be the proper way to approach *In Memoriam* from that perspective. How right Tennyson was to talk about 'weaving' the sections together.

> Known and unknown; human, divine;
>    Sweet human hand and lips and eye;
>    Dear heavenly friend that canst not die,
> Mine, mine, for ever, ever mine.          (129.1–8)

Can Arthur Hallam really be type and friend at the same time? Is the last line that I have quoted an expression of certitude or of desperation? Answers to these questions will differ, and they will depend upon each reader's interpretation, the general impression of design that Barbara Smith sees as crucial to our experience of closure. My own answer is that the poet cannot have it both ways, and that all his assertions to the contrary lead him to an impasse of anxiety because the formal requirements of elegy compel him to say both more and less than he means. ('It's too hopeful, this poem, more than I am myself,' Tennyson confessed to James Knowles some twenty years after *In Memoriam* was published.[6]) The Epilogue, with its generic change from elegy to epithalamium, provides the poet with a chance of escaping from his impasse and achieving closure.[7]

## IV

The Epilogue employs the trope of the bride leaving home in the same form as its first appearance in section 40. Again the figure of the bride mediates between the dead and the living, standing on the graves that form the floor of the church while 'the most living words of life' of the marriage service are recited. This bride is also destined to be a link among the days, joining the present stage of human development to a future of perfection. The Epilogue ends with the poet imagining the conception of his sister's child, 'a closer link / Betwixt us and the crowning race / Of those that, eye to eye, shall look / On knowledge' (lines 127–30).

However, the strength of the Epilogue lies less in its continuation of the main themes of *In Memoriam* than in the ways it can take the subsidiary anxieties of the sequence and close them off, one by one. Its tactic is diversion.[8] To begin with, the Epilogue is a palinode. The monument of love is complete, 'like a statue solid-set, / And

---

6. James Knowles, 'Aspects of Tennyson II: A Personal Reminiscence,' *Nineteenth Century*, 33 (January 1893), p 182.
7. Between the printing of the trial edition in March 1850 and the publication of the first regular edition on 1 June Tennyson added four new sections to the final movement: 119, 120, 121, 128. Section 124 was expanded by three stanzas, and sections 129 and 130 were transposed. See Ricks's textual notes to these sections, or the more detailed remarks by Susan Shatto and Marion Shaw in the commentary to their edition of *In Memoriam* (Oxford: Clarendon 1982), pp 285ff. No other part of *In Memoriam* underwent so many last-minute adjustments; nowhere else do Tennyson's revisions have such little effect.
8. Pattison, approaching in *In Memoriam* with the dominant assumption that idyll is Tennyson's major form, finds the Epilogue a formally satisfying completion of the elegy that precedes it. See *Tennyson and Tradition*, pp 111, 127.

moulded in colossal calm' (lines 15–16), and the poet proclaims the
changes in his own body and spirit that make him a different person
from the one who 'embalm[ed] / in dying songs a dead regret' (lines
13–14). Thus the Epilogue justifies bringing *In Memoriam* to publi-
cation. The marriage of Edmund Lushington and Cecilia Tennyson
is a surrogate for the cancelled marriage of Arthur Hallam and Emily
Tennyson that was lamented in section 84. The October wedding
responds to the autumn funeral procession with which *In Memoriam*
began. By giving away the bride, the poet (we might as well call him
Tennyson by this point) takes on the role of his own father, thereby
overcoming the conflicting feelings about the death of his father, as
well as Hallam's death, that animate sections 100–3 and 105. The
signing of the parish register, 'your names, which shall be read, / Mute
symbols of a joyful morn, / By village eyes as yet unborn' (lines 57–9),
is Tennyson's answer to his own previous doubts about the lasting
efficacy of the written word (see especially section 77). Finally, just
as Tennyson enacts his father's role at the wedding, so in the final
night-piece that concludes the epithalamium he takes on the role of
Arthur Hallam himself. The panorama of landscape and cosmos is
seen from the same perspective as Hallam's in his final apotheosis as
the 'dear spirit, happy star' of section 127.

The Epilogue is a wonderful display of poetic dexterity, but it
does not resolve the central anxiety of *In Memoriam*. None of its
stratagems, not Tennyson's 'conjecture' of Hallam as an invisible
guest at the marriage feast, not the marvelous *tour de force* of the
last sentence, eleven stanzas long in the *Eversley Edition*, not even
that sentence's approving use of 'link' (line 127) and 'type' (line
138), can finally divert us from the emptiness of heart with which
*In Memoriam* ends. For Arthur Hallam has not been recovered and
retained. If Hallam's personal presence is to be discovered any-
where in *In Memoriam*, it is back in section 89, the poem in which
Tennyson recalls his joy at Hallam's visits to Somersby. This lyric is
a concentrated summary of the whole pastoral tradition, with its
Theocritan format of feasting and song, its Virgilian concern with
public affairs, and, in the final couplet, the biblical promised land
flowing with milk and honey. Section 89 is unique among the *In
Memoriam* poems in being an idyll, not an elegy, perfectly resolved
and stable, with no hint of anxiety in its joy. It is unique also in
being the only place in *In Memoriam* where we actually hear Arthur
Hallam speak. What Hallam says is a warning against accepting
types in place of individual persons: 'For "ground in yonder social
mill / We rub each other's angles down, / And merge" he said "in
form and gloss / The picturesque of man and man"' (89.39–42). But
this version of pastoral is not definitive for the whole sequence, and
Hallam's warning slips by unheeded.

Several recent commentators have dealt with the ending of *In Memoriam* by describing the whole work as a poem in process, reaching out beyond its final lines to a fulfillment that transcends biography and history.[9] I do not see *In Memoriam* as transcendent in that way. The poem really does end at its last line, but I would draw a distinction between closing a poem and concluding it. The change of genre from elegy to epithalamium enabled Tennyson to close the sequence that he had written, but I doubt if he ever finished it. Outcroppings of its continuation appear in 'De Profundis,' 'In the Valley of Cauteretz,' 'In the Garden at Swainston,' and 'Vastness'; groundswells move through *Maud* and *Idylls of the King*.

*In Memoriam* has been compared * * * to *Piers Plowman* and to *Ulysses*.[1] I would like to reach my own closure with another comparison, to D.H. Lawrence's *Women in Love*. The action of *Women in Love* is a mirror-image of *In Memoriam*: it begins with a marriage and ends with a death—in Austria—and an English funeral. Like *In Memoriam*, *Women in Love* is eschatological without being transcendent, and it closes without really concluding. Furthermore, there is evidence that *In Memoriam* was somewhere in Lawrence's mind as he worked on *Women in Love*.[2]

When I try to imagine how Tennyson lived with *In Memoriam* after he had closed it, I am drawn to the final dialogue between Rupert and Ursula in Lawrence's novel. This would not be the conversation of Alfred Tennyson and Emily Sellwood, of course; but it might be the silent-speaking words of 'the poet' (for one last time) talking with his spirit as with a wife (cf section 97):

> 'Aren't I enough for you?' she asked.
>
> 'No,' he said. 'You are enough for me, as far as a woman is concerned. You are all women to me. But I wanted a man friend, as eternal as you and I are eternal. . . .
>
> 'Having you, I can live all my life without anybody else, any other sheer intimacy. But to make it complete, really happy,

---

9. E.g.: J.C.C. Mays, '*In Memoriam*: An Aspect of Form' *UTQ*, 35 (1965), 22–46; Henry Kozicki, *Tennyson and Clio: History in the Major Poems* (Baltimore: Johns Hopkins University Press 1979). The phrase 'poem in process' is from Culler, *Poetry of Tennyson*, p 217.

1. Mays, '*In Memoriam*: An Aspect of Form,' p 33, and Arthur J. Carr, 'Tennyson as a Modern Poet,' *UTQ*, 19 (1950), p 361.

2. In 'The Crown,' a group of essays that stands behind the final version of *Women in Love* as 'Study of Thomas Hardy' stands behind *The Rainbow*, Lawrence twice uses Tennyson's phrase 'the infant crying in the night' to describe and condemn a state of emotional immaturity that renders its victims incapable of fruitful struggle for the crown of love. The infant crying in the night finds its way into the text of *Women in Love* as part of Gudrun's railing against Gerald Crich in chapter 30. 'The Crown' also contains a reference to 'the delicate blue speedwells of childhood,' which sounds like Lawrence remembering 'The little speedwell's darling blue' of *In Memoriam* 83.10. See 'The Crown' in *Phoenix II*, ed Warren Roberts and Harry T. Moore (London: Heinemann 1968), pp 366, 414, 396.

I wanted eternal union with a man too: another kind of love,'
he said.

'I don't believe it,' she said. 'It's an obstinacy, a theory, a
perversity.'

'Well—' he said.

'You can't have two kinds of love. Why should you!'

'It seems as if I can't,' he said. 'Yet I wanted it.'

'You can't have it, because it's false, impossible,' she said.

'I don't believe that,' he answered.[3]

Better yet, let us give Tennyson himself the last word, the closing
lines of 'Vastness,' which he published in 1885, more than fifty
years after Arthur Hallam had died:

Peace, let it be! for I loved him, and love him for ever: the dead
are not dead but alive.

# JEFF NUNOKAWA

## *In Memoriam* and the Extinction of the Homosexual[†]

"So what do I know about being mature. The only thing mature
means to me is *Victor* Mature . . ."
                              —Mart Crowley, *The Boys in the Band*

"Descend, and touch, and enter; hear / The wish too strong for
words to name" (*In Memoriam*, 93.13–14).[1] It is difficult for a con-
temporary audience to read these lines, in which Tennyson prays for
Hallam's embrace, without thinking that the wish too strong for
words to name is the love that dare not speak its name. Tennyson's
critics have often resisted such interpretations by reminding us that
expressions of devotion must be situated historically. Gordon Haight,
for example, argues that "the Victorians' conception of love between
those of the same sex cannot be understood fairly by an age steeped
in Freud. Where they saw only pure friendship, the modern reader
assumes perversion. . . . Even *In Memoriam*, for some, now has a
troubling overtone."[2] As Haight's comment suggests, there is
often more homophobia than history in the traditional appeal to
the differences between Victorian and contemporary discourses of

---

3. D.H. Lawrence, *Women in Love* (Harmondsworth: Penguin 1960), p 541.

† From *English Literary History* 58.2 (Summer 1991): 427–38. © 1991 by The Johns Hop-
kins University Press. Reprinted by permission of the publisher, Johns Hopkins Uni-
versity Press.

1. *The Poems of Tennyson*, ed. Christopher Ricks (London: Longman, 1969). All subse-
quent citations of *In Memoriam* refer to Ricks's edition.

2. Gordon Haight, *George Eliot: A Biography* (New York: Oxford Univ. Press, 1968), 496.

desire. Christopher Ricks, no sympathizer with Hellenistic read-ings of *In Memoriam*, dismisses the claim that such readings are necessarily anachronistic: "As so often, the position of the histori-cal purist is itself unhistorical. . . . Some Victorians, who found Shakespeare's *Sonnets* troubling, found *In Memoriam* troubling."[3] *The Times*, for example, condemned *In Memoriam* for its "tone of amatory tenderness."[4] Tennyson's own trouble with this tone may be registered in his famous protest that while Hallam lived, he never called him "dearest."[5]

But the historical particularity of Tennyson's passion in the trou-bling passages of *In Memoriam* can be taken up to define, rather than deny, its homosexual character: what construction of the homosexual is registered and reproduced in the parts of *In Memo-riam* which Victorians themselves could designate as such?[6] I want to begin with the suppressed phrase which has elicited so much attention from critics interested in denying or affirming the homo-sexual character of Tennyson's poem. The invitation to matrimony that Tennyson excised from the manuscript version of section 93 ("Stoop soul and touch me: wed me") has been taken by various readers, including, perhaps, Tennyson himself, as a figure of homo-sexual desire. But it is the revision rather than the original, or better, the revision's relation to the original which we may more accurately designate as homoerotic: the site of homoerotic desire is consti-tuted as the negation of the heterosexual figure of marriage. To apprehend the homoerotic in *In Memoriam* as that which is defined *against* heterosexuality is to gain a sense of it as part of the nineteenth-century formation of sexual abnormality that Michel Foucault points to, a formation which is constituted by, and in turn constitutes its opposite: sexual normality.[7]

And if, according to a logic that Foucault has made familiar to us, the homosexual in *In Memoriam* is formed by its relation to the heterosexual, the heterosexual is formed by its relation to the homo-sexual. More specifically, *In Memoriam* proposes a developmental model of male sexuality which establishes the homoerotic as an

3. Christopher Ricks, *Tennyson* (New York: Macmillan, 1972), 219.
4. Quoted by Ricks, *Tennyson* (note 3), 219. [See p. 158 above—*Editor*.]
5. Quoted by Valerie Pitt, *Tennyson Laureate* (London: Barrie and Rockliff, 1962), 117. The point that I am rehearsing here, that the homoeroticism of *In Memoriam* has trou-bled even its first readers, is made most decisively by Christopher Craft, in his investi-gation of the poem's homosexual rhetoric, "'Descend, and Touch, and Enter': Tennyson's Strange Manner of Address," in *Genders* 1 (1988): 85–86. See also Craft's analysis of the sometimes complex strategies deployed by generations of Tennyson's readers to evade or contain the homosexual elements of the elegy (86–87). Craft's reading of *In Memoriam*'s "same gender eroticism" (87) touches my own. See note 8.
6. See, of course, Michel Foucault, *The History of Sexuality: Volume I. An Introduction*, trans. Robert Hurley (New York: Pantheon, 1978) for an account of sexual categories as the product of historically specific discursive practices, rather than timeless essences.
7. See especially part 2 of *The History of Sexuality*, "The Repressive Hypothesis."

early phase that enables and defines the heterosexual. "The wish too strong for words to name" is not a desire for matrimony, but rather a primary stage in the formation of the husband and the father:

> How many a father have I seen,
> A sober man, among his boys,
> Whose youth was full of foolish noise,
> Who wears his manhood hale and green:
>
> And dare we to this fancy give,
> That had the wild oat not been sown,
> That soil, left barren, scarce had grown
> The grain by which a man may live?
>                                   (53.1–8)

The "wild oats" and "foolish noise" which make up the patriarch's prehistory may be aligned with the boyhood love that Tennyson sets against the marital contract in section 59 of *In Memoriam*. This boyhood love is another version of early passion which makes way for, and a way for, heterosexuality:

> O Sorrow, wilt thou live with me
> No casual mistress, but a wife
> . . . . . . . . . . . . . . . . .
> My centered passion cannot move,
> Nor will it lessen from to-day
> But I'll have leave at times to play
> As with the creature of my love.
>                                   (59.1–2, 9–12)

Tennyson's post-Marlovian proposal of marriage is preceded and occasioned by the loss of his earlier pastoral play: his bride is a metonym for the loss of Hallam, and his heterosexual situation is thus defined as the ghost of prior passion; marriage is an elegy for earlier desire.[8]

I will seek shortly to demonstrate more specifically how *In Memoriam* identifies these early regions of passion as homoerotic, but before I do this, I want to recall the historical situation of Tennyson's ordering of male desire. The conception of the homoerotic as

---

8. Here is the most significant point of convergence between my reading of *In Memoriam* and Christopher Craft's. Like Craft, I locate the homosexual in Tennyson's poem as a primal moment in a developmental narrative that terminates with a form of heterosexual desire that appears removed from the earlier stage that precedes and enables it. But my sense both of the character of this developmental narrative and of its calibrations—the categories homosexual and heterosexual—differ from Craft's. While Craft emphasizes the status of this narrative as "a disciplinary trajectory" (95), more or less continuous with the project of sublimation that Havelock Ellis prescribed for same-gender desire, my reading takes up an evolutionary narrative in the poem, which casts the homosexual not as the target of proscription or aversion, but rather as something that a person, or population, naturally, necessarily, outgrows. ° ° °

an early term in the tutelary itinerary of the bourgeois British male, an itinerary which ultimately installs him in the position of husband and father, is a staple of Victorian and post-Victorian ideology. Certainly the definitive site of this erotic apprenticeship is the English public school where, in the words of one Etonian, "It's all right for fellows to mess one another a bit. . . . But when we grow up we put aside childish things, don't we?"[9]

In *Between Men: English Literature and Male Homosocial Desire*, Eve Kosofsky Sedgwick examines the ideological efficacy for the Victorian bourgeoisie of this evolutionary model of male desire. Sedgwick suggests that the social distinctions within the class of Victorian gentlemen were figured as different developmental stages within an individual psychic career in order to promote "the illusion of equality . . . within that class."[1] We may begin to sense that importance of such a softening of social distinctions for Tennyson in his relation to Arthur Hallam when we recall the difference between Tennyson's rather vexed and confused class and financial circumstances, and Hallam's far more secure possession of wealth and aristocratic position. The difference in their social circumstances, while perhaps not dramatic to our eyes, was sufficiently significant that, in the words of Robert Bernard Martin, "it is surprising that the most celebrated friendship of the century should ever have begun at all."[2]

Sedgwick argues that the Victorian narrative of individual psychosexual development served as the form in which economic and social distinctions within the bourgeoisie were made to appear. In Tennyson's poem, the figure of evolutionary scale not only promotes a con-

---

9. Michael Nelson, *Nobs and Snobs* (London: Gordon & Cremonski, 1976), 147, as cited by Eve Kosofsky Sedgwick, *Between Men: English Literature and Male Homosocial Desire* (New York: Columbia Univ. Press, 1985). In *The Worm in the Bud: The World of Victorian Sexuality* (1969; reprint, Harmondsworth, Middlesex: Penguin Books, 1983), Ronald Pearsall discusses the remarkable extent and intensity of homoerotic activity in the English public schools in the nineteenth century, and the comparatively tolerant or indifferent attitude of school authorities towards even overtly sexual relations amongst students (551–60). (See also Louis Crompton, *Byron and Greek Love: Homophobia in Nineteenth-Century England* [Berkeley: Univ. of California Press, 1985]). While the figuration of male homoerotic activity as schoolboy love, a term in the growth of the patriarch, casts this version of such activity as a part of, rather than apart from heterosexual hegemony, this is, of course, not to suggest that all instances of sexual intercourse between males in Victorian England were tolerated by or instrumental to heterosexual authority. Pearsall quotes William Stead's observation during the Wilde trial about the discrepancy between the prevailing attitude toward fleshy versions of schoolboy love and the fierce prosecution of homosexual behavior when it took place beyond the bounds of early development: "Should everyone found guilty of Oscar Wilde's crime be imprisoned, there would be a very surprising emigration from Eton, Harrow, Rugby and Winchester to the jails of Pentonville and Holloway. . . . boys are free to pick up tendencies and habits in public schools for which they may be sentenced to hard labour later on" (Pearsall, 555).

1. Sedgwick (note 9), 178. Sedgwick's book first alerted me to the activity during the Victorian period of the notion that homosexuality is "just a phase."

2. Robert Bernard Martin, *Tennyson: The Unquiet Heart* (New York: Oxford Univ. Press, 1980), 69.

ception of potential equality between terms situated at different
stages of development, but also replaces a model of social organization
where there is no such potential equality between vertically distinct
terms. In other words, in *In Memoriam*, we can witness the decision
to rewrite what the poem first designates as unchanging social differ-
ences as different moments in a narrative of development, a narrative
which includes, as one of its passages, the exodus of the male subject
out of the blighted pastoral regions of the homoerotic.

Throughout *In Memoriam*, Tennyson pictures the difference
between himself and his dead friend as an insuperable vertical
distance:

> Deep folly! yet that this could be—
> That I could wing my will with might
> To leap the grades of life and light,
> And flash at once, my friend, to thee.
>                                    (41.9–12)

In section 60, Tennyson describes this difference in height as a dif-
ference of class; the terms that he employs here to measure the
distance between himself and Hallam describe his sense of loss as
a sense of socioeconomic inferiority:

> He past; a soul of nobler tone:
> My spirit loved and loves him yet,
> Like some poor girl whose heart is set
> On one whose rank exceeds her own.
>
> He mixing with his proper sphere,
> She finds the baseness of her lot,
> Half jealous of she knows not what,
> And envying all that meet him there.
>
> The little village looks forlorn;
> She sighs amid her narrow days,
> Moving about the household ways,
> In that dark house where she was born.
>
> The foolish neighbours come and go,
> And tease her till the day draws by:
> At night she weeps, 'How vain am I!
> How should he love a thing so low?'
>                                    (60.1–16)

In the four sections of *In Memoriam* that follow, Tennyson enlists
various models of organic progression which recast and qualify the
class difference figured here. The distinction between Tennyson and
Hallam becomes, in section 61, the difference between a "dwarf'd . . .

growth" (7) and the "perfect flower of human time" (4). For Tenny-
son to define himself as a dwarfed growth is, implicitly, to attribute
to himself the unrealized potential for *full* growth. While the "soul of
nobler tone" is simply inaccessible to what is below and behind him,
the "perfect flower of human time" figures a completion of develop-
ment which the stunted plant could have attained. In section 63,
Tennyson collates the distinction between himself and Hallam with
differences between lower and higher species of animals, and if this
seems to substantiate rather than diminish their separation, we need
to remember Tennyson's endorsement of both phylogenic and ontoge-
netic versions of evolution. In section 118, for example, the forlorn
desire to "leap the grades of life" is rewritten as a prescription for a
personal practice of evolutionary process: "Move upward, working
out the beast, / And let the ape and tiger die" (27–8). And if the figure
of lesser development can rise to a higher stage, according to the
evolutionary models that Tennyson sets forth in sections 61 through
65, the higher rises by means of the lower. The inferior term of the
developmental hierarchy is cast as the seed that moves the superior
term to "noble ends" (65.12).

Tennyson thus relieves class differences by replacing the simple
social barrier between the "poor girl" and the "soul of nobler tone"
with a permeable boundary: the "dwarf'd growth" and the "perfect
flower of human time" are related as figures situated at different
stages of the same evolutionary narrative. I want to suggest that the
scenario of social ascent that Tennyson sets forth in section 64, in
which Hallam is pictured not as a noble, but instead as a case study
of upward mobility, registers the ideological force of these develop-
mental models. The description of Hallam as "some divinely gifted
man, / Whose life in low estate began . . . who breaks his birth's
invidious bar" (1–2, 5) is enacted by means of an implicit analogy to
the scenarios of natural evolution that surround it.

Identified with these evolutionary models, the scale from homo-
sexual to heterosexual is defined as another version of the develop-
mental range that displaces the class differences of section 60.
Here is Tennyson addressing Hallam in section 61:

> If thou cast thine eyes below,
> How dimly character'd and slight,
> How dwarf'd a growth of cold and night,
> How blanch'd with darkness must I grow!
>
> Yet turn thee to the doubtful shore,
> Where thy first form was made a man;
> I loved thee, Spirit, and love, nor can
> The soul of Shakespeare love thee more.
>
> (61.5–12)

When the stunted, shadowed growth locates his devotion to Hallam with Shakespearean love, he identifies his desire with a standard Victorian figure for the male homoerotic. It was the homoerotic reputation of the Sonnets which made some of Tennyson's contemporaries uneasy about his fondness for them. Benjamin Jowett, for example, was relieved by what he regarded as Tennyson's retreat from his devotion to the Sonnets. To do otherwise, Jowett, opined, "would not have been manly or natural. . . . The love of the sonnets which he [Tennyson] so strikingly expressed was a sort of sympathy with Hellenism."[3] Certainly it was the taint of Hellenism attached to the Sonnets which prompted Henry Hallam to "wish that Shakespeare had never written them."[4]

Tennyson begins section 62 by again affiliating his lower species of love for Hallam with Shakespearean devotion:

> Tho' if an eye that's downward cast
> Could make thee somewhat blench or fail,
> Then be my love an idle tale,
> And fading legend of the past.
>
> (62.1–4)

These lines allude to the conclusion of Sonnet 116: "If this be error and upon me proved, / I never writ, nor no man ever loved" (13–14).[5] We need now to notice what Tennyson does with Sonnet 116, and why he does it. If *In Memoriam* takes up the Victorian conception of the Sonnets as an exemplary figuration of male homoerotic passion, it revises the terms of Shakespearean desire to fit with the modern formation of the homosexual which gained hegemony in the nineteenth century. While Shakespeare's devotion is "the marriage of true minds" in Sonnet 116, it is defined as that which is *not* marriage in *In Memoriam*. In keeping with the construction of the homoerotic as an early point on the developmental agenda of male desire, a stage which *precedes* and is terminated by matrimony, Tennyson's poem draws marriage away from the form of devotion that Victorians attributed to the Sonnets and situates it at a height where that form has been transcended. Tennyson goes on in section 62 to compare his Shakespearean passion for Hallam with Hallam's own ascent to the higher species of heterosexuality:

3. Hallam Lord Tennyson, *Materials for a Life of Alfred Tennyson* (privately printed, no date). Quoted by Ricks (note 3 [p. 217]), 215. For a detailed discussion of the complicated career of "Hellenism" as a signifier of male homosexuality, see Crompton (note 9 [p. 219]), especially chapter 2.
4. Henry Hallam, *Introduction to the Literature of Europe* (1839), 3:501–4. Quoted by Ricks, *Tennyson*, 215.
5. *The Sonnets, Songs and Poems of Shakespeare*, ed. Oscar James Campbell (New York: Schocken Books, 1964), All subsequent citations of Sonnet 116 refer to this edition.

> And thou, as one that once declined,
> When he was little more than boy,
> On some unworthy heart with joy,
> But lives to wed an equal mind.
>
>                                   (62.5–8)

Shakespeare measures the permanence of his love in 116:

> Love's not Times fool, though rosy lips and cheeks
> Within his bending sickle's compass come;
> Love alters not with his brief hours and weeks,
> But bears it out even to the edge of doom.
>
>                                   (9–12)

But Tennyson, again subjecting the sonnet to the Victorian conception of the homoerotic as an early stage of male erotic development, declares the impermanence of the devotion that it expresses, casting it as a kind of schoolboy passion which "wholly dies" (10), or becomes "matter for a flying smile" (12) when boys put away childish things to become husbands and fathers.

Thus, Tennyson's claim that his passion for Hallam rivals Shakespeare's, works less to aggrandize his own passion than to diminish Shakespeare's. The constitution of the homoerotic in *In Memoriam* is most fully registered in its revision of Sonnet 116, a revision which converts Shakespeare's claim for the deathlessness of his desire into an announcement of its mortality.

I want now to examine a subtler announcement of the failure of Shakespearean devotion in *In Memoriam*. Tennyson alludes in section 62 to Shakespeare's designation of the permanence of his passion as the grounds upon which his writing rests: "If this be error and upon me proved, / I never writ nor no man ever loved." While Tennyson's echo of these lines slightly alters Shakespeare's contract ("if an eye that's downward cast / Could make thee somewhat blench or fail, / Then be my love an idle tale, / And fading legend of the past"), I nevertheless want to suggest that the connection that Shakespeare sets forth between the existence of his text and the permanence of his passion remains in place in Tennyson's poem, only now in a negative form. When he recasts the passion of the sonnet as temporary rather than permanent, Tennyson cancels the condition upon which Shakespeare's text depends. And the proof of Shakespeare's error is registered by the figure of Shakespearean devotion in section 61 that I referred to earlier, the figure who is "dimly character'd and slight." This fading legend of Shakespearean love is the negative realization of Shakespeare's covenant in Sonnet 116: here, the text disappears since the love that it represents is ephemeral, rather than eternal. The Shakespearean text is dimmed and slighted according to the

terms of its own contract and according to the Victorian concep-
tion of its content.

The negative version of the Shakespearean contract which inhabits
Tennyson's text suggests that "the wish too strong for words to name,"
another instance of desire contradistinguished from marriage, might
as well be called the wish too *weak* for words to name. In "the wish
too strong for words to name," the consequence of Tennyson's cancel-
lation of Shakespeare's claim for the durability of his love is fully real-
ized. The marriage of true minds is described now as the ephemeral
predecessor of marriage, a transitional, transitory, and thus wordless
"wish." Shakespeare's contract enables us to identify the place in *In
Memoriam* where the homoerotic is extinguished, the place where
Tennyson's love for Hallam is matured and his Shakespearean devo-
tion expunged. Tennyson's fear that Hallam's death left him a dwarfed
growth, permanently arrested at the stage of schoolboy love, is allayed
in section 81 of the poem, where Death declares that through its
intervention, Tennyson's devotion to Hallam was fully ripened:

> Could I have said while he was here,
> 'My love shall now no further range;
> There cannot come a mellower change,
> For now is love mature in ear.'
>
> Love then had hope of richer store:
> What end is here to my complaint?
> This haunting whisper makes me faint,
> 'More years had made me love thee more.'
>
> But Death returns an answer sweet:
> 'My sudden frost was sudden gain,
> And gave all ripeness to the grain,
> It might have drawn from after-heat.'
>                                               (81.1–12)

We may locate the repository of the ripened grain of Tennyson's
matured love when we gather together an allusion that is dispersed
in sections 81 and 82, an allusion to Keats's "When I Have Fears":

> When I have fears that I may cease to be
> Before my pen has gleaned my teeming brain,
> Before high-piled books, in charactery,
> Hold like rich garners the full ripened grain:
>                                               (1–4)[6]

Tennyson takes up not only the occasion of Keats's poem (the pros-
pect of premature death), but also two of its figures—the grain in
section 81 ("My sudden frost was sudden gain / And gave all ripeness

6. *The Poems of John Keats*, ed. Miriam Allott (London: Longman, 1972).

to the grain") and, in 82, the garner that Keats pictures as the container for that grain:

> For this alone on Death I wreak
> That wrath that garners in my heart;
> He puts our lives so far apart
> We cannot hear each other speak.
>
> (82.13–16)

By reconstituting the reference to Keats's text in these sections of *In Memoriam*, we can discern the harvest of Tennyson's matured love in the rancor of his heart, a rancor whose source is the impotence of speech.

The dispelling of the homoerotic in these lines becomes visible when the resentment that Tennyson garners in his heart is placed next to the *words* that Keats garners, the "high-piled books, in charactery," which "hold like rich garners the full ripened grain." Tennyson's wrath, which, I have suggested, may be identified with his ripened love, represents two linguistic failures; not only his inability to hear or be heard by Hallam, but also the absence of the words, the "charactery," that Keats pictures as the ripened harvest that fills the garners. And according to the Shakespearean formula active in Tennyson's poem, a formula which equates the termination of what the Victorians constructed as homoerotic desire with verbal disappearance, this absence tells us that the maturation of Tennyson's love is the conclusion of its homoerotic phase. The ripening of love is built upon the disappearance of prior characters, the proof of Shakespeare's error. This verbal absence appears at the conclusion of a section of *In Memoriam* which includes a survey of the stages of evolutionary progress:

> Eternal process moving on,
> From state to state the spirit walks;
> And these are but the shatter'd stalks,
> Or ruined chrysalis of one.
>
> (82.5–8)

The "wild oat" of section 53, an early version of male desire whose passing is defined by verbal effacement, may be construed amongst the "shatter'd stalks" and "ruined chrysalis" as something else abandoned by that which is ripe. The absence of any reminder of this early desire may be the poem's most eloquent elegy for the homosexual; unlike the grain and the butterfly, matured male love leaves behind no mark, no souvenir of a kind of devotion whose failure can have no trace.[7]

---

7. The psychosexual itinerary that I have sought to identify in *In Memoriam* is, of course, an exclusively masculine model of improvement. It is in section 60 of the poem, where the vertical distance between Hallam and Tennyson is figured as an impermeable boundary, that the difference between lower and higher is the difference between a

But if the homoerotic disappears within the course of male desire as it is charted by Tennyson, this inexorable early loss is incessantly rewritten in subsequent constructions of the homosexual, rewritten and transliterated. If the homosexual is a stage, fated for extinction in the nineteenth-century conception of the homosexual that *In Memoriam* helps to construct, the doom attached to it is visited upon a population as the category of the homosexual passes from stage to subject in the years that follow Tennyson's elegy.[8] The funeral that Tennyson hosts for his own puerile homoerotic desire in *In Memoriam* has its afterlife in the glamorous rumor of preordained doom that bathes the image of live-fast-die-young gay boys such as Dorian Gray, Montgomery Clift, James Dean, Joe Orton, and, most recently, a French-Canadian airline steward who came to be known as Patient Zero, the spoiled child in whom the dominant media apprehended the embodiment of the lethal effects of a new virus. The youthful fatality of homosexual desire, the youthful fatality which *is* homosexual desire in Tennyson's poem, prepares the way for the story of the bathhouse boy's frolicsome progress to an inevitable early grave. "Blanch'd with darkness" still, the figure "dimly character'd and slight" helps explain why the dominant media inaccurately identifies AIDS with, even *as*, the early death of gay men. The "dwarf'd" "growth of cold and night" haunts such representations of the current crisis, the "dwarf'd" "growth of cold and night" that defines the homosexual as that which dies young.

SARAH GATES

Poetics, Metaphysics, Genre: The Stanza Form
of *In Memoriam*[†]

The vacillation between opposite aspects of a theme or between opposing states of mind (such as hope and despair) that turn out

woman and a man. The replacement of "some poor girl" in section 60 with the figure of Shakespearean desire in the sections that follow reflects a crucial dimension of the strategy that Tennyson enacts in *In Memoriam*; to convert a masculine itinerary of desire into a social program for upward mobility is to confirm the position of women as a permanent underclass, excluded categorically from the potential for ascent. The embarrassed maiden of section 60 serves to remind us of who must be left behind by Tennyson's stairway scenario.

8. On the construction of homosexuality as a subject position, see Foucault (note 6 [p. 217]), and Jeffrey Weeks, *Coming Out: Homosexual Politics in Britain, from the Nineteenth Century to the Present* (London: Quarter Books, 1977). Eve Kosofsky Sedgwick considers how the discourse of evolution that I have sought to isolate in Tennyson's construction of the homosexual informs contemporary homophobic accounts of AIDS. See "*Billy Budd*: After the Homosexual," in *Epistemology of the Closet* (Berkeley: Univ of California Press, 1990), 185–190.

† From *Victorian Poetry* 37.4 (Winter 1999): 507–20. Reprinted by permission of *Victorian Poetry*.

not to oppose but to define each other is a crucial *modus operandi* in *In Memoriam*. In the past, critics tended to align themselves "in defense" of one side or the other. T. S. Eliot, for example, asserted of the faith/doubt theme that "its faith is a poor thing, but its doubt is a very intense experience,"[1] while Carlisle Moore argued, on the other hand, that this "doubt" really only serves the "faith" by proving its strength.[2] J. C. C. Mays synthesizes these positions by treating such apparent conflicts as interrelated and mutually constitutive dichotomous oppositions that animate the progress of the poem, arguing that each half only comes to know itself through the other half, so that the "whole progression of the poem is through opposition playing against itself" with the resolution occurring only in time.[3] In a similar tangle of apparently contradictory positions, studies of the poem that treat its structural form have tended to enlist it into the ranks of essentially narrative genres—"confession" or "autobiography," for example[4]—while others cast it as essentially lyric—as "fragment," "elegy," "sonnet sequence," "collection of aphorisms"—thus addressing each side of an apparent formal contradiction between the poem's lyric concentration and its narrative drift.[5] Although these formalist considerations seem less susceptible to the kind of synthesizing achieved in the thematic studies, David Shaw has made a detailed and illuminating examination into the generic affiliations of this narrative in lyrics and the ways in which Tennyson "tests" or expands the conventions of the genres he uses.[6] He suggests in *Tennyson's Style* that "even if there is no final generic reconciliation in *In Memoriam* (and I know of no study that convincingly demonstrates that there is), the poem as a whole does manage to achieve [a] kind of continuity in change" (pp. 146–147).

1. T. S. Eliot, "In Memoriam," in *Tennyson: In Memoriam: A Casebook*, ed. John Dixon Hunt (London: Macmillan, 1970), p. 135. [See p. 169 above—*Editor*.]
2. Carlisle Moore, "Faith, Doubt, and Mystical Experience in 'In Memoriam,'" in Hunt, pp. 241–259.
3. J. C. C. Mays, "*In Memoriam*: An Aspect of Form," *UTQ* 35 (1965): 28.
4. W. David Shaw discusses *In Memoriam* as a "confession" in "*In Memoriam* and the Rhetoric of Confession," *ELH* 38 (1971): 80–103 and later as "spiritual autobiography" in *Tennyson's Style* (Ithaca: Cornell Univ. Press, 1976), p. 132.
5. Donald Hair claims that "the fragment . . . is the essential form of the work" in *Tennyson's Language* (Toronto: Univ. of Toronto Press, 1991), a claim he supports in his analysis of the "theories of language" that "underwrite" the poem (p. 89). Peter Hinchcliffe analyzes *In Memoriam* as an "elegy" resolved at the end by an "epithalamium" in "Elegy and Epithalamium in *In Memoriam*," *UTQ* 52 (1983): 142–162 [see pp. 194–216 above]. He includes the list of "competing" "generic signals" the poem seems to provide which have been treated as "formal models" for understanding the poem in the past. Peter M. Sacks regards it as an "elegy" in his psychoanalytic study of the genre in *The English Elegy: Studies in the Genre from Spenser to Yeats* (Baltimore: Johns Hopkins Univ. Press, 1985). Shaw reads the poem as an elegy in *Elegy and Paradox: Testing the Conventions* (Baltimore: Johns Hopkins Univ. Press, 1994), in which he explores the ways *In Memoriam* "tests" the conventions of that genre, especially in its Darwinian context, which was undermining the spiritual kinds of consolation that had historically granted their resolutions.
6. See W. David Shaw, *Tennyson's Style*; *Elegy and Paradox*; and *Alfred Lord Tennyson: The Poet in an Age of Theory* (New York: Basil Blackwell, 1996); hereafter referred to as *ALT*.

In this essay, I would like to propose a way to understand this "continuity in change," by adapting some of Jean Starobinski's ideas about autobiography to a lyric format along the way, and especially by making a detailed exploration of poetics, of the peculiar appropriateness of Tennyson's *abba* stanza form as a vehicle for embodying and signifying his intellectual and spiritual conflicts (the thematic material), and his own journey through them (the autobiographical structure).[7] It seems clear to me that if we want to understand the "coherence" (the term Peter Hinchcliffe prefers, quite reasonably, to "unity" [p. 242]) of this extraordinarily self-contradictory, fluidly granulated work, we might start with a look at the only constant—and an obsessive constant it is—to be found in it.

Critics have often commented in passing upon the effect of the *abba* stanza form, which Christopher Ricks, for example, says "can 'circle moaning in the air', returning to its setting out, and with fertile circularity staving off its deepest terror and arrival at desolation and indifference." In his analysis, the *abba* form enacts in the outer rhymes the mourner's desire to "travel" rather than to "arrive," to continue missing Hallam rather than to cease loving him. The fourth line circles back to the first line via the rhyme; the stanza returns to its beginning; and thus, like the thoughts of the mourner,

> reced[es] from its affirmations, from what it momentarily clinches, so unlike the disputatious sequences of the heroic couplet: these very reasons make it the emblem as well as the instrument for poems in which moods ebb and flow, . . . in which hopes are recurrent but always then dimmed—though never shattered.[8]

This wonderful description itself enacts exactly the feel of the *In Memoriam* stanza. More recently, David Shaw has pointed out that the middle lines of the stanzas "contract the meaning, while the first and fourth lines tend to diffuse it," and "that the whole energy of the last line is directed forward, while the energy of the first line is directed back," a dynamic which produces "frequent stalemates . . . between forces of closure and delay" (*ALT*, p. 33), and Peter Sacks has mentioned that the self-enclosed quality of the stanzas enacts a kind of frozenness in the present that is symptomatic of melancholia (p. 169). These descriptions are helpful and put us on the right path, but more can be said about the *abba* form.

The fourth line does gesture back to the first, but it does not enact a complete return, for it can only do so after the reader has

---

7. My model for this study is John Freccero's "The Significance of *Terza Rima*," in John Freccero, *Dante: The Poetics of Conversion*, ed. Rachel Jacoff (Cambridge: Harvard Univ. Press, 1986), pp. 258–271, which explores the interaction of thematics and poetics in a specific verse form.
8. Christopher Ricks, *Tennyson* (New York: Macmillan, 1972), p. 228.

passed through the two middle lines whose couplet form gives so much strength to their rhyme. Thus, the outer rhyme of a- -a is distanced; the second "a" recollects only dimly the first "a," which by then has become a faint echo and seems, in spite of the rhyme, to have been something different than the "a" we are now reading. The effect of this pattern was aptly described by Charles Kingsley in 1850: "The mournful minor rhyme of each first and fourth line always leads the ear to expect something beyond."[9] The second "a" "returns," but it also leads "beyond" because it is different from the middle couplets and only faintly recollects its partner. The movement, then, is one of vacillation (a to bb, and back to a), of gesturing backward (a ←a), and of leading beyond (bb→ a). Rather than characterize this movement as a circle, I would call it a spiral, a figure that includes the backward forward gesturing of vacillation, the repetition risking stasis (the central concentration), but also the outer diffusion, the movement beyond. The ends do not quite meet: the first "a" raises the anticipation of the second, but the intervening couplet interrupts the closure, or deflects the rhyme, so that the second "a" recollects, but differs from, the first. The outer lines, therefore, gesture toward enfolding the inner lines, but at the same time, the inner lines break through, or refuse this enfolding gesture.

These enfoldings and interruptions can act upon each other in turns, especially if we expand our focus from individual stanza to the level of whole lyric: once the intervening middle deflects the closure of the enfolding ends, it becomes dominant. But then its very dominance becomes in turn vulnerable to deflection by the material it has interrupted. (Every "clinching" is in this poem ephemeral, as Ricks has already pointed out.) We can see this process quite clearly in section 127: the peace of the phrase "All is well" begins and ends the lyric, but is disrupted by the vivid and violent descriptions of revolution that fill the middle:

> And all is well, though faith and form
>   Be sundered in the night of fear;
>   Well roars the storm to those that hear
> A deeper voice across the storm,
>
> Proclaiming social truth shall spread,
>   And justice, even though thrice again
>   The red fool-fury of the Seine
> Should pile her barricades with dead.
>
> But ill for him that wears a crown,
>   And him, the lazar, in his rags:

9. Quoted in Christopher Ricks, *Tennyson*, p. 228.

> They tremble, the sustaining crags;
> The spires of ice are toppled down,
>
> And molten up, and roar in flood;
>     The fortress crashes from on high,
>     The brute earth lightens to the sky,
> And the great Aeon sinks in blood,
>
> And compassed by the fires of Hell;
>     While thou, dear spirit, happy star,
>     O'erlook'st the tumult from afar,
> And smilest, knowing all is well.[1]

The peace at the end prevails, in large part, because of the shifting placement of its imagery within the construction of the stanzas. It moves from the position of fragile enclosure in the outer lines of stanza 1 (the "And all is well, though" and "A deeper voice" in the first and fourth lines which surround, but fail to enclose, the "sundering" and "roaring" of lines 2 and 3) to the position of solid core in the middle couplet of stanza five ("While thou, dear spirit, happy star, / O'erlook'st the tumult from afar"). The violence which disrupts stanza 1 with the "sundering" and "roaring" possesses the middle of the lyric—stanzas 3 and 4—but enters only the first of the outer rhyming lines of the last stanza. Thus, what is at first an interrupting core of violence becomes an encompassing force, which is in turn interrupted and calmed (or settled) by a new core of peace which is ushered in by the "dear spirit, happy star" in the middle couplet of the last stanza. In the end, the last line, which fulfills the anticipatory "All is well, though" of line 1, is both a return and a movement beyond. The first "And all is well" is qualified by the subsequent "though" which introduces all the violence, while the last "all is well" follows strongly upon the "smiling" of this "happy star" and the overlooking "from afar" which immediately precede it. This chiastic structure is a larger version of the stanzaic *abba* in which the final rhyme gestures toward, yet recalls only faintly, its antecedent. The final "all is well," because it has conquered the middle disruption and because it comes from a heavenly plane that lies above both the disruptions and the peace that characterize the vicissitudes of earthly existence, recalls only faintly the first unsure "And all is well, though." Its context is much wider; its "well-being" has been earned. The spiral has swung next to, but past, its origin.

Moving from the level of individual lyric to broader theme, I would like to turn to sections 5 and 19, a pair of meditations on expression, silence, and grief which addresses the theme of "expressing the inex-

---

1. Citations are from *The Poems of Tennyson,* ed. Christopher Ricks (Berkeley: Univ. of California Press, 1987). Lyric and line numbers will appear parenthetically within the text.

pressible." Together, they yield the insight that the inexpressible nature of the mourner's grief comes from the inner intensity of feeling and the inadequacy of words. Characteristically, however, they make this claim in the sort of spiraling vacillation through opposite positions in an idea or state of mind, which the *abba* form so clearly enacts. At first, in section 5, "words" do not provide a channel for the release of inner feeling, but instead "half conceal" it:

> I sometimes hold it half a sin
>   To put in words the grief I feel;
>   For words, like Nature, half reveal
> And half conceal the Soul within.
>
> But, for the unquiet heart and brain,
>   A use in measured language lies;
>   The sad mechanic exercise,
> Like dull narcotics, numbing pain.     (ll. 1–8)

The outer garment of words, which in section 19 will allow the expression of grief, here prevents it. It enfolds, "half reveals and half conceals" the feeling, at best providing "dull narcotics" to "numb pain." As we might expect, these silencing (because inadequate) "words" and "language" appear interruptingly in the middle couplets, and hamper the expression of the "Soul's" feeling—the "sin," the "despair," the "pain," the "unquiet heart and brain" which extend uncertainly across the outer lines. But in the final stanza, "words" move into those outer lines:

> In words, like weeds, I'll wrap me o'er,
>   Like coarsest clothes against the cold:
>   But that large grief which these enfold
> Is given in outline and no more.     (ll. 9–12)

We begin a movement toward the other side of the spiral's loop, where "grief" will appear in the middle position and "words" in the outer. In the above stanza, "words" have begun a transformation into the early phase of expression—the "outline"; when we get to section 19, we will find a full exploration of this answering "opposite" (and at its close, the return "beyond"):

> There twice a day the Severn fills;
>   The salt sea-water passes by,
>   And hushes half the babbling Wye,
> And makes a silence in the hills.
>
> The Wye is hushed nor moved along,
>   And hushed my deepest grief of all,
>   When filled with tears that cannot fall,
> I brim with sorrow drowning song.     (19:5–12)

Now it is not the language (as container or garment), but the filling (the content) that silences. The fullness of grief imaged in the filling of the Severn and the Wye with "the salt sea-water" silences the surrounding hills just as the overwhelming ocean of unshed and unsheddable tears drowns the mourner's "song." Whereas in section 5 the inadequacy of words in the middles—words as concealment—had silenced, here at the far side of the loop, the density and concentration of grief in the middles—the tidal act of "filling"—"hushes." But in the last stanza we swing around once again, just beyond the point in section 5 where "words" became the "outline":

> The tide flows down, the wave again
>    Is vocal in its wooded walls;
>    My deeper anguish also falls,
> And I can speak a little then.          (ll. 13–16)

The draining allows "vocality," the "falling" anguish allows speech. Here, though, the "tide flows down" in the first outer line, almost as though the full stillness in the middle couplets has begun to drain into, or even through, those outer lines, as the mourner begins to "speak a little." He equates the tide's flow, the water's drainage, with his own speaking by setting "The tide flows down" and "I can speak" into the rhymed pair of outer lines—thus "draining" and relieving a too full container of its contents. Importantly, this means that the "flowing," "vocality," "anguish," and "speaking" occur in every line of the stanza, making this "expression" fuller. The anticipated "expression" given in "outline" in 5 is completed—but beyond—in this repetition with a difference. "Speaking a little" recollects "To put in words," but it is more "expressive"; it allows more grief to flow. In this thematic spiral of silencing-expression-silencing-expression, the anticipatory "outline" is "filled" and then "drained" in a more relieving expression "speaking" that "rhymes" with the first "outline" of expression but moves beyond it as well.

No doubt we could trace more loops in this theme, in which more grief, more reticence, or less adequacy would disrupt this newly won expression, for this process, like the spiral as a form, is potentially endless. However, I would rather trace such a longer set of revolving vacillations below, in the movements of Tennyson's general metaphysical discussion in *In Memoriam*. For now, I want to turn briefly to the recurrence of images and events in *In Memoriam*—the yew tree and the dark house, the Christmases, and the anniversaries of Hallam's death with which the mourner marks his emotional progress. In each case, the fulfillment "returns" to the motif established in anticipation, but also transcends the original scope. This pattern is perhaps clearest in the "Christmas" lyrics. Both section 28 and 104 begin with the same lines: "The time draws near the birth of Christ: / The moon is hid; the night is still" (28:1–2, 104:1–2), and continue with the same image of bells in the mist: "The Christmas bells from hill to hill / Answer each other in the mist" (28:3–4) and "A single church below the hill / Is pealing, folded in the mist" (104:3–4). But the cluster of images in section 104 has been replaced, in that the family has moved from the home of section 28, and re-felt, for the mourner has moved beyond the despair of sections 28–30 ("This year I slept and woke with pain, / I almost wished no more to wake, / And that my hold on life would break" [28:13–15]) and the quieter grief expressed in section 78 ("But over all things brooding slept / The quiet sense of something lost" [ll. 7–8]), to a larger sense of poetic vocation. The bells whose "merry, merry" "voices" bring "sorrow touched with joy" in section 28 can boldly "ring out the old, ring in the new" by section 106, signaling the mourner's readiness for higher poetic achievement: "Ring out, ring out my mournful rhymes, / But ring the fuller minstrel in" (ll. 19–20). Thus the vacillation and spiraling revolutions of the *abba* rhyme scheme, which characterize the individual stanzas, also characterize the broader movements among recurring images and events in the poem as a whole.

So, too, will it prove characteristic of the poem's metaphysical discussions. The vacillations between faith and doubt supply one of those "animating" forces that run through the poem—one that fails to settle even in the very frame that is supposed to resolve and close it. Before taking up this frame in detail, however, I would like to pick up the faith/doubt spiral in the famous central "trance" lyrics (sections 95 and 96), where we will see the spiraling vacillation characterized by the same enclosing/deflecting process I have been tracing. At first, doubt enfolds or encloses the possibility of faith while the mourner despairs. Then faith emerges from the center of this doubt, only to be struck through the center again by doubt, and so on. Beginning in section 95, the mourner's soul is swept up into Hallam's spirit, right out of the center of his heart's "hunger" (and at the center of the lyric—stanzas 7 and 8):

> A hunger seized my heart; I read
>   Of that glad year which once had been,
>   In those fallen leaves which kept their green,
> The noble letters of the dead:
>
> And strangely on the silence broke
>   The silent-speaking words, and strange
>   Was love's dumb cry defying change
> To test his worth; and strangely spoke

The faith, the vigour, bold to dwell
  On doubts that drive the coward back,
  And keen through wordy snares to track
Suggestion to her inmost cell.

So word by word, and line by line,
  The dead man touched me from the past,
  And all at once it seemed at last
The living soul was flashed on mine,

And mine in this was wound, and whirled
  About empyreal heights of thought,
  And came on that which is, and caught
The deep pulsations of the world,

Aeonian music measuring out
  The steps of Time—the shocks of Chance—
  The blows of Death. At length my trance
Was cancelled, stricken through with doubt.
                    (95:21–44)

It is a most powerful doubt, having struck through and "cancelled" such a rapturous, "empyreal" faith as is this one with which the spirit has "whirled" up the mourner. Moreover, true to the spiral pattern of enclosing and deflecting middles and ends, it is from the middle of this new rapturous faith—and the line—that the mourner is "stricken through," and returned to the earthly world, where the "doubtful dusk" shows the "knolls" and "the white kine" (ll. 50–51). It is a doubt, we could say, that "rhymes" with, yet moves "beyond" the earlier doubt—the "hunger" that begins the lyric. But out of this new doubt arises a new faith in section 96: "There lives more faith in honest doubt, / Believe me, than in half the creeds" (ll. 11–12). This recovered faith has a stronger quality because it, in turn, is wrung out of the powerful doubt just expressed in section 95, as the lyric goes on to recount (here, the mourner is speaking of Hallam, but is clearly using him as the model for his own process of regaining faith as well):

He fought his doubts and gathered strength,
  He would not make his judgment blind,
  He faced the spectres of the mind
And laid them: thus he came at length

To find a stronger faith his own.          (96:13–17)

Like the final "all is well" of section 127, the faith of section 96 has been regained on a different plane; it has lived through and encompassed the earlier doubt and now comes from the surer grounding in "judgment" which overcomes such "spectres of the mind" as, for example, the "spectral" experience recounted in section 95. Thus, this opening chime, the "spectral" faith of 95, has become only an echo to this new, surer faith that has come with the fulfillment of that early anticipation. But this new faith is, of course, susceptible to new doubts—the spiral does not stop—as we find in studying, for example, section 122. Here, the mourner runs up against that "judgment," which made the faith of section 96 so strong, in the doubts of "reason," expressed as anxiety about the reality of the experience reported in section 95: "Oh, wast thou with me, dearest, then?" (122:1) and "*If* thou wert with me" (122:9, emphasis added). However, by section 124 he spirals around again to another faith—one felt in the "heart," one which "melts" away the outer "freezing reason" from within, from a warmer center of feeling in the "breast":

> A warmth within the breast would melt
>   The freezing reason's colder part,
>   And like a man in wrath the heart
> Stood up and answered "I have felt."     (124:13–16)

The strength of the heart's "stand" rhymes with the earlier "judged" faith of section 96, but also moves beyond it: it has spiraled through and overcome the doubts produced by reason (and fed the "hunger" of the "heart" in section 95 as well).

These movements between faith and doubt and from Christmas to Christmas which trace the development from "mournful rhymes" to "fuller minstrel" bring me to another aspect of the poem, the mourner's evolution or "way of a soul." Alan Sinfield treats this idea thematically, as one of those dichotomies that animate the poem—this one between "Tennyson the private man" and "Tennyson the public poet," Tennyson the Romantic who expresses personal grief because he cannot help it ("piping but as the linnets sing") and Tennyson the Enlightenment classicist who makes a work of art by shaping his language carefully ("All as in some piece of art, / Is toil coöperant to an end"). These two natures struggle: the private man must turn his grief into art, thus allowing the public poet to appear; in turn, the "artifact" created by the public poet gives expression to the personal grief of the private man. One continually gives way to the other in a constant vacillation that, I would argue, is reflected in the *abba* stanza form.[2] However, I would like to cast my discussion of this issue in terms of genre rather than theme. For it seems to me that this development manifests itself in large part as a kind of *abba* spiraling

2. See the chapter "*In Memoriam*: The Linnet and the Artifact" in Alan Sinfield, *The Language of Tennyson's* In Memoriam (New York: Barnes and Noble, 1971), pp. 17–40.

vacillation between the fugal linearity and the centrifugal force of autobiographical "narrative" and the gravitational concentration and the centripetal force of lyric "moment." Studies of *In Memoriam* have wrestled with just this structural conflict between the basic narrative thrust of the whole and the (also basic) lyric stasis of the parts. Ralph Rader describes the first as "a sense throughout of the poem as a serially staged existential projection into time, in which the later stages were not for poet, any more than for speaker/actor, foreseen at the earlier stages,"[3] while Timothy Peltason evocatively describes the experience of reading each lyric moment:

> Reading a single section of *In Memoriam,* we fall into its lyric space only to pass through it and emerge blinking on the other side. Our experience as readers thus matches that of the poet, for whom consciousness is a constant series of repetitions, enchantments, and reawakenings.[4]

David Shaw addresses generic structure more formalistically, claiming variously that "individual sections have the concision of gravestone inscriptions but the poem as a whole is digressive. It has the amplitude of spiritual autobiography" (*Style,* p. 132), and that "Tennyson tries to accommodate elegy's high style and decorum to a diary's informalities and to the intimacies of a verse epistle" (*ALT,* p. 1). To my mind, it is exactly these opposing energies that propel what I would like to call its generic spiral, which is reflected in the *abba* stanza form. To clarify what I mean, however, I need to call upon some structural theory of autobiography—specifically, a passage from Jean Starobinski's "The Style of Autobiography," which articulates his notion of the "double deviation" of the autobiographical "I":

> The narrator describes not only what happened to him at a different time in his life but above all how he became—out of what he was—what he presently is. . . . The chain of experiences traces a path (though a sinuous one) that ends in the present state of recapitulatory knowledge.
> The deviation, which establishes the autobiographical reflection, is thus double: it is at once a deviation of time and of identity.[5]

I wish to secure two points from this passage: first, that the narrator is a present "I" who recollects the links in the "chain of experience" between him- or herself and the protagonist, the past "I";

---

3. Ralph Rader, "Notes on Some Structural Varieties and Variations in Dramatic 'I' Poems and Their Theoretical Implications," *VP* 22 (1984): 117.
4. Timothy Peltason, *Reading* In Memoriam (Princeton: Princeton Univ. Press, 1985), p. 84.
5. Jean Starobinski, "The Style of Autobiography," trans. Seymour Chatman, in *Autobiography: Essays Theoretical and Critical,* ed. James Olney (Princeton: Princeton Univ. Press, 1980), pp. 78–79.

second, that the "deviation" between narrator and protagonist is one of both time and identity. These points can help translate what have been the kind of experiential articulations of the poem's effect (such as those quoted above) into structural terms. Both deviations are at work in *In Memoriam*, although the lyric format of this "auto-biography" requires some adaptation of terminology. The speaker is not a present narrator, who, by recollecting a past self as protagonist gives his experience shape and coherence (or, as Starobinski says, the "contour of a life" [p. 73]), but is instead a present protagonist, who "speaks" these experiences and selves as they occur, in a series of lyric comments which slowly add up to something like a "contour of life." In other words, because of the lyric format of *In Memoriam*, the autobiographical deviations are dynamically reversed. Tempo-rally, we see the protagonist encounter his vicissitudes through his own eyes as they occur, and not through those of a resultant presid-ing consciousness recollecting them from a later time. The protago-nist raises his anticipations and voices his desires for his future self; his temporal deviation comes between the present "I" and the hoped for future "I": "Men may rise on stepping stones / Of their dead selves to higher things" (1:3–4). The deviation of identity is similarly reversed. The mourner does not cast back and examine the man he used to be and how he became the man he is, but instead longs for Hallam, the lost and future ideal self he would like to rejoin in either this world or the next. The "life" of *In Memoriam* or the mourner's "autobiography" is the story of "I" in a state of becoming, or, as Christopher Ricks says, of traveling rather than arriving.

Thus we can see, once again, the suitability of the *abba* stanza form. The mourner at the beginning, like the stanza in its first line, must live through the difficult experience of middle time in order to arrive at his final state, as the stanza arrives at its closing rhyme. Just as the first line raises the anticipation of its partner in the fourth line but then fades into a faint echo as that partner spins past closure, the mourner's hopes for himself and Hallam antici-pate their reunion, although when it comes, the "reunion" differs from the original anticipation. The double deviation created by the mourner at the beginning is never closed because the nature of the mourner himself changes through the experiences described—or more accurately, lived—in each lyric, just as the intervening bb couplets transform by interruption the a- -a rhyme. The mourner at the end "rhymes" with, but yet has evolved beyond, the earlier mourner. The spiritual reunion with Hallam in section 103, for exam-ple, fulfills its anticipation, but not as that anticipation had originally imagined. Hallam does not come back to earth, nor does the mourner die; rather, their "spirits" meet in the dreamed higher sphere that makes of the original desire a faint echo, or a dim recollection, of a past self, a "dead self"—the "stepping stone" to this higher place. The mourner at the end of *In Memoriam* desires neither an earthly reunion with Hallam nor a heavenly one (through death), any more than he desires to return to his early despair.

It is difficult to imagine a form better suited to accommodate both the evolutionary movement toward the "fuller minstrel" or the "higher race" and the self-enclosed, concentrated, individual lyric moments of fear, despair, or rage. However, its principle of spiraling revolution can also help to explain what Shaw (among others) has found to be "weak" closural gestures, for it is a form that seems particularly unsuited to the sealing and transcending requirements of "resolution." First, there is no interlacing between stanzas in the rhyme scheme (as there is in *terza rima,* for example)—a form that gives the stanzas what Peter Sacks calls a "self-encysted quality, an effect of being withheld from time" (pp. 168–169) and therefore, also, from time's discursive equivalents, narrative and the closures that mark its shapes. As in the flux of life (and the feel of *In Memoriam* seems to me closer to that flux than the most "realistic" of narratives), a sense of wholeness and overarching shape is difficult to perceive or to produce; the vacillations in thought, identity, or state of mind can continue forever, just as the stanzas can replicate themselves in self-enclosed, "lapidary" granules ad infinitum (*Style,* p. 132). Moreover, the spiral itself is an infinite, an endless, "closure-less," linear sort of "shape" that can only be brought to a stop arbitrarily (unlike other geometrical shapes that close themselves). This "stop" (the exact term is difficult to choose, for one cannot say "resolution," "closure," "conclusion," or even "finish" since none of these sealing actions takes place here) is just what the framing Prologue and Epilogue attempt to impose: an arbitrary stoppage to the spiraling doubts, faiths, expressions, silences, progressions, and regressions. (As David Shaw remarks: "The long elegy seems endlessly to end, and so never ends at all, except by a kind of optional stop rule that says, 'now we shall have an epithalamium that writes "finis" to our story'" [*ALT,* p. 32]). The frame itself gets swept up in the power, I believe, of the stanza form it shares with the rest of the poem and in its most intractable thematic incarnation, the vacillation between faith and doubt. So in the Prologue, we have a prayer to the "Strong Son of God, immortal Love" for faith, for a closing or bridging of the abyss between human and divine wisdom: "And in thy wisdom make me wise" (l. 44). In the Epilogue, this faith is forged, this abyss is bridged, from the earthly side by the child to be conceived on the wedding night, the "closer link / Betwixt us and the crowning race / Of those that, eye to eye, shall look / On knowledge" (ll. 127–130), and from the heavenly side by Hallam's spirit, the "noble type / Appearing ere the times were ripe / That friend of mine who lives in God" (ll. 138–140). This new bridge, the fulfillment of the prayer in the Prologue, has been earned in the interposing lyrics of *In Memoriam* which perform all the vacillating labor of doubting and finding faith, losing and regaining Hallam, so that, as fulfillment, it represents, like all the others, a movement beyond its anticipation. However, in the final stanza of the Epilogue, just as "That God" seems at last "one" with the creation (with no bridges needed), a new, wider abyss opens out:

> That God, which ever lives and loves,
>   One God, one law, one element,
>   And one far-off divine event,
> To which the whole creation moves.     (ll. 141–144)

Just at the end of the solid rhyming "oneness" invoked in the middle couplet, we find the fourth line once again pulling away, opening a gap. The "divine event" is suddenly "far off," and the "whole creation" just as suddenly lagging behind, having to "move," to cross another, vaster abyss which is signified in the assonance of the outer lines: God "loves" and it "moves." They reach, they yearn toward one another but cannot close, and we find ourselves swinging around another side of another loop, one whose "movement beyond" remains, this time, unrecorded—perhaps the only possible "stop" to this singular lyric narrative-narrative lyric.

# AIDAN DAY

## Tennyson's Grotesque[†]

In my 2005 study *Tennyson's Scepticism*, I wrote against an idea of Tennyson which casts him as, fundamentally, a religious and metaphysical conservative. It is true that a poem such as the 1850 *In Memoriam* has its speaker affirming, towards the end of the work, that there is a spiritual direction to human life. But I took the view—as, up to a point, have others before me—that there are major, subversively contrary elements in the poem which remain unaccommodated to that end. My main argument, however, was that Tennyson's long poem of 1855, *Maud*, subjects the kind of affirmation which closes *In Memoriam* to trenchant sceptical critique. What I did not focus on in *Tennyson's Scepticism*, and what I want to examine here, are some of the ways in which the grotesque, at the levels of both poetic content and manner, is a dimension of Tennyson's sceptical understanding of the nature of things.

† From *Tennyson among the Poets: Bicentenary Essays*, ed. Robert Douglas-Fairhurst and Seamus Perry (Oxford: Oxford University Press, 2009), pp. 76–86. Copyright © 2009 Oxford University Press. Reprinted by permission of Oxford University Press through PLSclear.

The expression 'Tennyson's Grotesque' is partly designed to call to mind Walter Bagehot's important essay of 1864 entitled 'Wordsworth, Tennyson and Browning; or, Pure, Ornate, and Grotesque Art in English Poetry'. In his essay, Bagehot said that 'grotesque art . . . deals . . . not with normal types but with abnormal specimens . . . It enables you to see . . . the perfect type by painting the opposite deviation . . . Of this art we possess in the present generation one prolific master. Mr. Browning is an artist working by incongruity' (*CH* 293).[1] In a 1969 essay which took Bagehot's notion of the grotesqueness of Browning's poetic style as its starting point, Isobel Armstrong observed:

> Since Walter Bagehot called Browning's art 'grotesque' this has become an indispensable word in the discussion of Browning's style—there are so many things which are immediately and strikingly ugly . . . the wrenching of metrical patterns, the heterogeneous vocabulary . . . Effects are exaggerated to the point of extravaganza.[2]

It is a dramatic, brilliant style. Armstrong notes in her essay that 'it is appropriate to call' it 'grotesque' (p. 93), and she argues that its power resides in the fact that it

> renders the structure of experience as a fluid, unfinished *process* on which we continually try to impose a shape, an order . . . A Tennyson poem is a burnished, meticulously finished object, demanding no more completion than it possesses; a Browning poem is organised so that the untidy, living immediacy of experience can be gone through and shaped as it is experienced. (p. 97)

In 1993 Armstrong rephrased this estimate of the nature and effect of Browning's style when, in the light of poststructuralist arguments that there is no necessary connection between language and referent, she read Browning's poetry in terms of

> the skewed gaze of Grotesque perception, the invasion of libido and desire which registers a sense of limit, the sense of something missing, as representation is incommensurate with what is represented . . . these are . . . structural elements in the poems. The poems seem to be presented as the scenes of restless secondary revision, an attempt to produce coherence, rather than as coherent representations in themselves.[3]

---

1. Quoted in *Tennyson: The Critical Heritage*, ed. John D. Jump (London: Routledge & Kegan Paul, 1967), 293 [*Editor*].
2. Isobel Armstrong, 'Browning and the "Grotesque" Style', in Isobel Armstrong (ed.), *The Major Victorian Poets: Reconsiderations* (London: Routledge & Kegan Paul, 1969), 93. Hereafter, page references given in the text.
3. Isobel Armstrong, *Victorian Poetry: Poetry, Poetics and Politics* (London and New York: Routledge, 1993), 294.

A Tennyson poem is 'a burnished, meticulously finished object, demanding no more completion than it posesses.' Browning's grotesque poems are 'presented as the scenes of restless secondary revision'. This may, up to a point, be an apt way of characterizing the manner of Browning's verse. But it is important to remember— taking a cue from Bagehot, when he writes that Browning's 'art . . . enables you to see . . . the perfect type by painting the opposite deviation'—that the attempt to forge coherence may value the coherence more profoundly than the attempt at it. By this kind of understanding, coherence emerges as the stable measure which haunts Browning's verse. It emerges as the implied, ever-present standard against which the surface grotesqueness of the poetry is produced and judged. Tennyson's poetry, I want to argue, frequently works and requires to be read in reverse manner. Formally, it may characteristically demand no more completion than it posesses. Tennyson's verse does, indeed, almost advertise completeness at its surface. But if Browning's poetic continually implies a coherence against which the grotesqueness of the style may be contrasted, Tennyson's exquisitely finished poetic manner often points—sometimes implicitly, sometimes explicitly—to a dissonance, an incoherence which contradicts and is unassimilated to the finish of the style. *In*coherence and *un*intelligibility emerge as the 'measure' against which the surface of the poetry pitches itself. By this kind of reading, Browning is, in the end, less troubling than Tennyson because Browning's grotesque remains more confident that it *can* map the incoherent. Tennyson is more disturbing because the perfection of his poetic manner frequently gestures beyond itself towards the unseemliness, the grotesqueness of that which cannot be ordered, that which *cannot* be mapped. If the grotesque does not manifest itself at a formal level in Tennyson as obviously as in Browning, then neither does Tennyson's grotesque compare directly with the idea of the grotesque formulated by the Victorian theoretician of the style, Ruskin. In *The Stones of Venice* (1851–3) Ruskin viewed different kinds of grotesque in Gothic art principally within moral, social, and cultural perspectives. The dominant frames of reference for Tennyson's grotesque are psychological and metaphysical.

This kind of grotesque is given something like an overt definition in section XXXIV of *In Memoriam*. In the first stanza of this section we hear:

> My own dim life should teach me this,
>     That life shall live for evermore,
>     Else earth is darkness at the core,
> And dust and ashes all that is . . .          (XXXIV.1–4)

The idea that earthly life engenders the hope of an afterlife, and that without that hope everything is meaningless, is expanded upon in the second stanza, where the poet takes the earth and the sun as tokens of the entire frame of things:

> Else earth is darkness at the core,
>     And dust and ashes all that is;
>
> This round of green, this orb of flame,
>     Fantastic beauty; such as lurks
>     In some wild Poet, when he works
> Without a conscience or an aim.
>                                   (XXXIV.3–8)

Life and a universe bereft of a higher moral structure and spiritual purpose amount to a *fantastic* beauty, where 'fantastic', as the *OED* tells us, carries the connotation of 'Perversely . . . imagined . . . grotesque in . . . conception'. It is not that Tennyson is prudishly condemning the amorality and purposelessness of the wild poet. The very expression 'Fantastic beauty' betrays Tennyson's own susceptibility to the intoxicating fascination of an alien, amoral universe. But to the extent that the comprehension of fantastic beauty displays Tennyson's empathy with the poet who works wild, outside of restrictive moral and spiritual codes, then such empathy is contradicted by that idea of a loving God which simultaneously haunts Tennyson throughout *In Memoriam*. Sensitive to fantastic beauty in all its raging glory, Tennyson in *In Memoriam* at once desires reality to be framed by a spiritual order that holds out the possibility of spiritual life. Tennyson's fantastic, his grotesque, is the horror of that which is not recuperable to such a sense of order, to such a sense of meaning, form, and purpose.

To see one way in which this may be, I want to look, first, at some further passages from *In Memoriam*. A composite of elegies on his dead friend, Arthur Hallam, *In Memoriam* is well known for its engagement with what, in the earlier nineteenth century, was the newly developing science of geology. In the 1830s Tennyson read the Scottish geologist Charles Lyell's great *Principles of Geology*, one of the founding texts of the modern science, first published from 1830 to 1833. Provoked by the death of his friend to write an elegy that takes up the question of the meaning of human existence, Tennyson found in Lyell a great deal that mesmerized him but no reassurance about the ultimate significance of human life.

At several points in *In Memoriam* Tennyson incorporated Lyell's perception that the physical nature of the earth itself exists in an inconceivably ancient and continuing process of formation and deformation. As I shall illustrate, this act of incorporation affected aspects of the form as well as the content of the verse. The vast temporal perspectives proposed in Lyell's work were a major factor in Tennyson's typical Victorian crisis of faith, since the *Principles* at once dissolved the account in Genesis of the creation of the world and helped to undermine belief in the idea of divine love as the energizing principle of the universe. In the *Principles* Lyell observed that 'We may divide the great agents of change in the inorganic world into two principal classes, the aqueous and the igneous';[4] the first involving the erosion of land by the action of water and the second involving the compensatory pushing up of new land mass through movement in the earth's crust. Lyell describes the erosive principle of running water with graphic efficiency: 'When earthly matter has once been intermixed with running water, a new mechanical power is obtained by the attrition of sand and pebbles, borne along with violence by a stream. Running water charged with foreign ingredients being thrown against a rock, excavates it by mechanical force, sapping and undermining' (p. 105).

It is a complementary principle of erosion in the case of the movement of the ice that slowly destroys mountain chains: 'The glaciers . . . of alpine regions, formed of consolidated snow, bear down upon their surface a prodigious burden of rock and sand mixed with ice' (p. 110). But if water and ice erosion endlessly '[d]raw down' the land to the sea, to use Tennyson's expression (*In Memoriam*, XXXV.11), then, as Lyell observes, 'the repair of land' is 'as constant as its decay' (p. 173). And it is restored from below. Describing the unending movements of the earth's crust—by which land masses are eroded only for their constituent materials to rise again, through igneous force, through the energy of volcanoes and earthquakes, as part of new land masses—Lyell speaks of 'the gradual conversion of part of the bed of an ocean into a continent' (p. 370).

Lyell's *Principles* adopts the stance and discourse of an Enlightenment text that is setting out rational truth. Its voice and perspective assume a universal authority. Even when there are gaps in the evidence used to sustain the general laws which the *Principles* propounds, the induction of rules from the surviving evidence is pursued as objectively grounded. A part of the strength of *Principles* lies, as James Secord has noted, in the way in which Lyell's 'highly-wrought depictions of grand scenery created the imaginative depth of past time which was at the heart of his message' (Lyell, *Principles*, p. xxvi). But Lyell's evocation of 'deep time' (ibid.), to use John McPhee's expression, does not foreground intellectual, emotional, and imaginative disturbance at the vistas he was opening up.

4. Charles Lyell, *Principles of Geology*, ed. James A. Secord (London: Penguin, 1997), 103. Hereafter, page references given in the text.

Not so in Tennyson. In *In Memoriam* Tennyson repeatedly nego-
tiates his own anxiety that there is no afterlife and that the human
experience of love, such as he feels for the dead Hallam, has no
ultimate sanction. In section XXXV, for example, the poet first pic-
tures an authoritative denial of the possibility of life after death. He
responds to that dramatized denial by trying to assert that, even if
it is true that there is no life after death in which his love for Hallam
could be vindicated, then love could at least be said to have a mean-
ing while there is an individual to keep a memory of it:

> Yet if some voice that man could trust
>   Should murmur from the narrow house,
>   'The cheeks drop in; the body bows;
> Man dies: nor is there hope in dust:'
>
> Might I not say? 'Yet even here,
>   But for one hour, O Love, I strive
>   To keep so sweet a thing alive:'
> But . . .                              (XXXV.1–8)

But this last pictured consolation withers in the face of the unimag-
inably long depredations of the earth described by the new geologi-
cal science. The new time-scale in which human affairs have to be
considered overwhelms the imagining of a meaningful consolation
for lost love in some human recollection of that love:

> But I should turn mine ears and hear
>
> The moanings of the homeless sea,
>   The sound of streams that swift or slow
>   Draw down Æonian hills, and sow
> The dust of continents to be;
>
> And Love would answer with a sigh,
>   'The sound of that forgetful shore
>   Will change my sweetness more and more,
> Half-dead to know that I shall die.'
>                                       (XXXV.8–16)

The difference between the merely fantasized voice that speaks of
hopelessness, on the one hand, and the articulation of geological
perspective, on the other, is that the geological orientation is not
preluded by an 'if' (XXXV.1). The perspectives of geological science
are not held conditionally in Tennyson's mind. Of the two voices of
hopelessness in section XXXV, it is the geological, not the specula-
tive, that can be and is trusted, its bleakness notwithstanding. The
representation of the humanly desolating temporal vistas of geo-
logical science, the portrayal of the endless slippage involved in

physical erosion, dramatizes the principle that *all* forms on earth, whether geological or poetic, are subject to erasure. It dramatizes simultaneously the undermining of any sense of a sustaining ground of love in the world. The proceses of wastage are caught, in part, through the profusion of the sibilant 's'. The insidious underminings dramatized by this sibilant across lines 8 to 12—ears, moanings, homeless, sea, sound, streams, swift, slow, hills, sow, dust, continents—are emphasized but not assimilated by the formal dimension of the verse. The sibilant 's', mimicking the flow of water, cumulatively suggests a drainage of both matter and meaning that exceeds the capacity of the verbal order to stem. There is nowhere for the 's' sound to go within the words and form, the units of meaning, of the section itself. The sound can only disappear into the inarticulate realm of untracked and untrackable waste that lies beyond words, beyond human order, including the order of this poem. Formally the poem may require no more completion than it possesses. But the completeness that it possesses does not exhaust its signification of that which lies outwith completeness.

It is the same, in these lines, with the aural tedium of the nasal consonant sound 'n'—turn, mine, moanings, sound, down, Æonian, continents. Consonants are phonetic elements that in themselves carry no verbal meaning. The drone of the 'n' sound—like the 's', which dramatizes unstemmable physical erosion and emotional and psychological loss—opens onto an abject space beyond words. The drone expresses, whilst not verbalizing, an area outside language, an area that escapes human meaning. It is the inane of a universe which neither speaks to nor recognizes human desires. This horror, Tennyson's grotesque, is very often intimated in the absence of order that he locates just beyond the limits of his verbal and formal control. Tennyson's sub-verbal way of defining, through the hypnotic repetition of the nasal consonant 'n', the mindless processes of an unselfconscious, unspiritualized universe, defines in the same breath the suffering of the human consciousness that contemplates such meaninglessness. Those narcotic consonant sounds capture the inarticulable stupidity, in the sense of the stupefaction, to which the mind is reduced in contemplating nothingness and purposelessness. One kind of Tennyson's grotesque, to repeat, lies not at the verbal surface of his art but in areas subliminally intimated which exceed artistic patterning. The consonantal sounds 's' and 'n' are common enough in English; but, here, Tennyson uses them in combination with the sense of his lines to engage an uncommon, disturbed understanding.

Tennyson returns repeatedly across *In Memoriam* to different expressions of the anxiety that reality is arbitrarily driven. In section III of the poem, for example, he admits that his grief at the loss of Arthur Hallam makes him vulnerable to a vision of the

meaninglessness of things. It is a vision which, before he has even
spelled it out, he tries to dismiss as an untruth:

> O Sorrow, cruel fellowship,
> > O Priestess in the vaults of Death,
> > O sweet and bitter in a breath,
> What whispers from thy lying lip?        (III.1–4)

Although, in the last line here, Tennyson characterizes as a lie what
we are about to learn is sorrow's negative vision, he has already, in the
third line, spoken of sorrow's message as simultaneously sweet and
bitter. There is in this use of the words 'bitter' and 'sweet' the sugges-
tion of a point of view which, while it may be disagreeable, remains
seductively solicitous. Tennyson thus acknowledges a force in sorrow's
perspective which he manages only rather peevishly to dismiss by
accusing sorrow of lying. Sorrow's vision, when it comes, across stan-
zas two and three, is apocalyptically disturbed. The grotesquerie of
an universal disharmony is stated here, even if, in this instance, there
is something slightly gothic, even formulaic about the terms:

> 'The stars,' she whispers, 'blindly run;
> > A web is woven across the sky;
> > From out waste places comes a cry,
> And murmurs from the dying sun:

> 'And all the phantom, Nature, stands—
> > With all the music in her tone,
> > A hollow echo of my own,—
> A hollow form with empty hands.'        (III.5–12)

In the last stanza of this section Tennyson no longer dismisses as a
lie this perception of the gracelessness of an unseeing cause. But
he still seeks to overcome the vision. The problem is that the nega-
tivity of sorrow's vision is countered only by a further negativity
when Tennyson speaks of mentally conquering the vision through
what looks like, metaphorically, some peculiarly unpleasant kind of
self-inflicted torture:

> And shall I take a thing so blind,
> > Embrace her as my natural good;
> > Or crush her, like a vice of blood,
> Upon the threshold of the mind?        (III.13–16)

The desperate, unresolved violence of this last, prospective image
of defeating the negative vision succeeds only in leaving that vision
in place. One negativity fuses fantastically with another.

   Glimpses of a blind undercurrent in the frame of things recur in
sections LVI and XXVI of *In Memoriam*. Section LVI opens with

the recognition that nature, defined in the preceding section of the poem as taking no care of individual life, also takes no care of species themselves, including the human. In section LV Tennyson had complained that nature 'lends . . . evil dreams' (l.6) because it seems to take care of the species (the 'type', l. 7) at the expense of individual members of the species: 'So careful of the type she seems, | So careless of the single life' (ll. 7–8). But LVI opens with one of the dawning recognitions of the later eighteenth and earlier nineteenth centuries—that fossil evidence in the rocks indicates the existence of many species on earth which have long since disappeared. The 'Nature, red in tooth and claw' which Tennyson famously speaks of a little later in this section carries no spiritual leavening:

> 'So careful of the type?' but no.
>   From scarpèd cliff and quarried stone
>   She cries, 'A thousand types are gone:
> I care for nothing, all shall go.
>
> 'Thou makest thine appeal to me:
>   I bring to life, I bring to death:
>   The spirit does but mean the breath:
> I know no more.' . . .                    (LVI.1–8)

The belief that humankind is unique in creation, the highest form of creation, is shattered by the recognition that it, too, is subject to the possibility of extinction and may one day be reduced to just another stratum in the fossil record. This recognition destroys any ability to believe in the Christian apparatus of belief where love, as the spiritual foundation of everything, makes it possible to negotiate, with a degree of optimism, the indecent nature of Nature:

> . . . And he, shall he,
>
> Man, her last work, who seemed so fair,
> Such splendid purpose in his eyes . . .
>
> Who trusted God was love indeed
>   And love Creation's final law—
>   Tho' Nature, red in tooth and claw
> With ravine, shrieked against his creed—
>
> Who loved, who suffered countless ills . . .
>   Be blown about the desert dust,
> Or sealed within the iron hills?
>           (LVI.8–10, 13–17, 19–20)

The idea that humanity breathes only physiologically and not spiritually, that it could be reduced to stone and nothing more, alienates

Tennyson. Viewed under the aspect of palaeontology, the human condition, bereft of a spiritual dimension, becomes a grotesque state, more grotesque than that of the animals, even the extinct dinosaurs ('Dragons of the prime'), because of its delusion of spiritual meaning:

> No more? A monster then, a dream,
>     A discord. Dragons of the prime
>     That tare each other in their slime,
> Were mellow music matched with him . . . (LVI.21–4)

Aching for some disclosure from the friend beyond the grave, the section ends without remedy:

> O life as futile, then, as frail!
>     O for thy voice to soothe and bless!
>     What hope of answer, or redress?
> Behind the veil, behind the veil.          (LVI.25–8)

Again, earlier in *In Memoriam*, in section XXVI, Tennyson had imagined an ultimate principle which is alien to humanity in its detachment from human concern. Tennyson indicates in this section that if he were convinced that such *is* the principle of reality, then a wish for death might overwhelm all other considerations:

> . . . if indeed that eye foresee
>     Or see (in Him is no before)
>     In more of life true life no more
> And Love the indifference to be,
>
> Then might I find, ere yet the morn
>     Breaks hither over Indian seas,
>     That Shadow waiting with the keys,
> To shroud me from my proper scorn.
>
>                    (XXVI.9–16)

Despair is never completely exorcized in *In Memoriam*. Tennyson tries to paper over his alienation with more positive assertions, particularly in the poem's closing stages; but, as T. S. Eliot observed in 1936, *In Memoriam*'s 'faith is a poor thing . . . its doubt is a very intense experience.'[5]

\* \* \*

5. T. S. Eliot, '*In Memoriam*', in John Dixon Hunt (ed.), '*In Memoriam*': *A Casebook* (London, Macmillan, 1970), 135. [See p. 166 above—*Editor*.]

## MATTHEW ROWLINSON

## History, Materiality and Type in Tennyson's *In Memoriam*†

This chapter aims to unpack and provide a context for the puzzling amalgam of organicism and historicism to be found in the last lines of Tennyson's *In Memoriam*. In those lines, the poem prophesies the evolution of humankind into a 'crowning race / [. . .] / No longer half-akin to brute' ('Epilogue' 128, 133).[1] With respect to the time of this future race, 'all we thought and loved and did, / And hoped, and suffered, is but seed / Of what in them is flower and fruit' (134–6). The tense shift in line 135, which contemplates the events of the poem and the grief and hope it expresses both in the present and from a standpoint of historical retrospect, dramatizes a split temporality which I will argue both characterizes the poem as a whole and also ultimately comes to define its representation of Tennyson's dead friend Hallam, the elegy's subject. In the poem's final mention of him, Hallam appears with respect to the crowning race to come as 'a noble type / Appearing ere the times were ripe' (138–9). In spite of its reference to ripeness, and the mentions of seed, flower and fruit in the lines immediately preceding, the temporality in which these lines set Hallam is not that of the vegetative cycle but that of history. The source of the phrase 'ere the times were ripe' is *Henry IV, Part 1*, when Worcester warns Hotspur—in vain, as it turns out—to set their plot against the King in motion only 'when time is ripe' (1.3.294).[2] The phrase thus aims to define an historical or political conjuncture; for the revolt to succeed, it must await the preparation of the necessary forces. In Tennyson's figure, Hallam, who resembles Hotspur in living and dying too soon, is represented as appearing out of his proper time, before his required conditions have been met.

---

† From *Darwin, Tennyson and Their Readers: Explorations in Victorian Literature and Science*, ed. Valerie Purton (London: Anthem Press, 2013), pp. 35–48. Reprinted by permission of the publisher.

1. Except where noted, citations of Tennyson's poetry are drawn from Christopher B. Ricks, ed., *The Poems of Tennyson*, 2nd ed., 3 vols, Longman Annotated English Poets (Harlow: Longman, 1987).

2. G. Blakemore Evans et al., eds, *The Riverside Shakespeare* (Boston: Houghton Mifflin, 1974). After the mid-nineteenth century, Shakespeare's phrase became a cliché, and it is now often used without any awareness of its source. Prior to 1850, however, I have not found any use of the phrase that does not make explicit reference to *Henry IV, Part 1*. The Shakespeare allusion can thus be assumed to be more active in Tennyson's lines than it appears now.

# I

The term 'type' is itself intrinsically historicist. Like its cognates in German, French and Latin, it derives ultimately from the Greek *tupos*, meaning impression. The root of *tupos* is a verb meaning 'to strike'; the underlying metaphor is thus from numismatics, the *tupos* being literally the impression of a seal in wax or the device hammered onto a coin. This etymology remains clearly visible in both of the term's main senses in current English usage. As part of the lexicon of print, the word 'type' retains its literal reference to a technology of impression—and also a crucial ambiguity about whether type is so called because it produces an impression or because it is produced by one.[3] When it refers to a class or kind within a taxonomical system, as in a blood type or a personality type, the term's reference to the idea of impression is more figural; in this sense, objects of a single type are formed according to a common pattern, of which they metaphorically bear the impression or stamp. In English, though not in other languages, this taxonomical sense of 'type' is recent, dating only from around 1840.

Before turning to nineteenth century senses of 'type', I would like to make two summary observations based on what we have seen so far. The first is that the impression constituting the type is the trace of an historical event. It comes into being in a conjuncture that imposes on a material object a shape or a mark previously alien to it. The type thus exists in a temporal order characterized by rupture rather than by organic growth; it comes into being by analogy with the contingent way metal is made into a coin—it could have been made into something else instead—rather than with the necessity by which an acorn grows into an oak. A second preliminary observation may seem to qualify the type's status as an historical trace, however; this is its characteristic of iterability. As the numismatic metaphor built into the term implies, the type reproduces a pattern that is always in principle subject to further reproduction. This is why the term was able to acquire a taxonomical meaning. Objects of the same type are all formed as iterations of a single pattern, like impressions of a single seal.

On the one hand, then, 'type' denotes the trace or impression of a specific event; on the other, a class of objects. For most of the term's history in English, its meaning has derived from the first of these denotations, which, as we will see, is the one at work in the

3. According to the *Oxford English Dictionary*, the word 'type' was incorporated into the lexicon of print only in the early eighteenth century. From the beginning of the print era, pieces of movable type were cast in matrices produced by striking with a punch. The punch was the original engraved form of which every piece of type was the impression. For a description of type-making see Philip Gaskell, *A New Introduction to Bibliography* (New York: Oxford University Press, 1972), 10–11.

idea of type that prevails in Christian and especially Protestant exegetical practice. The first two definitions of 'type' in Johnson's *Dictionary* (1756) as 1) An 'emblem [or] mark of something' and 2) 'that by which something future is prefigured' are directly rooted in typological exegesis.[4] In the 1830s Charles Richardson's *New Dictionary of the English Language* defined 'type' as 'A sign or mark (made or formed by *striking*), a form, an image [. . .]; a mark, figure, letter;'[5] giving the term's etymology more emphasis than had Johnson, but making no reference to the taxonomical sense then being imported from French and German. No British dictionary seems to have given this sense of the term before 1850, though as Paul Farber notes, Noah Webster did so in 1828 in his *American Dictionary of the English Language*.[6]

A full account of typology as a mode of exegesis is beyond my scope in this essay; even nineteenth-century typology is a vast topic.[7] So we continue in a reductive mode by citing the two passages from St Paul that Erich Auerbach, in a classic article, termed the 'basis' of typology. These are 1 Cor 10:6 and 11 'where the Jews in the desert are termed *typoi hemon* ("figures of ourselves"), and where it is written that "these things befell them as figures (*typicos*)."'[8] In these verses Paul establishes the schema for a mode of figural interpretation that became 'one of the essential elements of the Christian picture of reality, history, and the concrete world in general'.[9] In this schema, 'figural interpretation establishes a connection between two events or persons, the first of which signifies not only itself but also the second, while the second encompasses or fulfills the first. The two poles of the figure are separate in time, but both, being real events [. . .], are within time, within the stream of historical life.'[1] The crucial points here are that the type exists in historical time and that it links distinct events as instances of a single pattern.

4. Samuel Johnson, *A Dictionary of the English Language*, 2nd ed., 2 vols (London: printed by W. Strahan, for J. and P. Knapton; T. and T. Longman; C. Hitch and L. Hawes; A. Millar; and R. and J. Dodsley, 1755–56), 2:962.

5. Charles Richardson, *A New Dictionary of the English Language* (London: William Pickering, 1839), 825 (emphasis in the original).

6. Paul Lawrence Farber, 'The Type-Concept in Zoology in the First Half of the Nineteenth Century', *Journal of the History of Biology* 9, no. 1 (1976): 93.

7. The two major treatments of Victorian typology are Herbert L. Sussman, *Fact into Figure: Typology in Carlyle, Ruskin, and the Pre-Raphaelite Brotherhood* (Columbus: Ohio State University Press, 1979) and George P. Landow, *Victorian Types, Victorian Shadows: Biblical Typology in Victorian Literature, Art, and Thought* (Boston: Routledge and Kegan Paul, 1980). For an important discussion of language, natural history and the type in *In Memoriam*, see Isobel Armstrong, *Victorian Poetry: Poetry, Poetics, and Politics* (London: Routledge, 1993), 247–63.

8. Erich Auerbach, 'Figura', in *Scenes from the Drama of European Literature: Six Essays* (1959; repr., Minneapolis: University of Minnesota Press, 1984), 49.

9. Ibid., 33.

1. Ibid., 53.

Ambiguity in the term *tupos*, however, which it shares with the English 'type' and with related terms such as 'stamp' and 'seal', produces a crux in the typological conception of history. Any of these terms can equally denote either something that produces an impression or the impression itself as a product. The relation between a type in the history of the Jews and what from the seventeenth century on was termed its antitype in the Christian dispensation has thus always been open to different interpretations. Do we understand the type as a hammer and the antitype as its impression? Or do we by inversion think of the type as an impression that chronologically precedes its own cause? The prefix 'anti' makes the antitype an inversion of the type, as the idea that one is an impression of the other would imply; but the possibility for confusion is suggested by erroneous uses recorded in the *OED* from the seventeenth and the nineteenth centuries where 'type' refers to the Christian dispensation while the prefiguring event in Jewish history is termed an '*ante*-type'.[2] Or are both type *and* antitype the temporal impressions of a single transcendent pattern that reveals itself by iteration through historical time? This appears to be Auerbach's view when he asserts that typology not only establishes a relation between historical events but also points beyond history:

> Figural prophecy implies the interpretation of one worldly event though another; the first signifies the second, the second fulfills the first. Both remain historical events; yet both [. . .] have something provisional or incomplete about them; they point to one another and both point to something in the future [. . .] which will be the actual, real, and definitive event. [. . .] Thus history, with all its concrete force, remains forever a figure, cloaked and needful of interpretation.[3]

Typology thus deals above all with a real history in which events appear as letters or forms sequentially imposed on yielding matter. This history, however, can be read in different directions, a fact that in itself implies a split between the time in which it unfolds and the time in which it is interpreted. Whether we accept Auerbach's eschatological reading of the type or not, the split between the time of the typological event and the time when its meaning appears guarantees that it will occur only, in his terms, as 'provisional or incomplete'.

## II

In Britain in the 1830s and 1840s the crucial shift in the meaning of 'type' was its adoption into natural history as a term in morphology. This development had little to do with the exegetical sense of

2. I owe this reference to Peter Stallybrass.
3. Auerbach, 'Figura', 58.

the term I have been discussing but was rather the result of new British engagement with scientific developments on the continent, especially in Germany and France. In Germany the terms *typ, urtyp, urbild* and *bauplan*, among others, were used from the late eighteenth century to designate fundamental structures of organic morphology. In Kant, the existence of morphological types was the ground for what he termed a 'daring venture [. . .] of reason',[4] the speculation that similarities in structure between different organisms might be taken as evidence of actual kinship between them, though he conceded that no evidence had been found for the transmutation of one species into another. The *Naturphilosphie* of Schelling had as its central premise the idea that morphological types reveal themselves more perfectly in successive cycles of creation. Goethe wrote extensively on the morphology of plants, which he believed was defined by a single underlying pattern, the *urtyp*.[5] This position was shared with respect to vertebrates by Carl Gustav Carus, whose work on the vertebrate archetype was a largely unacknowledged source for Richard Owen in England.[6]

Natural science in early nineteenth-century France was if anything even more concerned with the significance of morphological types than it was in Germany, though without the idea of the type's temporal emergence that featured prominently in much German thought. Though he rarely uses the term 'type', Georges Cuvier's division of the animal kingdom into the four orders (*embranchements*) of vertebrates, invertebrates, mollusks and radiata effectively characterizes each of the great divisions by its typical features. In his last major work, the *Natural History of Fishes*, he proceeds by giving an exhaustive account of a single typical species, the perch, in whose conformation the essential features of fish are said to be summed up. Cuvier's apparently pragmatic adoption of a single species as the type of a genus lays the basis for William Whewell, in his *Philosophy of the Inductive Sciences* (1840), for a natural taxonomy in which classes are fixed not by a definition privileging certain functions or parts, in the Linnaean style, but by an example, which he termed the type: 'A type is an example of any class, for instance a species or genus, which is considered as eminently possessing the characteristics of that class.'[7]

4. Immanuel Kant, *The Critique of Judgement*, trans. James Creed Meredith, 2 vols (Oxford: Clarendon Press, 1952), 2:79.
5. On Goethe, and on plant morphology in German thought of the Romantic era more generally, see Robert J. Richards, *The Romantic Conception of Life: Science and Philosophy in the Age of Goethe* (Chicago: University of Chicago Press, 2002).
6. On Carus and Owen, see Nicholas A. Rupke, 'Richard Owen's Vertebrate Archetype', *Isis* 84 (1993).
7. William Whewell, *The Philosophy of the Inductive Sciences, Founded Upon Their History*, 2nd ed., 2 vols (London: John W. Parker, 1847), 1:494.

From Whewell's intervention stems the centrality of the term 'type' to British and American debates about taxonomy in the natural sciences during the nineteenth century. Different forms of the type concept provided a major bulwark against the Lamarckian view that the demarcations of species and genera in natural history were arbitrary. For Whewell, as for Cuvier of course, temporal development of the type was excluded; though each accepted the fossil evidence that species had in the past undergone extinction, both viewed the basic categories of animal morphology as immutable and believed that the traits defining them were preserved in the new species created to replace the old.

Nonetheless, the temporal status of the type in its theological sense does exert pressure on its uses in English-language scientific discourse. Charles Lyell, who like Whewell adopts Cuvier's conception of the type species, also uses the term in a chronological sense, referring to the typical species of a particular geological era.[8] The idea that a species is typical because it shows clearly the stamp of a particular time or place indeed becomes commonplace in nineteenth-century science; it plays a major role, for instance, in the polygenetic racial science of the second half of the century.

Even among transmutationists, where given the views of Cuvier, Whewell and Lyell one might not expect to find the concept of type, it is in fact pervasive. Robert Chambers's anonymously published *Vestiges of Creation* (1844) is a particularly clear example of the interaction of the natural-historical and the exegetical concepts of the type. Like Lyell, Chambers could write of a geological era as having its own 'master-form or type'.[9] Chambers's account of the progressive development of higher forms of life during the earth's secular history, moreover, presents the forms of life that have successively evolved as related to one another in a system that is repeated from age to age, so that there is a homology between the relations among the species that make up late-emerging and highly organized genera and the relations among earlier forms. Chambers took over this system, known as quinarianism, from W. S. Macleay and W. J. Swainson; it proposed that every division of the animal kingdom could be arranged into five classes, of which 'the most perfect with respect to the general character of the class' was termed the typical.[1] Other classes were subtypical or aberrant; the whole quinary structure was repeated 'throughout the whole of

8. Charles Lyell, *Principles of Geology, Being an Attempt to Explain the Former Changes of the Earth's Surface by Reference to Causes Now in Operation*, 3 vols (London: John Murray, 1830–33), 3:50.
9. Robert Chambers, *Vestiges of the Natural History of Creation* (1844; repr., Leicester: Leicester University Press, 1969), 84.
1. Ibid., 240.

the animal, and probably also the vegetable kingdom'.[2] The result, bearing in mind *Vestiges'* central argument regarding the successive appearance of the various orders of organic life, is that each form of life appears as a type—in the sense of a prefiguration—of others that are to follow it. Here is Chambers presenting this position with respect to 'the lowly [. . .] acrites', or polyp. The acrita, he asserts, 'were the first form of animal life on earth; and they appear like all of those which were to follow in five classes'. In the *Polypi natantes*, the *typical* form of polyp, 'we have a sketch of the *vertebrata*. The acrita thus appear as a prophecy of the higher events of animal development' and 'shew that the nobler orders of being, including man himself, were contemplated from the first'.[3] When humankind finally appears on the scene, as the typical species of the Mammalia, it is as 'the type of all types of the animal kingdom'.[4]

## III

The fusion of the senses of 'type' as taxon and as prophecy to be found in Chambers is most familiar today in a work strongly influenced by *Vestiges*, Alfred Tennyson's *In Memoriam*, published in 1850. Tennyson's poem is crucially concerned with the fossil evidence for the extinction of species, which it terms 'types', and it ultimately adopts Chambers's belief that extinction is a necessary part of the evolution of lower forms of life into higher ones. It also incorporates references to biblical types, like the image of water rising in the rock that organizes section 131. Its most systematic use of typology, however, is not as a source of images but as a formal principle; as the poem unfolds in time, it establishes multiple patterns of recurring events and motifs, each of whose appearances reinterprets all of the others. The interpretation of the meanings that these repetitions bring into being is at one level the poem's main action.

Tennyson's poem thus has a typological structure; as we saw earlier, one of the effects of such a structure is to split or multiply temporalities. Though the type is constituted by time, it exists in more than one present and belongs to temporal sequences that can run in different directions. This is why *In Memoriam* is structured by multiple and asynchronous internal calendars. As is well known, the poem presents a process of mourning that extends over three years, with the passage of time marked by the turning of the seasons and by the recurrences of Christmas and the anniversaries of Hallam's birth and death. This calendar compresses the actual period of Tennyson's work on the poem, which ran from the year of

2. Ibid., 242.
3. Ibid., 249–50 (emphasis in the original).
4. Ibid., 272.

Hallam's death in 1833 till shortly before its publication in June of 1850. This second calendar, however, does not simply remain outside the poem; rather, it is incorporated into it, establishing a second principle of organization that operates alongside the temporal markers I have just mentioned. At the poem's initial publication in a stand-alone volume, the title page naturally bore the year of publication. After this it opened with an untitled section—which A. C. Bradley later made it conventional to term the 'Prologue'—that makes a retraction of the poem to follow, referring to it as the 'confusions of a wasted youth' (42). This section, uniquely in the poem, bears a date, 1849, in Arabic numerals, marking its retrospective view of what follows. In the authorized editions of the poem—on a separate page in the stand-alone editions—there then follows a dedication: 'In Memoriam A. H. H.', with the year of Hallam's death in Roman numerals.[5] From this second beginning the poem then proceeds in both directions: forward along its three year calendar and also back to the dated retraction we have already read, and ultimately back to the title page, where the dedicatory act performed by the formula 'In Memoriam' is cited to become the poem's title.

*In Memoriam* is by no means the only mid-Victorian text with conflicting chronologies. The trait may appear wherever we find explicit or implicit reference to the forms of biblical narrative. Dickens's *Bleak House*, for instance, features a typological structure in which the old Bleak House prefigures and is superseded by the new; this apparently simple temporal logic is, however, complicated by the novel's two narrators, who use different tenses, and by the way the narrative is shot through with hints of anachronism, like the fantasy of a 'megalosaurus' on Holborn Hill in the opening paragraph,[6] and recurrent allusions to a coming apocalypse in a world where nothing ever seems to change.

The conjunction of different temporal systems in *In Memoriam* is the topic of a section where the poem reflects explicitly on its own structure and meaning. Passages like this one, where the poem appears as its own interpreter, necessarily have the character I have been discussing, of belonging to more than one temporal schema, since they occupy a position at once within the poem's diegesis and outside it. In section 121, the conjunction in a single textual moment of multiple temporal systems is the topic of the poem's auto-exegesis. The section's major trope is apostrophe, the figure of presence *par excellence*, in which the direct address of speaker to

5.  For this dedicatory page, which Ricks's edition of Tennyson does not reproduce, and for other details of the poem's publication history, see Alfred Tennyson, *In Memoriam*, ed. Susan Shatto and Marion Shaw (Oxford: Clarendon Press, 1982).
6.  Charles Dickens, *Bleak House*, ed. Stephen Gill (Oxford: Oxford University Press, 1996), 11.

auditor presumes their coexistence in a single place and time. The addressees in this poem are themselves in part personified moments in time, in part celestial bodies—Hesper and Phosphor, the morning and evening stars, each of which is represented as watching and listening to the characteristic events of the hour at which it appears. Nonetheless, their character as personified moments in time notwithstanding, both Hesper and Phosphor, morning and evening, have a temporal existence that is principally defined as the mediation of another moment, of the full presence or absence of the sun in the coming day or night.[7] In this sense both Hesper and Phosphor are types—the point is clearest in the address to Phosphor: 'Behind thee comes the greater light' (12). Hesper and Phosphor are thus equally lights whose meaning is given by their relation to the greater light that either follows or precedes them, as antitype to type.

More fundamentally, the typological ordering of section 121 appears in its mythological and linguistic syncretism. Typology has been since St Paul the dominant Christian approach to Hebrew scripture. It is necessarily an exegetical practice of translation and refiguration in which putatively erroneous or partial texts are read as anticipating their fulfillment or completion by true ones. The difference between texts in a typological scheme is always, as we have seen, understood as a difference between historical moments. If section 121 begins by personifying the morning and evening stars, its eventual argument depends upon the knowledge that these personifications are merely different names and figures for a single celestial body: 'Sweet Hesper–Phosphor, double name / For what is one' (17–18). The argument also requires us to recognize that Venus, the modern name of this body, was previously the Latin name of the goddess of love. Behind the Greek names of the personified morning and evening, there appears the name in a different language of one of the archetypal mourners of the elegiac tradition, whose grief over the dead Adonis is an explicit *topos* in the genre from its beginning in Moschus's 'Lament for Bion' up to Shelley's 'Adonais' and is an implicit point of reference for the series of female mourners in Tennyson's own poem.[8] Finally, behind Venus as goddess and mourner, there appears Venus as a planet, whose shining by the reflected light of the absent sun makes it a figure for the elegist himself.

The central figure of *In Memoriam* section 121 links past and present as repeated appearances of the same thing, using a typological schema to assert the continuity of the poet's identity and,

7. For a study of mediation in the English 'Hesperian' poem, see Geoffrey Hartman, 'Poem and Ideology: A Study of Keats's "To Autumn"', in *The Fate of Reading and Other Essays* (Chicago: University of Chicago Press, 1975).

8. On the female mourner in male elegy, see Peter M. Sacks, *The English Elegy: Studies in the Genre from Spenser to Yeats* (Baltimore: Johns Hopkins Press, 1985). Sacks's chapter in this book on *In Memoriam* is the fullest treatment of the poem's typological structure.

therefore, the formal coherence of the poem by which that identity is represented. If its primary concern is with coherence within the temporal span of a single human life, though, the typological schema the poem elaborates nonetheless also encompasses a history whose phases—we might term them animist, theological and scientific— are made to appear as types of one another and ultimately of the poet's life in the present.

Our reading, though, shows this present's indeterminacy. We began with the claims that section 121 has apostrophe as its organizing trope and that this trope guarantees and indeed constitutes for the poem a series of presents and presences. The opening two stanzas are set at evening and addressed to Hesper as evening's personification; the next two are set at morning and addressed to Phosphor. What time, however, is the setting of the final stanza, addressed to 'Sweet Hesper–Phosphor' (17)? Here the poem reveals the succession of present moments apparently constituted by apostrophe as a fiction and sets itself in a temporal order of a different, apocalyptic, kind where present and past coexist. This consequence of the type's temporal schema extends beyond the borders of this single lyric to disturb or render indeterminate the entire diegesis of Tennyson's lyric sequence. When this section asserts the unity of the speaker's past and present, it is radically unclear what past and what present it refers to. Is the poem's present a morning of joy that has succeeded the evening of mourning in which the poem's opening sections are set? Or is the section's present defined by its opening stanzas, which would then appear in contrast to the joyous dawn of the poet's life with Hallam? In light of its double address neither reading of the section will suffice, and we are led to view it as locating within the poem a position from which its structuring narrative can be seen from outside. An apocalyptic view—indicated as such by the allusion to Revelation 22:16 in the identification of Hesper–Phosphor as the double name 'for what is one, the first, the last' (18)—thus emerges as the only one in which the type can appear as fulfilled or complete.

## IV

*In Memoriam* closes—if we ignore the opening, also a kind of close—by anticipating a 'coming race' ('Epilogue', 128) that is to close the evolutionary sequence. The passage echoes Chambers, who concludes his chapter on 'Animated Nature' by speculating that 'our race' might be 'but the initial of the grand crowning type' (276). Chambers's odd figure, with its clutter of terms of art from printing, at once imagines the coming race as closing an evolutionary narrative and as the final character in a passage of print—that is to say it represents 'our race' and the one to come as existing both in temporal succession and simultaneously. Though humanity may be best adapted to the present state of things, Chambers writes, the external world will in time undergo change, whereupon 'there may be occasion for a nobler type of humanity, which shall complete the zoological circle on this planet' (276). The figure of the circle here, which anticipates the coincidence of beginning and ending in the unnumbered first section of Tennyson's poem, again leaves it equivocal whether Chambers is referring to the completion of a temporal narrative or of a taxonomical schema.

In the final stanzas of Tennyson's poem, he echoes Chambers's speculations and makes a last reference to Hallam, remembering him with reference to the form of humanity that is to come as 'a noble type / Appearing ere the times were ripe' ('Epilogue', 139–40). In taking over Chambers's narrative, Tennyson shifts the term 'type', as we have seen is always possible, from the future to the past and supplements its natural-historical sense with its earlier reference to prefiguration. He makes Hallam, as it were, the type of a type; appearing before the proper moment in Chambers's 'zoological circle', he can only prefigure the class of which he is an example. With this ending the poem revises a figure that goes back to the beginnings of elegy, the association of the lost friend with the cycle of plant life, so that in death he can be represented as a flower cut down too soon. In Tennyson's final version of the figure, though, it is not Hallam's death but his birth, and indeed his entire earthly existence, that happen too soon. Moreover, in spite of the references to ripeness, as well as to seed, flower and fruit, in the lines immediately preceding, the temporality in which the epilogue sets Hallam is not that of the vegetative cycle at all but that of history. Though Tennyson's usage refers to both the morphological and the theological senses of 'type', neither sense allows for the idea of the type as premature, which transforms the idealist and theological ideas of history that the concept brings with it into something more ironic.

As we have seen, *In Memoriam* is structured by multiple internal time-schemes. As a result, with respect to the different calendars that the poem incorporates, none of its events occur at a proper time. This characteristic prefigures the view of Hallam's life that it reaches at its close. It also points to a general feature of Tennyson's historical poetics. His works are often striking in their topicality or in some way endowed with what we could call a dateline. In its representation of domestic life, and in its political references— updated before publication to refer to the events of 1848[9]—*In Memoriam* is much more directly a poem of its time than, say,

9. After the trial edition, Tennyson revised section 127 so that it referred to 'The red fool-fury of the Seine' (7) as coming 'thrice again' rather than 'once'—presumably recalling the three revolutionary years of 1789, 1830 and 1848.

'Adonais', 'Thyrsis,' or 'Ave atque Vale', three other hypercanonical elegies of the nineteenth century. Rather than linking Tennyson's poems to a single historical date of origin, however, their topical specificity more characteristically produces in them a kind of internal difference or anachronism. Much has been written on the problem of actually assigning a date to many of Tennyson's poems, which were often composed over decades. Contradictory or ambiguous temporal positions are moreover a recurrent formal and thematic preoccupation in his work. In major dramatic monologues, what we call the dramatic situation can often also be read as the rehearsal or repetition of a situation, a problem that divides the very notion of a 'situation' against itself. I am summarizing here claims I've made elsewhere with respect to 'Ulysses' and 'Tithonus';[1] these two monologues also offer particularly elaborate instances of a trope that preoccupies Tennyson throughout his career, that of the double star Hesper–Phosphor and the chiastic interchange of morning and evening, beginning and ending.

Tennyson's poems can thus have a contradictory relation to any specification of a time or date. One manifestation of his interest in the temporal location of his poems is the prominence among them of anniversary observances; these include official poems such as 'On the Jubilee of Queen Victoria', late poems commemorating the 600th anniversary of Dante's birth and the 1900th of Virgil's death, and also birthday epistles to friends and contemporaries, such as those to Edward FitzGerald and W. G. Palgrave. The addressees of both of these epistles died before receiving them; the poem to FitzGerald moreover got his age wrong, complimenting him on a 75th birthday he never in fact saw. Tennyson's response to FitzGerald's death was to add a pendant to his poem, transforming it into an elegy and incorporating into it a figure for its own belatedness: their addressee's death has 'made the rhymes, / That missed his living welcome, seem / Like would-be guests an hour too late, / Who down the highway moving on / With easy laughter find the gate / Is bolted, and the master gone' (67–72).[2] Without being reductive, it is worth saying that Tennyson could have suppressed the original poem to FitzGerald; he could also have published it without modification and allowed the fact of publication itself to sever it from its original context and addressee. In print, the address of a birthday or other epistle becomes to a greater or lesser extent a fiction; as a fiction the poem survives and can indeed be said to presuppose the death of the figure whose birth it putatively commemorates.

1. Matthew Rowlinson, *Tennyson's Fixations: Psychoanalysis and the Topics of the Early Poetry* (Charlottesville: University of Virginia Press, 1994).
2. The poem frames 'Tiresias', which is also about words as dead letters.

For Tennyson, however, the poem's connection to its original occasion is sufficiently strong—the poem is so topical—that the forestalling of its address to FitzGerald transforms it not into a fiction but into a dead letter. The double temporality of a poem that is at once inseparable from its occasion and too late for it gives a paradigm that has a broad application in Tennyson's work, especially *In Memoriam*.

Poems of direct lyrical address and poems of anniversary commemoration indeed play important roles in *In Memoriam*, functioning as structuring devices in the sequence as a whole. *In Memoriam* comprises 131 numbered lyrics, framed by an unnumbered proem and an epilogue. The great majority of these lyrics are in the present tense; their status as utterances having a specific temporal location is in many cases emphasized by Tennyson's use of the figure of address to endow a section with a specific dramatic situation: 'Dark house, by which once more I stand [. . .]'. This line, the opening of section 7, reminds us how frequently, moreover, the situations in *In Memoriam* repeat an earlier situation or commemorate a past event. Tennyson stands before Hallam's house as he often stood while Hallam was alive; later in the sequence, in section 119, he will return again to the same place, initially to address the house once more but ultimately to address Hallam himself, who in the earlier section appears only as an absence: 'He is not here' (9).

This kind of repetition-with-a-difference is the fundamental principle by which *In Memoriam* links its component sections, with their discrete lyric presents, into a narrative. Every event in the poem is thus a kind of commemoration, so it is not surprising that prominent among them are several explicit commemorations of anniversaries. As we know, the sequence dramatizes a process of mourning that extends over three years; *In Memoriam*'s sheer length entails a significant revision of elegiac convention. In a departure both from the genre's Classical models and from Milton's Christianized version, neither the natural nor the sacred calendar is found in Tennyson's poem to be a source of consolation. The poem marks the observation of three Christmases, but without the Christian promise of personal immortality. Nor does it find any promise of individual rebirth in the natural world; by its structure and its length, it affirms that the natural cycle leading from death to life also leads back to death again. The poem's calendar measures the homogeneous empty time of bourgeois history; the meanings of its most important dates, like the anniversaries of Hallam's birth and death, are contingent rather than motivated by theology or cosmology. As Tennyson notes in section 99, the date of Hallam's death is for some people a birthday or a wedding anniversary. Even the three sections set on successive Christmases represent it as a secular family gathering rather than a religious observance. The sacred calendar, like the solar one, functions as an apparently neutral ground that does not determine the events the poem superimposes on it.

The poem's contents are thus arrayed along several distinct and incompatible temporal axes. By dating the dedication and the proem, Tennyson allows the retraction performed by the latter to encompass the whole chronological scheme organizing the material that follows, which it proleptically exposes as a poetic fiction. Like the anniversary poem for FitzGerald, individual sections of *In Memoriam* are occasional poems whose occasions don't take place. In this respect the whole sequence remains in the traumatic situation described in section 6, where the poet recalls writing before the news has come of Hallam's death and compares his work, 'wrought / At that last hour to please him well' (17–18), to the self-adornment of a young girl dressing to meet her lover—all unknowing that 'the curse / Had fallen, and her future Lord / Was drowned in passing through the ford, / Or killed in falling from his horse' (37–40). The poem itself participates in the illusion it exposes, referring to the girl's 'future Lord' even as it makes clear that the future in question no longer exists. Though Tennyson writes here in the past tense of his preparations for the reunion with Hallam that never came, the poem nonetheless still occupies a present structured by a missed occasion.

In the middle decades of the nineteenth century, the term 'type' designated in one field the imprint *on* history of an ideal form and in another the working out *in* history of a providential design. Tennyson's type, like his poetry, *has* a proper time with respect to both of these concepts of history—but *misses* it. With respect to these concepts it designates something lost, a conjuncture that they foreclose. Given the source of the phrase 'ere the times were ripe' in *Henry IV, Part 1*, we can see in this foreclosure not only the trace of a traumatizing personal loss but also the possibility of an oppositional or even revolutionary relation to history.[3]

3. The cardinal event of Tennyson's friendship with Hallam was their trip to the Pyrenees in the summer of 1830 to bring money and dispatches in support of an abortive rising against the absolutist monarchy of Ferdinand VII. Recollections of the landscape through which they travelled recur throughout Tennyson's subsequent poetry, most vividly in 'In the Valley of Cauteretz', written on the occasion of a return to the Pyrenees in 1861. This poem explicitly memorializes the original trip with Hallam, whose date it mistakes. For details of this trip and of the disastrous outcome of the movement it supported, see A. J. Sambrook, 'Cambridge Apostles at a Spanish Tragedy', *English Miscellany* 16 (1965). On revolutionary bad timing, see Slavoj Žižek, *The Sublime Object of Ideology* (London: Verso, 1989), 58–64.

# MICHELLE GERIC

# [The Geological Model]†

\* \* \*

Despite the difficulties Lyell's strategy of division posed, other patterns of change expounded in *Principles* were sympathetic to *In Memoriam*'s thematic expression. For example, Tennyson discovered in *Principles* the virtue of repetition. Lyell's uniformitarianism was a premise from which to argue 'scientifically' that the laws of geological change should be assumed to be unvarying.[1] Lyell encouraged a perception of change as uniform across time, and a sense of the repetition of types of actions pervades *Principles*. He used repetition to his advantage; his aim was to convert readers to a uniformitarian cast of mind via the replication and reinforcement of material evidence, and to alert them to the profound effects that can be wrought from geological processes operating in the present. James Secord argues that "The sheer length of the *Principles*—over 1400 pages in the original edition—was essential to this programme of perceptual reform." Lyell used a rich array of observed data from many diverse sources, as well as literary references, all designed to overcome resistance to uniformitarian theorising. Thus, the "calmative effect of hundreds of examples, made readers into witnesses to the power of modern changes".[2] Readers were gradually converted to a uniformitarian perspective as the evidence mounted and uniformitarian thinking itself became an established way of seeing and knowing in the minds of readers. Just as geological processes operated imperceptibly to change the entire landscape,

† From "*In Memoriam*'s Uniformitarian Poetics" in *Tennyson and Geology: Poetry and Poetics* (London: Palgrave, 2017), pp. 119–125. © Michelle Geric 2017. Reprinted by permission of SNCSC. Page numbers in brackets refer to this Norton Critical Edition. Like earlier critics such as E. B. Mattes (see p. 170 above), Geric examines the influence of Charles Lyell's *Principles of Geology* (1830–33) on Tennyson's poem. This section focuses on Lyell's "uniformitarianism," the theory that changes in the earth's surface occur not primarily through cataclysmic events but through constant gradual processes such as erosion.

1. Hallam Tennyson acknowledges that his father was "deeply immersed in . . . Lyell's *Principles*" in 1837 (*Memoir*, I, 162). It is generally agreed that the first sections to be written, and those that definitely pre-date Tennyson's reading of *Principles*, were XXX, IX, XVII, XVIII, XXXI–XXXII, LXXXV and XXVIII. See, for example, Christopher Ricks, *Tennyson* (1972), 121, Susan Shatto and Marion Shaw, eds., *Tennyson: In Memoriam* (1982), 6. Shatto and Shaw suggest that dating the composition of the lyrics is particularly difficult because "Tennyson was in the habit of re-using old notebooks, and two adjacent poems may in fact have been composed at widely different times" (7). However, there is evidence that he was reading Lyell earlier in 1836, as a letter to Richard Monckton Milnes attests, where he refers to Lyell's theory of climate change as given in chapter eighteen, volume two of *Principles* (*Letters ALT*, I, 145). More significantly, Dennis Dean demonstrates that Tennyson was familiar with Lyellian ideas much earlier than 1836 from his reading of his "favorite periodical", the *Quarterly Review* (*Tennyson and Geology*, 1985, 5).
2. Charles Lyell, *Principles of Geology*, ed. James A. Secord (1997), xx.

diligent readers would be worn down—subtly eroded by wave after wave of evidence while simultaneously a new perspective gradually arose in them—thus, they would find themselves, by the end of the three volumes, inhabiting an entirely new conceptual landscape. And this is certainly the way Darwin famously read Lyell as "alter[ing] the whole tone of one's mind".[3] Fittingly, the major geological processes that Lyell advocated in *Principles* (in order to demonstrate that present processes operating in deep time were sufficient to account for all past change) were, like his rhetoric, largely slow acting and accumulative. Thus, there was an elegant and powerful symmetry in Lyell's science and rhetorical strategy— the former offering an understanding of geological change through the accumulative effects of processes presently visible, the latter attempting to gradually erode readers' received perceptions through the accumulation of evidence for uniformitarian change.

In similar fashion, repetition becomes the major pattern for the expression of the speaker's out-of-proportion grief.[4] *In Memoriam*'s abba-rhymed quatrains work to extend indefinitely the grief that a more conventional elegy, in its function as a paradigm for recovery, specifically seeks to end. Where the use of quatrains becomes distinctive, even eccentric, is in terms of quantity; over seven hundred such quatrains, all unvarying in their metre and rhyme scheme, is unprecedented and almost alarming in its persistence. Such rigid and uniform repetition gestures towards the interminable—towards Lyell's fixed laws of change operating against a backdrop of geological time. So small a unit as the quatrain seems to be absurdly extended beyond what it might be expected to sustain, and in this it shares with Lyell's uniform laws a sense of the power of small actions in extended time. On a wider level, the poem produces its effect via gathered evidence, mobilising one after another numerous scenarios and vignettes that assess and reassess the power of love and the meaning of death, the effects of doubt and the quality of faith, that work to form and reform the speaker's experience of grief, continually keeping it present. Calmative evidence allows readers to view the speaker's emotion from various angles, and makes them witness to a grief so powerfully present that it has the potential to reshape perceptions of the past. Thus, as Lyell assembled evidence to argue that the present allows us to understand the past, *In Memoriam*'s accumulated lyrics make present grief the arbiter of a past, now seen entirely differently in the light of loss, as

3. Darwin to Leonard Horner, August 29, 1844, *Correspondence of Charles Darwin*, 3 vols., Fredrick Burkhardt and Sydney Smith, eds. (1987) III, 55.
4. A. Dwight Culler, observing connections between Lyellian geology and *In Memoriam*, notes that "if we think that Tennyson requires a long time to move from grief to reconciliation, we should consider what Lyell required for the formation of mountains and seas." *The Poetry of Tennyson* (1977), 150.

in section XXIV * * *, where a speaker specifically located in the present wonders if the past really was "As pure and perfect as I say?" (2). Thus, the speaker is converted to uniformitarian thinking not only in terms of the structure of Lyell's argument—the repetition and accumulation of evidence—but also in Lyell's methodological approach which sees the 'present as the key to the past'.

The poem's length has always been an issue. Tennyson famously asserted that the *In Memoriam* lyrics were not written "with a view to weaving them into a whole, or for publication"; it was only after he found that he "had written so many" lyrics around his grief for Hallam that he felt they might be brought together as a single poem (*Memoir*, I, 304), which suggests that there was no premeditated linear structuring of the poem. *In Memoriam* seems to have developed from the initial resolve to write about the loss of Hallam in a particular form; as Michael Mason suggests, "Tennyson's decision, whenever it occurred, to reserve the special ABBA stanza for all poems on Hallam's death, and only those poems, must have followed on some kind of plan to assemble these as a group."[5] Christopher Ricks argues that the poem's proposed title, *Fragments of an Elegy* implies "with frankness and probably with truth, that the poem as a whole does not possess a firm focus". The fitness of *In Memoriam*'s form, however, lies in part in its fragmentation, as the lyrics capture the small units of feeling that surface in the mourner; the short stanzas and brief lyrics match the grieving experience, the mind interrupted from the demands of routine life by memory, the intervals of forgetfulness pierced by the sharp remembrance of loss. For Ricks, "the most important critical question about *In Memoriam* remains the first and most obvious one: in what sense do the 133 separate sections, ranging in length from 12 lines to 144 lines, constitute a whole, a poetic unity, a poem?"[6] The compulsion to keep producing elegiac lyrics, however, seems to have outstripped concerns for the kind of unity Ricks expects.[7] However, the poem's stanzaic form itself seems to offer a unity of kinds; as Sarah Gates suggests, the stanza form is the "only constant—and an obsessive constant it is—to be found" in the poem.[8] Tennyson's knowledge of Lyellian geology also implies a rationale for seeing

5. Mason, "The Timing of *In Memoriam*" in *Studies in Tennyson*, Hallam Tennyson ed. (1981), 60.
6. Ricks, *Tennyson* (1972), 212.
7. T.S. Eliot found *In Memoriam* to have "only the unity and continuity of a diary" but a diary, nevertheless, "of which we have to read every word", while Eric Griffiths suggests "*In Memoriam*'s unity principally stems from a feature which would be surprising if ever found in a diary: it is written throughout in the same stanza." Eliot, *Essays Ancient and Modern* (1932), 196 [167]. Griffiths, "Tennyson's Idle Tears" in *Tennyson Seven Essays*, Philip Collins ed. (1992), 46.
8. Sarah Gates, "Poetics, Metaphysics, Genre: The Stanza Form of *In Memoriam*" (1999), 508 [226].

unity in ever-repeating stanzas. Already versed in the uniformitarian perspective, on reading Lyell's full text, Tennyson was exposed to the formal cohesion of *Principles* indicated by uniformitarian laws that figure the natural, consistent and repetitive patterns against which human concerns play out. The formal structure of *In Memoriam* constitutes the level at which these laws rule human perception and circumscribe the material limits of human experience. The completed poem emerged from the gathering up and ordering of the lyric sections originally unfixed from any particular sequence.[9] The final version, its length, its repetitive quatrains and unwavering abba rhyme scheme, feel entirely fitting, as many critics have suggested, for the expression of a mental state in which the psyche is stuck within the trammels of grief.

The discursive microdialogue of the poem, however, and its movement between faith and doubt also encodes Lyellian patterns of displacement. Like James Hutton before him, Lyell's aim was to suggest an overall harmony in the system of nature. On the surface, this aim would have been attractive to Tennyson. The earth, according to Lyell, is governed by strict uniformitarian laws that preserve its delicate harmony. Lyell spends the largest part of volume one of his *Principles* offering evidence for the far-reaching effects of igneous and aqueous geological forces working in unison. His aim is to show that there is a balance in these operations that keeps the ratio of land and sea constant. For example, in his treatment of aqueous agents, Lyell writes:

> The sediment carried into the depths of the sea by rivers, tides, and currents, tends to diminish the height of the land; but, on the other hand, it tends, in a degree, to augment the height of the ocean, since water, equal in volume to the matter carried in, is displaced. The mean distance, therefore, of the surface, whether occupied by land or water from the centre of the earth, remains unchanged by the action of rivers, tides, and currents. (*PG*, I, 475)

Erosion and sedimentation describe a process of 'displacement' in which the same materials appear continually to exchange places. Change occurs, but it is non-progressive change that keeps the system in balance. Surface land is eroded or destroyed in one place, only for there to be a corresponding uplift and re-formation elsewhere in the system. Thus, the earth shifts continually in the repeated play between

---

9. Sections XXX, IX, XVII, XVIII, XXXI–XXXII, LXXXV and XXVIII, Christopher Ricks points out, were of a type: "The striking thing about this early group is that it evinces the less perturbed calm which *In Memoriam* mostly intimates to be an achievement slowly won rather than immediately entered upon." *Tennyson* (1972), 121.

ruin and renewal and, paradoxically, everything is in continual flux, constantly changing places, while the wider picture suggests that everything "remains unchanged". Similarly, faith and doubt, hope and despair shift continually in the poem as the speaker moves from the heights of meaning, for example, in the ecstatic lyric of XCV when Hallam's "living soul was flash'd on mine" (36), into the troughs of despondency when faith is "cancell'd, stricken thro' with doubt" (44). Displacement is the rule in all the movements between faith and doubt in the poem; what can never be achieved while this formal pattern prevails is a dialectic synthesis that might activate progress. An acknowledgement of the significance of displacement is found early in the poem, where the speaker wonders if there can be a corresponding gain in loss; if we can "find in loss a gain to match?" (I, 6).

In the shifting landscape of Lyell's system of displacement, however, there is only ever a finite quantity of matter in the system. The earth shapes and reshapes itself continually in the present, and there is something very poignant about the process of displacement in which the same materials are continually rearranged, whether geological materials, or the finite gamut of signifiers that constitutes *In Memoriam*'s language of love and loss, as they foreground respectively the limits of physical existence and the insufficiency of language. The speaker searches the bounds of these finite systems in the agonising quest for a certainty that neither can offer, as nothing can be added or taken away, no progress or gains can be made in the closed system of continual displacement. The continual forming and re-forming of finite materials in displacement helped to envisage Hallam's physical self—his remains—as permanently remaining. However, they are only available in a form now teasingly unsatisfactory. The loved other is "turn'd to something strange" (XLI, 5) and what remains must enter the geological system of displacement which is the fate of all remains. From here there can be no reconstitution of remains, no return to a former state, however much lyric themes rehearse those possibilities. Sifting through the vestiges of remains—remembered touches, gestures, words, letters—in Lyell's humanly unmeaning landscape, is merely a continual attempt to reconstruct the same materials in different but always equally inadequate forms.

Repetition is a well-documented literary device in *In Memoriam*. There is regular use of anaphora, for example: "Thou madest" and "Our wills" in the opening section; "Peace and goodwill, goodwill and peace, / Peace and goodwill" (XXVIII), and "Ring out" and "Ring in" of CVI to name only a few. And the doubling of words: "hand-in-hand", "each at each", "orb to orb", "veil to veil", "Rise, happy morn, rise, holy morn" in section XXX alone, with other examples too numerous to mention.[1] Repetition evokes a sense of being outside linear time. For example, in section XXII and XXIII the past spent with Hallam is envisaged as a complete and unchanging past:

> The path by which we twain did go,
> Which led by tracts that pleased us well,
> Thro' four sweet years arose and fell,
> From flower to flower, from snow to snow:
>
> And we with singing cheer'd the way,
> And, crown'd with all the season lent,
> From April on to April went,
> And glad at heart from May to May.          (XXII, 1–8)

While the seasons may change, the doubling of words foregrounds sameness as they move "From flower to flower, from snow to snow", "April on to April", "May to May" (4, 7–8). Paradoxically, change appears to effect no change whatsoever. However, the next lines describe how a catastrophic but unforeseen change—Hallam's forthcoming death—lurks in the future:

> But where the path we walk'd began
> To slant the fifth autumnal slope,
> As we descended following Hope,
> There sat the Shadow fear'd of man;

The 'descent' towards death is marked by a shift in the landscape as the "path we walk'd" "slant[s]" downwards. The unchanging seasons, thus, belie a deeper imperceptible change occurring in the landscape as larger movements of displacement range below seasonal adjustment, effecting much broader and far-reaching change. The path, which represents the passage through time, 'descends', taking everything that moves through time further into the dark geological world of dead matter where meaning is lost in an eternity of repetitive processes of displacement. By the next section the speaker, "looking back to whence I came / Or on to where the pathway leads", finds that all has changed entirely: "How changed from where it ran / Thro' lands where not a leaf was dumb" (XXIII, 7–10). Figured by uniformitarian patterns of displacement in which the material landscape shifts almost imperceptibly on a global scale, Hallam's death is nevertheless envisaged as a transformation of geological proportions, one that delivers the speaker onto an alien landscape that has been struck dumb, having been emptied out of human meaning by Lyell's strategy of division. The change is suitably subtle as while it represents catastrophe in the human world, in Lyell's material world it is no change at all.

1.  On repetition see, particularly, Alan Sinfield, *Alfred Tennyson* (1986), 114.

## References Cited

Burkhardt, Fredrick, and Smith, Sydney, eds. *Correspondence of Charles Darwin*. Cambridge: Cambridge University Press, 1987.

Culler, A. Dwight. *The Poetry of Tennyson*. New Haven and London: Yale University Press, 1977.

Dean, Dennis R. *Tennyson and Geology*. Lincoln: Tennyson Research Centre, 1985.

Eliot, T. S. *Essays Ancient and Modern*. New York: Hardcourt, 1936.

Gates, Sarah. "Poetics, Metaphysics, Genre: The Stanza Form of *In Memoriam*." *Victorian Poetry* 37 (1999): 507–520.

Griffiths, Eric. "Tennyson's Idle Tears," in *Tennyson: Seven Essays*, edited by Philip Collins. London: Palgrave Macmillan, 1992.

Mason, Michael. "The Timing of *In Memoriam*." In *Studies in Tennyson*, edited by Hallam Tennyson. London and Basingstoke: Macmillan, 1981.

Ricks, Christopher. *Tennyson*. Basingstoke: Macmillan, [1972,] 1989.

———. ed. *Tennyson: A Selected Edition Incorporating the Trinity College Manuscripts*. Berkeley and Los Angeles: University of California Press, 1989.

Secord, James, ed. *Charles Lyell, Principles of Geology*. 1830–33. London: Penguin, 1997.

Shatto, Susan, and Marion Shaw, eds. *Tennyson: In Memoriam*. Oxford: Clarendon Press, 1982.

Sinfield, Alan. *Alfred Tennyson*. Oxford: Blackwell, 1986.

Tennyson, Alfred. *Letters of Alfred Lord Tennyson, I, 1821–1850*, edited by Cecil Y. Lang and Edgar F. Shannon, Jr. Oxford: Clarendon Press, 1982. [Abbreviated *Letters ALT*]

Tennyson, Hallam. *Alfred Lord Tennyson: A Memoir by his Son*, 2 vols. London: Macmillan, 1897. [Abbreviated *Memoir*]

# MICHAEL D. HURLEY

## [Faith and Form in *In Memoriam*][†]

\* \* \*

Coming to *In Memoriam* after the Wellington Ode[1]—which is inevitably the opposite of what usually happens—we are primed to hear how far it likewise thrives through its resistance to the formal rationalizations of theology, and to the settled traditions of verse elegy itself. Lineation, rhyme and rhythm are essential to *In Memoriam*, as they are for the Wellington Ode, but in a different way. Tennyson explained how his poem's one hundred and thirty-one sections (plus Prologue and Epilogue) were written 'at many different places, and as the phases of our intercourse came to my memory and suggested them': 'I did not write them with any view of weaving them into a whole, or for publication, until I found that I had written so many'

---

[†] From "Alfred Tennyson: Word Music" in *Faith in Poetry: Verse Style as a Mode of Religious Belief* (London: Bloomsbury, 2018), pp. 53–57, 63–66. © Michael D. Hurley, 2018. Reprinted by permission of Bloomsbury Academic, an imprint of Bloomsbury Publishing Plc. Hurley's citations of the poem's sections have been changed.

[1]. "Ode on the Death of the Duke of Wellington," which Tennyson wrote in 1852, two years after the publication of *In Memoriam* [*Editor*].

(*Memoir* i. 304–5). Yet after an early period of experimentation (in which manuscripts show a variable stanza length of between four and five lines, and some stanzas with an alternating rhyme scheme), he established a consistent form to run through each of his separate sections, implicitly unifying the poem's diverse episodes and tones. Sections vary in length, but each shares the same stanza, according to the same rhyme scheme and metre. Pastoral and other literary elements in the poem invite associations with the elegy tradition, but rather than employ the so-called elegiac quatrain (abab), Tennyson rhymes abba. He also composed by tetrameter rather than pentameter, further distancing his poem from the formal dignities of the elegy genre, aligning his poem instead with the oral outpourings of the ballad and song, or even the nursery rhyme.

Little changes, but hardly trivial in a poet so accomplished as a stylist and in a poem so self-aware about the workings of poetry itself. Tennyson was after all the man who boasted he knew the quantity of every word in English except 'scissors'; and he had, with virtuosity, already turned his hand to the long line, from the classical-cum-medieval form of 'Leonine Elegiacs', to the breathlessly extensive catalectic trochaic octameters of 'Locksley Hall'. Styling *In Memoriam* as he does, by tumbling tetrameters and bite-sized quatrains, was, then, a highly conscious decision; and indeed he did so because he believed that his stanza form was his own innovation. He was wrong on that front (Ben Jonson, Philip Sidney and others had got there before him), but the point stands that he did not wish to compose by default: he wished to reimagine elegy's orotundities, as well as his own.[2] His stanza's comparatively short lines (four rather than five main stresses) tend to brief and incomplete suggestions, while also offering ready opportunities for post-modifying enjambments. The Prologue immediately sets a tone of firm resolve, in such stanzas as:

> Strong Son of God, immortal Love,
>   Whom we, that have not seen thy face,
>   By faith, and faith alone, embrace,
> Believing where we cannot prove
>                      (Pro. 1–4)

And:

> We have but faith: we cannot know;
>   For knowledge is of things we see;
>   And yet we trust it comes from thee,
> A beam in darkness: let it grow.
>                      (Pro. 21–4).

2. For a fuller account of the workings of Tennyson's stanza, see Sarah Gates, 'Poetics, Metaphysics, Genre: The Stanza Form of *In Memoriam*', *Victorian Poetry* 37 (1999), 507–19. [See p. 226 above—*Editor*.]

End-stopped, confident, propositional. The emphatic caesura of that last line quoted above exemplifies the Prologue's steady, summative purpose. Composed after the rest of *In Memoriam* had been completed, it frames and thereby also seeks to forgive the haverings and heterodoxies that follow ('Forgive' is indeed the request issued at the start of each of the Prologue's final three stanzas). How different that steady start is to the opening of the poem proper, in section I, which hazes its syntax, twice running over the lines, feeling its way along:

> I held it truth, with him who sings
> To one clear harp in divers tones,
> That men may rise on stepping-stones
> Of their dead selves to higher things.
>
> (I.1–4)

That stanza immediately gives way to others that acerbically turn against its sentiment, from the very first word of the very next line: 'But'. Even the Prologue is a poem of productive scepticism, however, such that John William Colenso cited part of it as the epigraph to his radically controversial *The Pentateuch and Book of Joshua Critically Examined*—'as though', Kirstie Blair convincingly argues, 'Tennyson's poem provided part of the inspiration (and indeed authorization) for his exploration of biblical history'.[3] For in spite of the Prologue's assuredly end-stopped bracing, like the rest of *In Memoriam*, its prefatory reflections reaffirm a kind of faith that must be tested on the pulse of experience, rather than something readily expressed by doctrines of science, philosophy or theology: 'Our little systems' all come and go, and are 'but broken lights' of the divine image (Pro. 17, 19). What follows, then, are fragments and broken lights, which means a kind of 'faith' that 'has centre everywhere, / Nor cares to fix itself to form' (XXXIII.3–4). Faith is frisked through diverse channels, that is, and by restless revisions, according to the vagaries of personal testimony, rather than by the rehearsal of universal, settled wisdom. At one point 'Urania speaks with darkened brow' at the poet's presumption to trench into matters of religion:

> 'Thou pratest here where thou art least;
> This faith has many a purer priest,
> And many an abler voice than thou.'
>
> (XXXVII.1–4)

3. Kirstie Blair, *Form and Faith in Victorian Poetry and Religion* (Oxford: Oxford University Press, 2012), 163. Blair's claim here helpfully directs the reader to further argument by her on this subject: 'Alfred Tennyson', in Rebecca Lemon, Emma Mason, Jonathan Roberts and Christopher Rowlands, eds, *The Blackwell Companion to the Bible in English Literature* (Oxford: Blackwell, 2009), 496–511. On Tennyson's wider relation to higher criticism, see also Charles LaPorte, *Victorian Poets and the Changing Bible* (Charlottesville: University of Virginia Press, 2011).

Instead of seeking to 'prate' on theology, or indeed philosophy or science, the poet's soundings in these domains for knowledge and comfort leave him empty-handed; and so he returns again and again to the one unshakeable conviction of his love, which alone proves sustaining, even when it appears counter to other, mounting evidence. In one scene, where he contemplates the decaying bodies of the dead that threaten the possibility of love's endurance, he resists this objective reality in the only way he can, by cussedly asserting his subjective faith:

> Might I not say? 'Yet even here.
> But for one hour, O Love, I strive
> To keep so sweet a thing alive:'
> (XXXV.5–7)

Striving—effortfully performed across the line-break here, into the thin air of the page's white space—seems fragile ('But for one hour'), if not actually futile. The rest of this section answers its own hopeful question by heaping more fears of hopelessness, in the decay of the earth itself across geological time, a theme that recurs throughout the poem (notably, CXXIII).[4] 'Ulysses', written earlier than *In Memoriam*, but also informed by his immediate grief for Hallam, ends with an obdurate commitment 'To strive, to seek, to find, and not to yield' (70). Tennyson explained that the poem was 'written under the sense of loss and that all had gone by, but that still life must be fought out to the end', and that it 'gives the feeling about the need of going forward and braving the struggle of life'. It certainly does; though it is far more convincing about the 'strong' 'will' of the speaker (that persists though he has, physically, been made 'weak by time and fate' (69, 70)) than the likelihood that his striving, seeking and finding will be successful. We trust the sincerity of the speaker's faith, while doubting its objective foundation. In comparable ways, faith in *In Memoriam* is not predicated on the elimination of doubt but on the scoping of faith; and while doubts threaten to enervate, they ultimately spur faith, as something not proven by objective fact but willed into being. Among the poem's most quoted lines are:

> There lives more faith in honest doubt,
> Believe me, than in half the creeds.
> (XCVI.11–12)

The affront to creedal authority here is consistent with what is well known of Tennyson's religious convictions, as summarized in his grandson's essay on 'Tennyson's Religion'. Namely, that he held to a

---

4. For excellent studies of the particular tussle between faith and doubt in the poem, with special reference to science, see Eleanor Bustin Mattes, *In Memoriam: The Way of the Soul* (New York: Exposition Press, 1951), 55–63 [pp. 170–83 above]; Basil Willey, *More Nineteenth Century Studies* (London: Chatto & Windus, 1956), 79–105.

few cardinal beliefs—in God and His providential goodness, in the revelation of God's love and laws through Christ, and in the immortality of the human spirit and the immutability of free will—but that he scanted further ecclesiastical details, and was indeed sceptical about attempts by established religions to claim complete authority. Although he put some store in revelation, the Bible, miracles and the authority of the Church, he was most concerned with and convinced by faith founded on lived experience.[5] Hence the pushback that comes through his parenthetical pause in that second line, which turns from recommending honest doubt to issuing his own certain testimony, 'Believe me': a rival faith authenticated by personal feeling, even if such faith sits on a knife's edge, as Seamus Perry describes it, for being 'at once a claim of conviction ("believe me, I know what I'm talking about"), and also a plea to be believed ("you must believe me"), an appeal that admits the very real possibility of a reader's frank incredulity about faith on these terms'.[6]

The honesty in Tennyson's faith is thus determined by the honesty of his doubt. It is governed by a sense of scruple that (in an analogous context) Herbert F. Tucker describes as Tennyson's 'peculiarly undogmatic certitude',[7] and it expresses itself as a kind of irreverence that is at once epistemological and poetic. When Milton mourned the death of his Cambridge college mate several centuries earlier, Dr Johnson complained that his subsequent elegy (*Lycidas*), decked with mythic figures, was too ornately contrived to be convincing: 'Where there is leisure for fiction there is *little grief*.'[8] A dubious kind of cavilling (a category 'confusion', as C. S. Lewis showed),[9] but Tennyson could not at any rate invite the same, since he resists not only the systems of prefabricated thought but also the settled poetic mode of elegy itself, striking out—as he did in his Wellington Ode—to present grief, and the faith required to reconcile it, as the very opposite of leisure. He implicates his readers instead in the hard-won immediacy of what Freud called 'the work of mourning'.[1]

\* \* \*

5. A number of scholars have advanced this position, but I am indebted here to Donald Hair's lucid overview, in his 'Tennyson's Faith: A Re-Examination', *University of Toronto Quarterly* 55, no. 2 (1985–6), 185–203.
6. Seamus Perry, *Alfred Tennyson* (Tavistock: Northcote House, 2005), 10.
7. Herbert F. Tucker, *Tennyson and the Doom of Romanticism* (Cambridge, MA: Harvard University Press, 1988), 25.
8. [Samuel Johnson,] *The Lives of the Poets*, 3 vols. ed. John H. Middendorf (New Haven and London: Yale University Press, 2010), vol. 1, 175–6.
9. The 'confusion' Lewis identifies is between 'the organization of a response and the pretence of a response', and it is abetted by 'Romantic Primitivism . . . which prefers the merely natural to the elaborated, the un-willed to the willed': C. S. Lewis, *A Preface to 'Paradise Lost'* (New York: Oxford University Press, 1965), 55.
1. Sigmund Freud, 'Mourning and Melancholia' (1917), trans. Joan Riviere, in *General Psychological Theory*, ed. Philip Rieff (New York: Macmillan, Collier Books, 1963), 164–79.

This poem's seven hundred and twenty-five stanzas are, then, not only marked by what Perry nicely characterizes as Tennyson's 'scrupulous imprecision' at the level of the word and phrase,[2] its words and phrases are also perpetually in flux: narratively, tonally, figuratively, and so on. Whatever poised equivocations play on his deployments of modals and semi-modals, these are doubled by his sequiturs and semi-sequiturs that join them up. At a global level, the poem's formal subdivision into sections marks a structural inconclusiveness, and allows it to take a less predictable path than is usual in classical or even English elegy. From Sidney to Spenser to Milton to Gray to Shelley, grief is negotiated in a broadly linear movement towards consolation, but Tennyson discomposes this generic trajectory for the elegy form, threatening the very possibility of its expected *peripeteia*. Loosely (and liturgically) cycling through three years marked by Christmases (XXX, LXXVIII, C), *In Memoriam* traverses in often unexpected ways, back and forth between sections, from reconciliation to renewed grief, as it also diverts from the focus of mourning itself, notably towards related questions of religious faith. There is no wrinkle in our reading when Tennyson refers to his poetic activity as 'chanting hymns' (CVIII.10), given not only the formal similarity of his sections to hymnody,[3] but also the spiritual saturation of these sections. Nor is it a shock to learn that other titles he considered for the poem include 'Fragments of an Elegy' and 'The Way of the Soul': the former emphasizing the extent to which the poem is consciously incomplete in its elegiac account; the latter, how far the poem exceeds a meditation on mourning to be a testimony of the spirit in the broadest sense.

Still, Tennyson worried that the poem might be overdetermined by its Epilogue, making it 'too hopeful' ('more than I am myself', he suggested to James Knowles.[4] There was certainly a danger that the ending might, together with the Prologue, have compressed the textures of the sections between them. But these bookending sections—starting with a funeral, ending with a marriage—do not serve as fixed points in a straight narrative. They were both written late in the compositional process, and they are to some extent separate from the rest of the poem, and they mark a definite 'drift'. Yet they are also of a piece with the governing narrative strategy of the main poem, which is defined above all by its unfixity, its (almost Blakean) destabilizing 'No'. That is the animating principle of

2. Perry, *Alfred Tennyson*, 139.
3. See Marion Shaw, '*In Memoriam* and Popular Religious Poetry', *Victorian Poetry* 15 (1977), 1–8.
4. Although Hallam Tennyson denied that his father ever expressed such a quandary (see Philip L. Elliott, *The Making of the Memoir* (2nd edn, Lincoln: Tennyson Society, 1995), 20, n.), the poem itself does, insistently and repeatedly.

Tennyson's faith in the poem that needs to be grasped above all, and before anything else can be. Scholars have noted that Tennyson carefully revised the final sequence of the poem's sections to ensure that 'faith wins out over doubt',[5] but he also latterly added new verses (XCVI), to affirm the value of doubt in quickening faith. The poem's final outcome is by no means smoothed into a steady or inevitable progress of consolation and optimism.

Ragged narrative style can mean and can do different things, of course; but in reading Tennyson, the *ne plus ultra* of orbicular euphony, we may at least be assured that his formal deformities were conscious imperfections. Charles LaPorte brilliantly parses the fragmentariness and conflictions of *Idylls of the King* as an intervention by Tennyson on the nature, value and dangers of contemporary hermeneutical criticism (whose biblical source material was likewise fragmented and dispersed).[6] But unlike that later poem (or indeed his 'Ode'), *In Memoriam* engages religious faith in a way that is in the end more personal than universal, tracing the straits of an individual psychology more than the general state of faith, whether inflected by 'higher criticism', or anything else. *In Memoriam* certainly does have an epic range and scope, and engages the theological pressures of its moment, but its formal instabilities are focused through its troubled speaker. Verse serves not so much as an emblematic intervention in contemporary religious debates as an individuated, line-by-line tussle with such debates, stained by the pain of personal circumstances.

Correspondingly, the poem's affective power inheres not so much in the satisfactions that come where faith wins out—as if doubt were progressively chipped away—but rather in the ways doubting persists through the poem, acting as the driver through which faith is refined and emboldened. Doubt is not progressively subtracted, in other words, it is turned to positive ends. Even the stylistic feature that most conspicuously unites *In Memoriam* as a whole, its stanza scheme, has been read as expressing that same ongoing negotiation between faith and doubt, as the end-rhyme from the first line of each stanza is momentarily stranded. Tennyson suggested that *In Memoriam* 'was meant to be a kind of *Divina Commedia*' (*Memoir* i. 304), but though Dantean influence is strongly evident thematically, and through many of his borrowings, analogues and allusions,[7] the two poems strongly diverge when it comes to the defining feature of their poem's rhyme scheme. This divergence

---

5. See Helen Small, 'Tennyson and Late Style', *Tennyson Research Bulletin* 8 (2005), 226–59 (232).
6. LaPorte, *Victorian Poets and the Changing Bible*, Ch. 2.
7. See Gordon D. Hirsch, 'Tennyson's Commedia', *Victorian Poetry* 8, no. 2 (1970), 93–106.

is not an isolated, aesthetic difference: the purposeful way *terza rima* rolls inexorably, if also uncertainly forward, gathering itself up as it goes, indicates and endows a different theological mode.[8] For the *In Memoriam* stanzas necessarily fall back on themselves. Their abba structure looks like the opening of a Petrarchan sonnet, but one that never makes it to its octave 'turn'.[9] These stanzas may only re-turn, through perpetual cycles. The fourth-line rhyme offers a delayed sonic closure that does not propel the poem forward but instead remembers its beginning. As here:

> I wrong the grave with fears untrue:
>  Shall love be blamed for want of faith?
>  There must be wisdom with great Death:
> The dead shall look me through and through.
>  (LI.9–12)

With the 'a' rhyme reprisal, untruth is clarified, and thereby made true, as it were, in the echoing 'through and through', which insists that the dead friend does after all know the veracity of the speaker's love, and returns it undiminished. Such elegant economy in the poem's thinking here is rarely seen in the Wellington Ode. But the strategy of unsteadying and reprisal through rhyme, and of refusing easy sweetness and the apparent stupidities of onomatopoeia, is consistent across both poems. If these poems charm, they are also verses of gritty endeavour. *In Memoriam* is 'Perplext in faith', but over the course of almost seventeen years of grief-induced doubt, 'At last he beat his music out' (XCVI.9–10).

Tennyson walks a fine line here, perhaps a blurred one. *In Memoriam* finally allayed Emily Sellwood's misgivings as to his faith, such that she agreed to marry him soon after its publication. Charles Kingsley declared the poem to be 'the noblest Christian poem which England has produced for two centuries'.[1] For other readers, though, Tennyson's honest doubting has seemed dishonestly uncommitted. 'We remain undecided as to Mr Tennyson's faith,' *The English Review* concluded in 1850, 'though we opine, that, strictly speaking, *he has none,* whether negative or affirmative, and advise him, for his soul's good, to try to get one!'[2] Such a response is at once reasonable but at the same time as misguided as it is possible

8. For further discussion of the theo-poetics animating *terza rima*, see Michael D. Hurley, 'Interpreting Dante's Terza Rima', *Forum for Modern Language Studies* 43, no. 3 (2005), 320–31.

9. For an ingenious argument on the sonnet-like halo of the *In Memoriam* stanza, see Denise Gigante, 'Forming Desire: On the Eponymous *In Memoriam* Stanza', *Nineteenth-Century Literature* 53, no. 4 (1999), 480–504.

1. Quoted in Laurence W Mazzeno, *Alfred Tennyson: The Critical Legacy* (New York: Camden House, 2004), 16.

2. Quoted in Ricks, *Tennyson*, 296 n.

to be. It is correct to say that the poem's faith is not wholly nor straightforwardly either negative or affirmative, but it is wrong to conclude that this was because Tennyson was firmly undecided either way. For he was in fact firmly committed—as the reviewer would have him be—to *trying* to work through his position, which he attempts through the measure of verse itself, engaging doubt to clarify his faith, by the mode that only verse might allow.

\* \* \*

# Alfred Tennyson: A Chronology

1809    Born (August 6) in Somersby, Lincolnshire.

1811    Arthur Henry Hallam born (February 1); sister Emilia (Emily) Tennyson born.

1827    Together with two of his brothers publishes a small volume of poetry.
Enters Trinity College, Cambridge.

1828    Hallam arrives at Trinity.

1829    Meets Hallam sometime in the spring; invites him to Somersby (December), where Hallam meets Emily.

1830    Publishes *Poems, Chiefly Lyrical*.
Travels with Hallam in southern France (summer).

1831    Death of his father, George Tennyson (March); returns to his family in Lincolnshire without finishing his degree at Cambridge.
Hallam publishes a favorable review of *Poems, Chiefly Lyrical*.

1832    Hallam's engagement to Emily finally recognized by Hallam's parents.
Publishes *Poems* with Hallam's encouragement.

1833    Hallam dies in Vienna of a stroke (September 15). Tennyson receives the news in early October; begins writing sections of *In Memoriam* later that month.
Ship bearing Hallam's body arrives in England in late December; the funeral, which Tennyson does not attend, takes place in early January 1834.

1837    Arranges for his family to move from Somersby to High Beech, Epping.
Engaged to Emily Sellwood.

1840    Engagement broken off.

1842    Publishes *Poems* in two volumes, his first book of verse since Hallam's death.
Marriage of sister Cecilia Tennyson (born 1817), described in the Epilogue to *In Memoriam*.

1850    Publishes *In Memoriam* to great critical acclaim (early June).
Marries Emily Sellwood (June).
Named Poet Laureate by Queen Victoria (November).

1852    Birth of son Hallam.

| 1854 | Birth of son Lionel. |
|------|----------------------|
| 1855 | Publishes *Maud*. |
| 1859 | Publishes first portion of *Idylls of the King*. |
| 1864 | Offered a baronetcy but refuses (as will happen three more times). |
| 1883 | Accepts offer to be made a baron, thus becoming Lord Tennyson. |
| 1886 | Son Lionel dies. |
| 1892 | Dies (October 6) and is buried in Westminster Abbey. |

# Selected Bibliography

• indicates items included or excerpted in this Norton Critical Edition

## Editions

The major editions of the poem are as follows (in order of publication):

*In Memoriam*. London: Moxon, 1850.
>  The first edition, like all separately printed editions that appeared in Tennyson's lifetime, was published anonymously. It did not include two sections that appear in the final version: LIX (added 1851) and XXXIX (added 1870).

*The Works of Alfred, Lord Tennyson*, ed. Hallam, Lord Tennyson. London: Macmillan, 1907–08 (the "Eversley Edition").
>  This posthumous edition incorporates Tennyson's final revisions to his poems. It also includes a number of previously unpublished explanatory notes, both by Tennyson and by his son Hallam.

*The Poems of Tennyson*, ed. Christopher Ricks. 2nd ed. Berkeley: University of California Press, 1987.
>  This landmark in Tennyson scholarship, first published in 1969, is the standard edition for all of Tennyson's poetry; it contains a full textual apparatus and a concise and informative introduction to the poem. There is also a one-volume *Selected Poems* drawn from the Ricks edition (Longman, 2006), which contains all of *In Memoriam*.

*In Memoriam*, ed. Susan Shatto and Marion Shaw. Oxford: Clarendon Press, 1982.
>  This is the most complete edition of the poem available. It includes extensive notes on each section, a detailed description of all the manuscripts and printed texts, and appendices containing additional poems that were once part of *In Memoriam* but were not included in the final version. The introduction describes the growth of the poem and very usefully discusses classical analogues.

## Biographies and Background

The most useful sources include the following (in order of publication):

• Hallam, Lord Tennyson. *Alfred Lord Tennyson: A Memoir*. London: Macmillan, 1897.
>  Hallam Tennyson's memoir of his father has been an indispensable resource for subsequent Tennyson studies. The chapter on *In Memoriam* contains extensive comments by the poet concerning his intentions.

T. H. Vail Motter, ed. *The Writings of Arthur Hallam*. New York: Modern Language Association, 1943.
>  Motter's edition reproduces Hallam's poems, criticism, and theological writings, many of which directly influenced the writing of Tennyson's poem.

Sir Charles Tennyson. *Alfred Tennyson*. London and New York: Macmillan, 1949.
This biography by the poet's grandson fills in gaps left by the *Memoir*, including details of the poet's troubled boyhood with his brooding father.

Robert Bernard Martin. *Tennyson: The Unquiet Heart*. New York: Oxford University Press, 1980.
The best of several good modern biographies, by a writer who was also a respected critic of Victorian literature.

James A. Hoge, ed. *Lady Tennyson's Journal*. Charlottesville: University Press of Virginia, 1981.
Emily Sellwood married the poet shortly after the publication of *In Memoriam*. Her journal offers a fascinating insight into their lives in the years 1850–74.


## Criticism

Critical literature on the poem is extraordinarily extensive and represents a wide range of different approaches. The following is a selection of some of the most interesting and influential works.

Adams, James Eli. "Woman Red in Tooth and Claw: Nature and the Feminine in Tennyson and Darwin." *Victorian Studies* 33 (1989): 7–27.
Adams astutely analyzes the gendering of the poem's evolutionary models, particularly the personification of Nature as a betraying "demonic woman."

Albright, Daniel. "The Muses' Tug-of-War in *In Memoriam*." *Tennyson: The Muses' Tug-of-War*. Charlottesville: University Press of Virginia, 1986, pp. 176–213.
In a fresh take on an old theme, Albright explores the polarities of Tennyson's poem, particularly the binaries of heavenly and earthly, expressive and inexpressive.

Allison, Kiera. "The Repression of the Return: Tennyson's *In Memoriam* and the Art of the Unheard Echo." *Victorian Poetry* 53 (2015): 41–56.
Argues that the poem's many repetitions represent not a sign of repressed psychological trauma (as many earlier critics suggest) but a more conscious playing and experimenting with memory.

Armstrong, Isobel. "Tennyson, the Collapse of Subject and Object: *In Memoriam*." *Language as Living Form in Nineteenth-Century Poetry*. Brighton: Harvester, 1982, pp. 172–205.
A brilliant, densely written analysis of the poem's consciously self-thwarting language and consequent conceptual complexities.

———. "Tennyson in the 1850s." *Victorian Poetry: Poetry, Poetics and Politics*. London and New York: Routledge, 1993, pp. 252–83.
As her book's title indicates, Armstrong explores the intersection of poetry and history, and particularly of poetic form and political ideology. The chapter on *In Memoriam* considers the influence of Victorian science and language theory on Tennyson's notion of "type."

Barton, Anna. *Alfred Lord Tennyson's* In Memoriam: *A Reading Guide*. Edinburgh: Edinburgh University Press, 2012.
This very useful handbook for students offers a complete text of the poem together with an extended commentary explaining its different movements and major themes.

Blair, Kirstie. "'Raving of dead men's dust and beating hearts': Tennyson and the Pathological Heart." *Victorian Poetry and the Culture of the Heart*. Oxford: Oxford University Press, 2006, pp. 181–224.
Blair finds images of the heart pulsing through both the language and rhythms of the poem and traces the speaker's development from heartsickness to healthy circulation.

———. "'Beyond the Forms of Faith?' Tennyson and the Broad Church." *Form and Faith in Victorian Poetry and Religion*. Oxford: Oxford University Press, 2012, pp. 163–96.

Examines the tension between the poem's devotion to a single stanza form and its skepticism about the need for particular religious forms and rituals.

• Bradley, A. C. *A Commentary on Tennyson's* In Memoriam. London and New York: Macmillan, 1901.

Bradley's was the first important book-length study of *In Memoriam*. In addition to a section-by-section commentary, it contains an excellent introduction outlining the overall structure of the poem.

Christensen, Allan C. "Navigating in Perilous Seas of Language: *In Memoriam* and 'The Wreck of the Deutschland.'" *Victorian Poetry* 47 (2009): 379–401.

Offers a persuasive account of the poem's worries about the limits of verbal expression, with a particular focus on the ship poems (sections 9–18).

Cole, Sarah Rose. "The Recovery of Friendship: Male Love and Developmental Narrative in Tennyson's *In Memoriam*." *Victorian Poetry* 50 (2012): 43–66.

Cole traces a development in the poem's representation of the speaker's relationship to Hallam, from static, feminine images (often involving marriage) at the outset to images of progressive, evolving male-male friendship at the end.

Corbett, Mary Jean. "No Second Friend?: Perpetual Maidenhood and Second Marriage in *In Memoriam* and 'The Conjugial Angel.'" *ELH* 81 (2014): 299–323.

Corbett contextualizes the poem's figures of betrothal and marriage, focusing on the triangular relationship between Tennyson, his sister Emily, and Arthur Hallam.

Craft, Christopher. "'Descend, and Touch, and Enter': Tennyson's Strange Manner of Address." *Genders* 1 (1988): 83–101.

An excellent reading of the link between death and homoerotic desire in *In Memoriam*. Craft lucidly summarizes earlier critical anxiety about the sexuality of the poem, and his reading has strongly influenced later gender-based readings.

• Day, Aidan. "Tennyson's Grotesque." In *Tennyson among the Poets: Bicentenary Essays*. Ed. Robert Douglas-Fairhurst and Seamus Perry. Oxford: Oxford University Press, 2009, pp. 76–94.

In keeping with the mainstream of criticism on *In Memoriam* since the 1950s, Day suggests that the poem's progressivist viewpoint is constantly called into question by its vision of a world devoid of deeper meaning.

• Eliot, T. S. "In Memoriam." *Essays Ancient and Modern*. London: Faber & Faber, 1936, pp. 175–190.

Eliot's brief but enormously influential essay discusses the nature of Tennysonian doubt and memorably analyzes the poem's confessional structure.

• Gates, Sarah. "Poetics, Metaphysics, Genre: The Stanza Form of *In Memoriam*." *Victorian Poetry* 37 (1999): 507–19.

Gates relates the poem's most distinctive formal feature, its *abba* stanza, to larger structural units—individual sections, groups of sections, and finally the whole evolutionary narrative.

• Geric, Michelle. *Tennyson and Geology: Poetry and Poetics*. London: Palgrave, 2017.

Geric's chapter on *In Memoriam* examines the influence particularly of Charles Lyell's *Principles of Geology* on Tennyson's poem, showing how the verse form of *In Memoriam* mimics the constant, repetitive, non-teleological geological forces Lyell described.

Gigante, Denise. "Forming Desire: On the Eponymous *In Memoriam* Stanza." *Nineteenth-Century Literature* 53 (1999): 480–504.
> Beginning with Tennyson's Renaissance precursors, Gigante argues persuasively that the *In Memoriam* stanza encapsulates a form of desire that is simultaneously thwarted, endless, and anonymous.

Gold, Barri J. "The Consolation of Physics: Tennyson's Thermodynamic Solution." *PMLA* 117 (2002): 449–64.
> Gold explores the similarities between *In Memoriam* and the developing science of thermodynamics in the mid-nineteenth century, focusing on the balance between the laws of conservation of energy and entropy.

Gray, Erik. *The Poetry of Indifference, from the Romantics to the* Rubáiyát. Amherst: University of Massachusetts Press, 2005.
> The chapter on Tennyson focuses on the three Christmas sections of *In Memoriam*, arguing that they exemplify the poem's surprising resistance to transcendent ambitions, whether religious or poetic.

———. "Polyptoton in *In Memoriam*: Evolution, Speculation, Elegy." *Studies in English Literature* 55 (2015): 841–60.
> Considers the poem's frequent use of polyptoton, or repetition of the same word in variant forms, arguing that it embodies the elegist's ability and willingness to imagine alternative possibilities.

Griffiths, Devin. "Spooky Action in Alfred Tennyson's *In Memoriam A.H.H.*" *The Age of Analogy: Science and Literature between the Darwins*. Baltimore: Johns Hopkins University Press, 2016, pp. 129–65.
> In a wide-ranging analysis Griffiths examines the poem's tendency to speculate about the unknown, especially the afterlife, through historical and scientific analogies.

Haggerty, George E. "'O Sorrow, wilt thou live with me': Love and Loss in Tennyson's *In Memoriam*." *Queer Friendship: Male Intimacy in the English Literary Tradition*. Cambridge: Cambridge University Press, 2018, pp. 41–51.
> Haggerty's chapter considers *In Memoriam* less as a poem of queer desire than as a passionate love poem in the tradition of classical elegy.

Hair, Donald S. "Tennyson's Domestic Elegy." *Domestic and Heroic in Tennyson's Poetry*. Toronto: University of Toronto Press, 1981, pp. 7–46.
> The poem's domestic imagery, Hair suggests, functions as pastoral conventions do in earlier elegies: as a means of rendering the speaker's private grief familiar and universal.

Henchman, Anna. "The Globe We Groan In: Astronomical Distance and Stellar Decay in *In Memoriam*." *Victorian Poetry* 41 (2003): 29–45.
> Henchman argues that the astronomical imagery that pervades Tennyson's poem emphasizes the inevitable gap between perception and conception, what we see or experience and what we know or believe to be true.

• Hinchcliffe, Peter. "Elegy and Epithalamium in *In Memoriam*." *University of Toronto Quarterly* 52 (1983): 241–62.
> Noting that one of the characteristic elements of elegy is the transformation of the dead into a transcendent archetype, Hinchcliffe argues that *In Memoriam* resists this depersonalizing trope by combining elegy with its generic opposite, epithalamium or marriage song.

Hsiao, Irene. "Subtraction and Division: Calculating Loss in *In Memoriam*." *Victorian Poetry* 47 (2009): 173–96.
> Hsiao explores Tennyson's quantification of love, loss, and time, particularly in section 85.

• Hurley, Michael D. *Faith in Poetry: Verse Style as a Mode of Religious Belief*. London: Bloomsbury, 2018.
> Hurley's chapter on Tennyson describes how the form of *In Memoriam* expresses his strenuous working out of faith both in God and in poetry.

Joseph, Gerhard. "Producing the 'Far-Off Interest of Tears': Tennyson, Freud, and the Economics of Mourning." *Victorian Poetry* 36 (1998): 123–33.
    Joseph offers a succinct analysis of the poem's conscious quest to derive gain from loss.

Kolb, Jack. "Hallam, Tennyson, Homosexuality and the Critics." *Philological Quarterly* 79 (2000): 365–96.
    Surveys the history of queer readings of *In Memoriam* in the twentieth century, noting the many inaccuracies and omissions in the work of critics who claim a biographical basis for their readings in the relationship between Tennyson and Arthur Hallam.

• Mattes, Eleanor B. *In Memoriam: The Way of a Soul.* New York: Exposition Press, 1951.
    Mattes considers various influences on Tennyson's poem, including Hallam's own writings. The most important chapters are those that analyze how Tennyson's study of science affected his faith and gave rise to the poem's idiosyncratic treatment of the concept of evolution.

• Nunokawa, Jeff. "*In Memoriam* and the Extinction of the Homosexual." *English Literary History* 58 (1991): 427–38.
    Along with that of Christopher Craft, this article provides one of most persuasive queer readings of the poem. Nunokawa suggests that sexuality, like everything else in *In Memoriam*, follows an evolutionary model, in which schoolboy homoeroticism eventually gives rise to normative heterosexual marriage.

Peltason, Timothy. *Reading* In Memoriam. Princeton: Princeton University Press, 1985.
    Peltason's reader-response approach sets itself against generations of critics who have sought a unifying theme in the poem (or objected to the lack of one) by celebrating the moment-by-moment vacillations that the reader necessarily shares with the poet.

Ricks, Christopher. *Tennyson.* 2nd ed. New York: Macmillan, 1989.
    First published in 1972, Ricks's lively, penetrating study set the standard for critical biography of Tennyson. The chapter on *In Memoriam* has significantly influenced subsequent formalist and queer readings of the poem.

Rosenberg, John D. "Stopping for Death: Tennyson's *In Memoriam*." *Elegy for an Age: The Presence of the Past in Victorian Literature.* London: Anthem, 2005, pp. 33–65.
    Offers an extremely informative and comprehensive introduction, addressing questions of autobiography, genre, sexuality, and the poem's place in literary and cultural history.

Rovee, Christopher. "Secrets of Paper." *Word & Image* 30 (2014): 388–400.
    A meditation on the parallels between *In Memoriam* and photography, an elegiac art invented around the same time as the poem's composition.

• Rowlinson, Matthew. "History, Materiality and Type in Tennyson's *In Memoriam*." In *Darwin, Tennyson and Their Readers: Explorations in Victorian Literature and Science*. Ed. Valerie Purton. London: Anthem, 2013, pp. 35–48.
    Rowlinson reconsiders the poem's treatment of science, religion, and time, all through an illuminating analysis of its use of the key word "type."

Sacks, Peter M. "Tennyson: *In Memoriam*." *The English Elegy: Studies in the Genre from Spenser to Yeats.* Baltimore and London: The Johns Hopkins University Press, 1985, pp. 166–203.
    Sacks moves through the poem from Prologue to Epilogue, illuminating the poet's work of mourning at each stage in the context of the elegiac tradition.

Sendry, Joseph. "*In Memoriam*: Twentieth-Century Criticism." *Victorian Poetry* 18 (1980): 105–18.

    Sendry's article surveys the poem's critical history through the first eight decades of the twentieth century, offering analyses of all of the major contributions. The same issue of *Victorian Poetry* that contains this article also contains five further essays on *In Memoriam*, all of them valuable, concentrating on such issues as the poem's descriptions of writing, its metaphors, and its prosody.

• Shannon, Edgar Finley, Jr. *Tennyson and the Reviewers*. Cambridge: Harvard University Press, 1952.

    The chapter on *In Memoriam* forms the culminating point of this study of Tennyson's reputation and of the influence that reviews of his early poetry had on his revisions and his subsequent writings.

Shaw, W. David. "The Autobiography of a Mourner: *In Memoriam*." *Tennyson's Style*. Ithaca, NY, and London: Cornell University Press, 1976, pp. 132–67.

    Shaw enumerates the forms of catharsis Tennyson achieves, concentrating on the paradox that although *In Memoriam* uses the conventions of personal confession, it nevertheless relies upon indirect or "veiled" language.

———. "The Paradox of Genre: Impact and Tremor in Tennyson's Elegies." *Elegy and Paradox: Testing the Conventions*. Baltimore and London: Johns Hopkins University Press, 1994, pp. 212–35.

    Shaw's sophisticated analysis puts Tennyson's poem in its generic context by examining traditional elegiac binaries that *In Memoriam* embodies without ever resolving.

Sinfield, Alan. *The Language of Tennyson's* In Memoriam. Oxford: Basil Blackwell, 1971.

    Sinfield provides often brilliant close analyses of syntax, imagery, sound, and rhythm, all contributing toward a sustained reading of the poem's double voice: immediate, yet carefully controlled.

———. *Alfred Tennyson*. Oxford: Basil Blackwell, 1986.

    An important Marxist reading. The chapter on *In Memoriam* contains a concise account of the poem's social and political self-positioning; it describes how *In Memoriam*, though in so many ways a private elegy, nevertheless became a work of central importance to "the bourgeois state."

Smith, Robert Rowland. "Forgetting Tennyson's Memory." *On Modern Poetry: From Theory to Total Criticism*. London: Continuum, 2012, pp. 105–16.

    Offers an extended close reading of a single section of *In Memoriam* (section 7), teasing shades of meaning out of every phrase.

Tate, Gregory. "Tennyson's Unquiet Brain." *The Poet's Mind: The Psychology of Victorian Poetry 1830–1870*. Oxford: Oxford University Press, 2012, pp. 91–123.

    Tate reads the poem's explorations of psychology in the context of contemporary theories about the mind and the brain.

Tomko, Michael. "Varieties of Geological Experience: Religion, Body, and Spirit in Tennyson's *In Memoriam* and Lyell's *Principles of Geology*." *Victorian Poetry* 42 (2004): 113–33.

    Countering the notion that Victorian scientific developments consistently threatened religious faith, Tomko argues that Charles Lyell's treatise offered Tennyson a model of reconciling spiritual and physical truths.

Tucker, Herbert F. "*In Memoriam A.H.H.*: Transient Form." *Tennyson and the Doom of Romanticism*. Cambridge: Harvard University Press, 1988, pp. 376–406.

    Tucker's rich and witty book offers extraordinary close readings of major poems from the first half of Tennyson's career. The chapter on *In Memo-*

*riam* describes "the reciprocal, historically conditioned impingement of self and society."

Wheeler, Michael. "Tennyson: *In Memoriam*." *Death and the Future Life in Victorian Literature and Theology*. Cambridge: Cambridge University Press, 1990, pp. 221–64.

Wheeler considers Tennyson's heartfelt universalist hope—that every individual will live on after death—in the context of Victorian theology.

Williams, Rhian. "Shakespeare, His Sonnets, *In Memoriam* and the Reviewers." *Tennyson Research Bulletin* 8.3 (2004): 178–89.

Argues that the reputation of Shakespeare's sonnets, which were generally held in suspicion in the early nineteenth century because of their expression of love for a man, benefited by their association with Tennyson's much admired poem.

Wilson, William A. "Victorian Philology and the Anxiety of Language in Tennyson's *In Memoriam*." *Texas Studies in Literature and Language* 30 (1988): 28–48.

Wilson connects the poem's frequent worries about the inadequacies of language to the linguistic theories of Tennyson's contemporaries.

# Index of First Lines